Civility

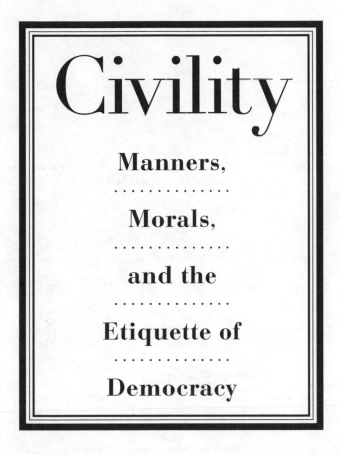

Civility

Manners,
. . . .
Morals,
. . . .
and the
. . . .
Etiquette of
. . . .
Democracy

Stephen L. Carter

Basic Books
A Member of Perseus Books, L.L.C.

Author's Note: All Biblical quotations, unless otherwise noted,
are from the New Revised Standard Version.

PUBLISHED BY BASIC BOOKS
A Member of Perseus Books, L.L.C.

LIBRARY OF CONGRESS CATALOGING-IN-PUBLICATION DATA
Carter, Stephen L., 1954–
Civility: manners, morals, and the etiquette of democracy / by Stephen L. Carter
p.—cm.
Includes bibliographical references and index.
——*ISBN 0-465-02384-3 (alk. paper)*
1. Civil society. 2. Etiquette. 3. Democracy. I. Title.
—*JC336.C35—1998*
—*321.8—dc21*   *97-44099*

98   00   02   01   99
1   3   5   7   9   10   8   6   4   2

For Sara,
and for George and Loretta,
three heroes of civility

The laws that govern manners contain many true and unchanging principles mingled with much that is untrue, unimportant, and transitory.

OLIVER WENDELL HOLMES JR.,
The Common Law

CONTENTS

Contents

PREFACE

DURING the fall of 1996, I happened to hear on the radio an interview in which an academic from Eastern Europe scoffed at the idea that his country should adopt American-style democracy. Pointing to the bickering and partisan posturing that often stifle serious dialogue in the United States, he asked what exactly was so good about our system. As we watch the collapse of civility in America, he is hardly the only one asking that question. From visitors to volunteers to voters, everybody seems to be wondering why Americans treat each other so shabbily.

Georges Clemenceau once referred to the United States as "the only nation in history which has miraculously gone directly from barbarism to degeneration without the usual interval of civilisation." He was, as usual, overstating, but he also captured an attitude that Americans have held about their own nation (and that Europeans have held about Americans) almost from the nation's inception: civility is in a decline. And Americans today are like Americans of every era. We think our nation's manners are falling apart. Some three out of four of us think civility has declined over the past decade. An even greater number think drivers are particularly uncivil. As for our politicians, they finish below professional athletes when the public is asked to rank different groups according to civility. In short, although we Americans have always thought civility is collapsing, I think, this time, we might be right.

In this book, I try to analyze what has happened to civility in the United States, why it matters, and what we can do about it. This book represents the second in a series that began with *Integrity*, which was published in 1996. My idea is to write a series of books exploring elements of good character that are, as I wrote there, "pre-political," by which I mean that we should all struggle to exemplify them, whatever our philosophical or partisan differ-

ences. I began with integrity because it is a virtue without which
the others have no meaning. Integrity helps us understand what is
right and do it, even when there is cost: if I have no integrity, there
is no point in asking me what I stand for.

Civility is next because, having developed integrity as a tool for
creating our own moral selves, we must next develop tools for
interacting with others. I do not consider civility synonymous with
manners (although I do think manners matter). I have in mind an
attitude of respect, even love, for our fellow citizens, an attitude, as
we shall see, that has important political and social implications.
Moreover, civility is a moral issue, not just a matter of habit or
convention: it is morally better to be civil than to be uncivil.

This book should not be considered a sequel to *Integrity*;
although the books have overlapping themes, one need not read
the first to appreciate the second. Like *Integrity*, this book is not a
formal work of legal scholarship. It is, rather, an investigation into
both our yearning for and our inability to achieve a society marked
by true civility. Like *Integrity*, this book has important Christian
themes—I am, after all, a Christian—and many religious examples. But one need not be a Christian, or religious at all, to follow
the argument. And, like *Integrity*, *Civility* tries to balance a discussion of philosophy and theology with examples drawn from law,
politics, and everyday life.

This book is in a sense a prayer—a prayer for understanding
and for our strength, as a nation, to build a society in which we act
with, rather than talk about, genuine respect for others. In
researching and writing the book, I have learned a tremendous
amount about the history of civility as a concept and about the
important battles over whether it is valuable and, indeed, what it
means. But I make no claim to possess more civility than anybody
else, and I do not think of myself as an expert in it: I am no Miss
Manners. Rather, I think of myself and the reader as fellow students of civility—and so I am inviting the reader to accompany me
on a journey. I do not pretend to know where it ends. I only insist
that the trip is an important one if we are to preserve the moral
discipline that distinguishes human beings from other animals.

I should add a point about my sources. Readers will quickly
note my reliance on American sermons delivered in the eighteenth

and nineteenth centuries. This era differed from our own in two important respects: first, theology was determinedly public, and its accessibility to lay folk mattered, rather than, as now, the property of a handful of sophisticates in divinity schools who too often seem to write only for each other; and, second, television had not yet destroyed the attention span, so congregations had the patience to listen as preachers wove complicated arguments that went on for forty-five minutes or an hour or sometimes more. In consequence of these two factors, marvelous sermons were delivered and often published to be read more widely. Many of those sermons have survived, and they form a rich and fascinating record of the public religious mind during an era in which, because of chattel slavery, the entire ethic of Christianity was the battlefield for a war over the American future. Fortunately, the right side won. The sermons I quote here—most of them commentaries on the biblical command to love the neighbor, the favorite abolitionist text—provide an important moral record of the struggle and illuminate for the student of civility just how difficult it can be to put into practice the principles most of us know in our hearts to be right.

. . . .

This book, of course, is not my work alone. I discussed earlier versions of some of these arguments in lectures or workshops at Boston College, DePaul University, Samford University, Seton Hall University, the College of William and Mary, and William Mitchell College of Law. I also made presentations based on the research for this book to the annual meeting of the presidents of the universities of the Evangelical Lutheran Church in America and to the Grand Rapids Area Council on Ecumenism. And, as always, I had the benefit of many a lunch or office visit with my colleagues at the Yale Law School, including Bruce Ackerman, Akhil Amar, Robert Ellickson, Tony Kronman, Alan Schwartz, and Kate Stith. I have also benefited from close and careful readings of the draft by Ronald Feenstra and George Jones and from a spirited conversation on civility with Austin Sarat. I wish to offer special thanks to Ian Ayres, for pointing out the counterintuitive relationship between home burglar alarm systems and incivility; to Paul Gewirtz, for his gentle admonitions that incivility is no new thing; to Rod Rinnell, for reminding me that we are all characters in the same story even if none of us see it through to the end; and, with deepest affection, to Margaret Farley, who, during the book's lengthy middle age, warned me about the writer's temptations.

Of course, none of this would have been possible without the generosity of Anthony Kronman, dean of the Yale Law School, and the remarkable efforts of my research assistants over the past several years: Deborah Baumgarten, Kali Bracey, Amy Campbell, Heidi Durrow, Dina Friedman, Daniel Goldschmidt, Goodwin Liu, and Lewis Peterson, all students at the Yale Law School, all of whom contributed greatly. I also learned a great deal on the subject from Layaliza Klein, another student at the school.

Finally, and most important, I give thanks to God for the love of my family, and for their willingness to let me love them back. I thank my children, Leah and Andrew, for helping me to remember that civility begins at home, and, most of all, my wife, Enola Aird, not only for wise and tireless readings of the book's many drafts, but for teaching me the relationship between the secular ideal of civility and the Christian ideal of awe.

S.L.C.
Cheshire, Connecticut
September 1997

I

The
Collapse
of the
Three-Legged
Stool

I
. . . .
Barbarians Running Late

After being cut off by another driver in traffic and slamming on your
brakes, you stop at the next service station for gas, your adrenaline still
pumping, only to be made to wait by a clerk who is busy flirting with
a girlfriend but who finally, after finishing a cigarette, emerges from
his grimy booth and saunters sullenly to your car and stands outside
the window, not speaking, barely glancing your way, waiting for you to
state your needs, which he fulfills silently, neither cleaning your wind-
shield nor checking your oil, and when he is done, he speaks his first
words, "Sixteen-fifty," and glowers at you when you lack exact change,
but at last, after a period of further flirtation, drops a few greasy, torn
dollars and some dirty coins into your palm, and now your blood is
boiling, so you pull out of the station a little too fast, narrowly missing
another motorist, who raises his middle finger and mouths an obscen-
ity at you . . .

. . . .

In the middle of the unruly nineteenth century, there were no
automobiles, but America was agog over railroads. For the first
time in human history, horseback was not the fastest way to travel.
An entrepreneur named Leland Stanford hammered a golden spike
into a rocky Utah plateau, and the coasts were connected by three
thousand miles of track. Everybody wanted to ride. Everybody
suddenly had someplace to go. The owners of the railroads grew
wealthy. Naturally, the passengers were divided into classes; that
was the American way. The first-class coaches often had gold

fittings, and the third- or fourth-class cars might have no more than hard wooden benches, but all the trains were full.[1]

Travel in those days was necessarily in groups. Nobody but the very rich could afford to travel alone. One bought a ticket and sat down in a train car full of strangers. Doubtless the excited passengers jostled each other for space, but although the Europeans were already looking down on American manners,[2] it was not yet the nation's fashion to be rude. On the contrary, this remarkable new technology worked as well as it did, moving the citizenry from city to city, because the travelers understood their obligation to treat each other well. They purchased guides to proper behavior, like *Politeness on Railroads* by Isaac Peebles, and tried to follow its sensible rules: "[W]hispering, loud talking, immoderate laughing, and singing should not be indulged by any passenger" was one. "Passengers should not gaze at one another in an embarrassing way" ran another.[3] Conductors were soon cracking down on passengers who "indulg[ed] personal preferences at the expense of other passengers."[4]

Well, of course: to travel so far together, packed shoulder to shoulder like chess pieces in their little box, everybody had to behave or the ride would become intolerable. Everyone followed the rules for the sake of their fellow passengers, and they did so, as one historian has noted, out of a spirit of "self-denial and the self-sacrifice of one's own comfort for another's."[5] Alone of God's creation, human beings can make those choices, setting aside their own needs and desires for the sake of living in society with others. And so this nineteenth-century understanding captures two of the gifts that civility brings to our lives: First, it calls on us to sacrifice for others as we travel through life. And, second, it makes the ride tolerable.

But nowadays we have automobiles, and we travel both long and short distances surrounded by metal and glass and the illusion that we are traveling alone. The illusion has seeped into every crevice of our public and private lives, persuading us that sacrifices are no longer necessary. If railroad passengers a century ago knew the journey would be impossible unless they considered the comfort of others more important than their own, our spreading illusion has taken us in the other direction. We care less and less about our fellow citizens, because we no longer see them as our fellow passengers. We may see them as obstacles or competitors, or we may not see them at all, but unless they happen to be our friends, we rarely think we owe them anything.

When I ponder the shape of this incivility crisis, I think of a boy wearing droopy pants (whom we encounter in chapter 4), the link between the New York Yankees and Levittown (which we discuss in chapter 3), and the obsessive Danish chess genius Aron Nimzovich (whom we will meet in chapter 17). But, perhaps because I am speaking of the way we travel, I most often think about the man at Houston Intercontinental Airport who skipped his security check and literally shut the place down.

You may remember the story. In July 1995, a man raced past the security gates in Houston without bothering with such formalities as walking through the metal detector or having his carry-on luggage screened. The guards, taken by surprise and perhaps not as well trained as they should have been, were unable to stop the man—let us call him Selfish Passenger—who swiftly disappeared into the crowd. Probably Selfish Passenger was simply being selfish, but the airport authorities, rather than risk the chance that the man was armed, decided to evacuate both Continental Airlines terminals, requiring every individual in the two buildings—some seven thousand people—to leave and then to be screened again before reentry. This process took the better part of four hours. Selfish Passenger's rush through the gates delayed at least forty flights, caused thousands of fellow passengers to miss connecting flights, and generally made lots of people's day miserable.

Why did he do it? Said a spokesman for the Houston police, "We're guessing he was late for a flight and just didn't want to fool around by going through the metal detectors."[6] Indeed, with two entire terminals shut down while everybody was rescreened, it is likely that Selfish Passenger made his plane. And although the anger and frustration quotient in the airport was doubtless raised by many degrees, there was no point in taking it out on the people running the place. One who was made to wait put it this way: "I'm glad they're making sure everyone is safe, but it's too bad all of us had to suffer like this just because of one person."[7]

Now, it strikes me that what Selfish Passenger did was enormously uncivil, and I suspect that you agree. Still, it is worth pondering for a moment what precisely was so uncivil about it. Not the fact that it was illegal: sometimes, as we shall see, breaking the law can itself be a civil act, and following it uncivil. And not the fact that some people were inconvenienced: I imagine that shoppers are inconvenienced by a striking union's picket line outside a supermarket, but picket lines are not necessarily uncivil.

No, what was uncivil was that Selfish Passenger acted like a selfish passenger: thinking only of his own need to be on time, uninterested in any harm he might do to others. The notion that morality might require him to sacrifice his own interest or desire for the benefit of others, even briefly, probably did not occur to him at all.

This is scarcely surprising. Selfish Passenger's behavior was only a more extreme form of what most of us do all the time. Perhaps it is because our society is so market-driven that we behave that way; markets exist, after all, to satisfy individual desire. Thus, we live in a world in which charitable giving is way down. So is volunteerism. Asserting our constitutional rights is way up. Negative political advertisements are up. So is the use of vulgar language.[8] And vandalism motivated by racial or religious hatred.[9] We do business with little thought for others. Firms looking for ways to control their budgets decide to cut training, even though the predictable result is that customer service gets worse.[10] A basketball star kicks a photographer and is rewarded with a multimillion-dollar endorsement contract. A CEO fires thousands of workers and is rewarded with a multimillion-dollar bonus. Sacrifice? What sacrifice? We have no fellow passengers; we are in this struggle we call life for ourselves alone.

In pursuit of selfishness, we glorify the viciously offensive. In 1996 critics enthused over a film about the fight to protect the First Amendment rights of Larry Flynt, whose magazine, *Hustler*, features drawings of women bound, tortured, and crawling with maggots. (Somehow those images did not make it into the film.)[11] That same year, civil libertarians rushed to the defense of a "death metal" group with the charming name of Cannibal Corpse, whose song "Necroebophile" (from an album entitled *The Tomb of the Mutilated*) was singled out for special criticism by William Bennett of Empower America and C. Delores Tucker of the National Political Congress of Black Women, who have recently led an effort to persuade the music industry to exercise a degree of restraint—or perhaps of morality. The song describes, among other things, masturbating with the severed head of a child. It is difficult to imagine anything more unthinkably vicious to which young people might be exposed, but the companies that market such music are blithely unconcerned. Mere viciousness, even when combined with moral vacuousness, will hardly dissuade a corporation from using the First Amendment as a shield while pursuing the dollar. Like the film industry, which reserves some of its highest salaries for actors who specialize in portraying angry, remorseless killers, and like the television networks, which for a time adopted a voluntary "rating" system that gave parents absolutely no information about the content of programs, the firms in the music business evidently believe that the social costs of the stream of gore and horror and lonely despair that flows over the nation's children are somebody else's problem . . . because we have no fellow passengers.

Even when we do have fellow passengers we misbehave. The airlines have lately seen a rise in hostile and abusive conduct by passengers, and Selfish Passenger was hardly the worst of the bunch. A man who was angry at missing a flight connection threw his suitcase at an eight-month pregnant airline employee. A woman who learned that there were no more sandwiches on her flight to Las Vegas punched the flight attendant and pushed her to the floor.[12] Airline critics say that passengers are mad because service has become so inept. I am a frequent traveler, and I agree about how bad service is. When passengers respond with aggression, however, we simply see another sign of how our narrow focus on our own interests is making us uncivilized.

As for the automobile itself, it seems an almost diabolical tool, in the traditional sense of the word—a thing of the devil, made to bring out the worst in us. A Colorado funeral director complained to his local paper about impatient drivers darting in and out of funeral processions rather than waiting for them to pass, ignoring both law and tradition in their zeal to get where they are going— to say nothing of showing disrespect for the deceased. Cars kill far more people every year in America than handguns—about forty thousand a year, far greater than the population of Cheshire, the Connecticut town where my family lives—and the most common cause of fatal accidents is a driver who is going too fast or wanders out of the proper lane.[13] An uncivil driver, we might say, who disbelieves in rules of the road. And not all the deaths are accidents. A grim 1997 report from the American Automobile Association reported a sharp rise in the use of cars as weapons—that is, running people over on purpose. The authorities seem helpless. The city of Los Angeles, confronted with more and more drivers who refuse to stop (as California law requires) for pedestrians in crosswalks, has decided to try . . . eliminating crosswalks!

On the railroad trains, all the passengers together were a community, called by a shared moral understanding to sacrifice for each other. But if, as we now seem to think, there are no other passengers, there is no community. And if there is no community, we can do what we like, not just on the roads but everywhere. The illusion that we travel life alone is ruining us all. The proper name of the illusion is incivility.

· · · · · · · · · · · · · ·

. . . and now your blood is boiling, so you pull out of the station a little too fast, narrowly missing another motorist, who raises his middle finger and mouths an obscenity at you, but still there is no escape, your business is not done, you swing into the next fast-food joint for a quick bite, and you wait in line behind two bickering kids, continuing in their loudest and most irritating whine an argument that has obviously been with them for some days or weeks or years, and then you jump two inches into the air because across the room there is a terrific crash as somebody knocks over a display of some cartoon character whose countenance never bothered you before but does now, and the person who walked into the sign, booming with laughter, walks on out the door, making no move to pick it up, but nobody who works in the restaurant moves either, and now it is your turn at the counter, and once more there are no words of welcome, only a glassy, empty stare from a teenager who would rather be doing anything else, legal or illegal, than spending a few minutes serving a customer . . .

· · · · · · · · · · · · · ·

8

Suddenly, everybody is worrying about our growing incivility. Public intellectuals are writing about it: the subject has lately occupied thinkers from Gertrude Himmelfarb to Robert Bellah to Michael Sandel to Amitai Etzioni. Robert Putnam, a Harvard sociologist, publishes an article about the decline of bowling leagues and sparks a nationwide debate over why we seem to be joining less.[14] And our woeful political debates! A mass of data affirms that the unwillingness of our leaders to be civil to each other adds to the voter alienation that is sweeping the nation. A 1996 survey shows that Americans, by a huge margin, believe that politicians are less civil than other groups not noted for their politesse—professional athletes, for example.[15] A 1997 study by the Annenberg School of Communications concluded that the level of civility on the floor of Congress has reached its lowest point since 1935.[16]

The concern has spread into popular culture. Maybe it is unsurprising that Miss Manners has written a book about how our nation can regain its civility. But Ralph Reed, until recently director of the Christian Coalition, has also taken up the cry. So has Jim Wallis, his co-religionist and political opponent. Scott Peck, author of *The Road Less Traveled*, devoted a book to the problem. It has captured the attention of virtues guru William Bennett. And of Senator Daniel Patrick Moynihan. Magazines feature it on their covers, newspapers run front-page stories: Why are we so rude? they demand.[17] Anxious journalists appear on television to ask each other whether it is all just a fad, worried perhaps that if politicians stop calling each other names, the media might have nothing to report but the news. And in official Washington, everybody is for it: President Clinton, House Speaker Newt Gingrich, Senate Majority Leader Trent Lott, whoever. All are calling for more civility. In March 1997, members of the Congress, on both sides of the aisle, held a retreat in Hershey, Pennsylvania, to talk about how to get more of it. At this writing, about a dozen national commissions are considering the problem of incivility, and private foundations—ever the bellwethers of trendiness—are all at once coughing up money to study it.

And all these people are right to be concerned, because the crisis, trendy or not, is real. Some of the signs receive much press: the relentlessly negative character of our political campaigns, the nastiness of public moral argument, the viciousness of our campus debates over everything from curriculum to rules for student behavior. After the accident that killed Diana, Princess of Wales, the press began to point to the incivility of ... the press. The paparazzi who evidently hounded Diana to her death, in refusing to accept any bounds that might mark a sphere of privacy, illustrate perfectly the consequences of our incivility crisis: there are no bounds because there are no fellow passengers whose lives or needs or hopes we must respect. Some of the signs of crisis are so mundane that we scarcely notice them any longer: the clerk who will not address customers as *Sir* or *Ma'am*; the political activist whose only interest in the other side is to drown it out; the late-night driver who, thinking only of his own desires, sits on the tail of the car ahead, high beams all aglow. And some significant signs are ignored: our growing use of depersonalizing stereotypes, for example, or what has been dubbed the new informality: perfect strangers (particularly those who are selling something) call people they have never met before by their first names, a practice that used to be considered disrespectful.

Manners are dying in part because technological change makes them seem less necessary (see chapter 11), and in part as a consequence of the second American revolution that erupted in the 1960s (see chapter 3), but they are also a casualty of the illusion generated by our wealth and privilege, that in our luxury we have no fellow passengers. If we are alone in life, why bother to be polite? Especially to those who disagree with us: our causes are far too pressing for us to bother respecting our opponents (chapter 8). And not only have we become rude, we have become oddly ungenerous. We give less time and money to charitable causes. Few of us can be bothered any longer to involve ourselves in self-governance: we are voting less, we are joining less, we are evidently discussing the issues of the day with our fellow citizens less. Thus, our growing incivility becomes a threat to our democracy. (How embarrassing that the President must call a national summit to remind us to volunteer.)

Our children are mimicking the incivility of the adult world. In one survey, an astonishing 89 percent of grade school teachers and principals reported that they "regularly" face abusive language from students.[18] Violence in the schools has increased steadily in recent decades, and, in my adopted state of Connecticut, a solid majority of high school students say they could get a gun if they wanted one. We see our young people killing one another over articles of clothing and casual insults, the way people did in less civilized times. So alarmed is the American Academy of Pediatrics that it has urged its members to talk to parents about violence prevention along with diapers and immunizations. No wonder opinion shapers are worried.

Fortunately, most of those who think about the subject of civility agree that we need more of it. (We will meet some of the dissenters in chapter 2.) They cannot quite agree, however, on why we have so little of it and whether the decline is recent. Thus, writers have looked for causes in the collapse of community, the dearth of moral education, our lurch toward radical individualism, and the fast-paced, thoughtless argument style of the media age. But all of these are only symptoms; they are not themselves the disease.

Similarly, despite the growing concern, we seem to have trouble agreeing on exactly what civility *is*. Some people, when they think of civility, think of manners. Others think of proper standards of moral conduct, or a set of standards for conducting public argument. Still others think of willing participation in the institutions that enable our democracy to thrive, what has come to be known as the movement for civic renewal. Some long for a golden past. Others imagine a platinum future. And all of these views are partly correct: like the blind men and the elephant, the many observers of civility are talking about different parts of the same animal.

Civility, I shall argue, is the sum of the many sacrifices we are called to make for the sake of living together. When we pretend that we travel alone, we can also pretend that these sacrifices are unnecessary. Yielding to this very human instinct for self-seeking, I shall argue, is often immoral, and certainly should not be done without forethought. We should make sacrifices for others not simply because doing so makes social life easier (although it does), but as a signal of respect for our fellow citizens, marking them as full equals, both before the law and before God. Rules of civility are thus also rules of morality: it is morally proper to treat our fellow citizens with respect, and morally improper not to. Our crisis of civility, then, is part of a larger crisis of morality. And because morality is what distinguishes humans from other animals, the crisis is ultimately one of humanity.

In the nineteenth century, rules of etiquette—manners—were thought to carry moral content. Among the classes that thought manners important, a person who followed the rules was considered morally superior to a person who broke them. Obviously, this view has not lasted. The historian Arthur Schlesinger traced the change in attitude to the period following the First World War, when a new middle class arose, "intent on aping the ways of those whom they had formerly deemed to be of finer clay." Writes Schlesinger: "Etiquette now managed to disentangle itself from ethics, taking on its modern meaning of a generalized pattern of behavior designed to lubricate social intercourse."[19] Rules of behavior, then, moved from the realm of morality to the realm of pragmatics: they were encouraged not because they were independently good, but because they seemed to produce good results. The task of those who would construct a society based on civility—and of this book—is thus to re-entangle etiquette and ethics.

. . . .

. . . no words of welcome, only a glassy, empty stare from a teenager who would rather be doing anything else, legal or illegal, than spending a few minutes serving a customer, and when she gets your order wrong and then blames you for it, expression finally coming into her voice as she says, "You didn't tell me that," and you want to snap at her, but you restrain yourself, making excuses, accepting this treatment, as though because she is a mere child and not well raised she can do what she pleases, and so you make your uneasy way out of the restaurant, your blood pressure elevated more by the ill treatment than by all the salt, and you return to your car, under the wiper of which some unknown entrepreneur has placed a flyer encouraging you to come in for a free reading of your palm, and with your hands full of fast food and the refuse containers in the parking lot already bursting with debris, you face the classic urban dilemma, add to the trash in the car or add to the trash on the street, and you decide to be good, you fold the flyer between your fingers and drop it on the seat, and then you are once more on the way to work, and you try the radio, and on one station the host is call-

ing everyone who disagrees with him idiotic, and on the next, the candidates for Congress are accusing each other of corruption, but the third station, at least, carries music, even if the principal subjects seem to be drugs and rape, and so you select the all-news station and are told in gleeful detail of what murders and molestations occurred overnight, and borne on by these glad tidings, you at last arrive at your job, where you are expected to be polite.

. . . .

And if instead you arrive exhausted, then you have experienced our national crisis of incivility at its most debilitating level: not the way our politicians scream or the way talk shows poison the air, but the way we drag ourselves through endless unfriendly days. You see and perhaps feel the need for what Isaac Peebles sold in the nineteenth century: a set of rules on how passengers should treat each other. Perhaps you long for a shared sense that we citizens are together on our journey, and that, although we may jostle and shove a bit for small advantages, we are all passengers on the same train, headed in the same direction. If so, what you really feel is the need for greater civility. And that puts you smack into the mainstream.

CIVILITY AND DESIRE
. . . .

The idea that we need more civility is, as they used to say, no new thing. As the nineteenth century drew to a close, arbiters of social custom threw up their hands, wondering what had happened to the good manners of earlier generations.[20] And, like the commentators who wonder the same thing today, the critics lacked a sense of the broad sweep of history. For we Americans, it must be conceded, have long been famous for our bad manners. Even winning the Revolutionary War was evidently considered bad form—at least by the losers—for the British commanders reported back on the rudeness of the colonists. We were world-famous for our bad manners. After Fanny Trollope, wife of the novelist, visited the new nation in the 1830s, she wrote a popular book arguing that

Americans had none. (This three-hundred-page polemic, entitled *Domestic Manners of the Americans*, was especially scathing in its treatment of American men, whom Trollope had seen chewing tobacco and spitting in public.) A few years later, as the Congress debated the slavery issue, we had shouting matches on the floors of both Houses, and, in a notorious episode, one member of the House used a cane to beat Senator Charles Sumner bloody and senseless.[21] Theater audiences routinely hissed bad performances by tossing fruit, rotten eggs, even the carcasses of animals to chase actors from the stage. Sometimes disagreements over the merits of different thespians exploded into violence, most notably in the Astor Place riot of 1849, in which twenty-two people died.[22]

But the complaint is older than America. It goes back to the sixteenth century, when the scholar Desiderius Erasmus of Rotterdam wrote the first important work on the subject of civility, a celebrated little book entitled *De civilitate morum puerilium* (On civility in children). Although it is for his writing on theology that historians consider Erasmus one of the leading scholars of the Renaissance, it is his concern about the world in which children were being raised that commends him to the student of civility. His book was an effort to settle the debates then raging over whether and why proper behavior should matter. He wrote for a public concerned about the proper behavior of a child confronted with everything from the wiles of a prostitute to a chair on which the previous occupant had defecated.[23] Although the idea goes back to ancient Greece, it was Erasmus who popularized the notion that some people were civilized and others uncivilized—and that the difference might have moral consequences. Erasmus was the first to propose that we measure a mode of behavior to set those who were civilized apart from those who were not. And if this argument by the pacifist Erasmus later helped supply, albeit indirectly, justifications for everything from slavery to imperialism, it also leads, rather more directly, to the happy possibility of a community (or a nation, or perhaps a world) bound together by shared norms of proper conduct.

Writing in 1530, Erasmus addressed a Europe in which the satisfaction of immediate desire—whether for food, wealth, revenge, or sex—was the primary basis for human action. It is not easy for the modern reader to envision his world. People ate with their hands from a common plate. They urinated in the street and defecated at the dining table. They killed over small disagreements and maimed over unpaid debts. In other words, they acted on impulse. Erasmus warned that unless humans were willing to discipline their desires, there would be nothing to distinguish them from other animals. Self-discipline was the mark of civilization, he maintained; anything less was mere barbarism.

Erasmus popularized the concept of *civilité*, from which our word *civility* is most directly descended. *Civilité* is often translated as *politeness*, but it means something more. It suggests an approach to life, a way of carrying one's self and of relating to others—in short, living in a way that is civilized. The ideal arose "at a time when chivalrous society and the unity of the Catholic church were disintegrating," so that Europeans were casting about for guidance on how to avoid killing each other.[24] The word *civilité* shares with the words *civilized* and *civilization* (and the word *city*, for that matter) a common etymology, an Indo-European root meaning "member of the household." Of course: civility, as Erasmus understood, is what enables us to live together. To be civilized is to understand that we live in society as in a household, and that within that household, if we are to be moral people, our relationships with other people (our fellow citizens, members of our civic household) are governed by standards of behavior that limit our freedom. Our duty to follow those standards does not depend on whether or not we happen to agree with or even like each other.

Use the metaphor of the household, use the metaphor of the train, but the point is the same: we are required, for the sake of our shared community, to follow certain rules of behavior. We must, however, be cautious in our enthusiasm for civility. Civility is not all of a piece. Rules are not good rules just because they are rules. Sometimes what are described as rules of etiquette may demand exactly the opposite of seeing others as our equals before God. Feminist scholars have pointed out how many traditional rules of etiquette worked to the disadvantage of women: for example, the nineteenth-century social norm that a lady did not walk along the street alone.[25] And the trains that so excited America in the nineteenth century were segregated: black passengers rode in the Jim

Crow car. That was what led to the Supreme Court's infamous 1896 decision in *Plessy v. Ferguson*,[26] which established the pernicious "equal but separate" doctrine as fundamental but uncivil constitutional law, which it remained for half a century. Meanwhile, black parents taught their children to use segregated rest rooms and to step aside on the street for white adults, and black men were warned not to make eye contact with white women— simple matters of politesse.

So, yes, the rhetoric of civility and manners has been used for wicked purposes, and any effort to reconstruct civility must study those eras and learn from them. But that historical fact should not blind us to the basic point Erasmus tried to make, that rules of behavior are what distinguish civilized humans, who are willing to discipline their desires, from barbarians, who do not even try. And if we apply Erasmus's test to ourselves, we might discover that we are becoming uncivil because we are becoming uncivilized. Obsessed with grabbing what we want and keeping what we have—and very certain that we travel life alone—we are forgetting the need for the moral discipline that, as Erasmus pointed out, distinguishes humans from animals. Here we come to the heart of the matter. The rudenesses we have been discussing, although they are genuine and they matter, are the merest scratches on the surface of the crisis; they are, one might say, merely the evidence of our growing incivility.

The deeper problem is the disintegration of social life. We live in an era when the values of the market and of politics—both of which are characterized by an amoral emphasis on *getting* what we want—are crowding into the social life of the nation, where we are supposed to engage in the moral reasoning that helps us to *decide* what we want. Because of the well-documented decline of the structures that traditionally helped sustain moral norms—most notably the three-legged stool of family, religion, and the common school—we enter the market or politics with flimsy moral armament. We lack the tools to consider what we *should* value or *should* want, to say nothing of how we should act, and thus more and more tend to follow our impulses. And both the political world and the market are more than happy to cater to our baser instincts. People of my age and older (I am in my forties) often express dismay at the acquisitiveness—not to say selfishness—of the rising generation. But young people are only doing what we have, through our example, taught them: lacking a solid moral grounding that would teach them to do anything else, they are acting on impulse instead.

CIVILITY AND THE COMMON GOOD

. . . .

The idea that we should use our freedom to the common good rather than to seek our own pleasures has long been at the center of Christian and Jewish ethics. On this point, at least, Augustine and Maimonides were in full agreement. It goes back at least to Aristotle and was central to the defense of human freedom by such Enlightenment philosophers as John Locke. But it is not one of those ideas so old and venerable and self-regarding—like the profit motive—that we cannot imagine life without it. It is, and has always been, an idea so fragile that, if not carefully nurtured, it will certainly die.

Unfortunately, we are not nurturing it at all. We are not preserving the institutions of social life that mediate between politics and the economy, on the one hand, and our flimsy moral selves, on the other. We still join organizations, but they tend to be groups like the National Rifle Association or Planned Parenthood or the American Association of Retired Persons, groups that affirm (and lobby for) our views rather than form or challenge them—and that ask their members not to gather together to think through the difficult issues of the day, but only to send in their checks.[27] They do not call on us, for the sake of our fellow passengers, to control our impulses; instead, they promise to defend our right to exercise them.

Living in a democracy requires hard work that we seem less and less willing to do. To take a simple example, too many of us cast uninformed votes, making the choice for what political scientists call "rational ignorance"—that is, we decide that adding to our store of knowledge about the candidates is not worth the trouble.[28] Or we vote for political candidates who spread the most slimy untruths about their opponents and the most noble untruths about themselves. Meanwhile, the candidates themselves, desperate to catch our attention, raise obscene amounts of money in return for goodness knows what secret promises. But we citizens behave no better than our politicians. We squabble over our rights and ignore our obligations. We believe the function of government is to give us the goodies we desire. We ignore the organizations that make civil society function. We do not vote in the local elections that affect our daily lives far more than the contests over the Congress and the Presidency that occupy our attention. We do not know the names of our city council members. (We do not even know the names of our neighbors.)

In short, we Americans behave as though we can no longer recall what sacrifices freedom demands or why they are important. Surrounded by unparalleled wealth and power, the envy of the world, we are indulging in an act of national forgetting that is turning us into the barbarians Erasmus worried about.

It is not too late, however, to rediscover civility and thus to preserve both our humanity and our civilization. The purpose of this book is to defend the ideal of civility and to propose a path toward restoring it to its vital status as a central feature of our republic. As we prepare to enter a new century, the role of the student of civility is not to call for a return to a mythical Golden Age, but to press for a reconstructed civility that preserves what is highest and best in our traditions of acceptable behavior, demands of us that we rein in our desires, and yet at the same time avoids the repressive results of our traditions at their worst.

The key to reconstructing civility, I shall argue, is for all of us to learn anew the virtue of acting with love toward our neighbors. Love of neighbor has long been a tenet of Judaism and Christianity, and a revival of civility in America will require a revival of all that is best in religion as a force in our public life. Only religion possesses the majesty, the power, and the sacred language to teach all of us, the religious and the secular, the genuine appreciation for each other on which a successful civility must rest. Critics who insist that religion is a danger to civility are misreading both America and religion—and generally have no better ideas. The current level of incivility is morally intolerable. And it is getting worse. Without the aid of the nation's religious traditions, we will continue our slide away from a world in which we are able to discipline our desires and toward a world in which the only values that matter are the selfish and acquisitive values of politics and the market.

. . . .

Let me offer the reader a small map of where this journey will take us. After defending the concept of civility against its recent debunkers, the first part of the book considers the nature of civility and incivility and traces some of the causes, and history, of the crisis. Part one concludes with the suggestion that the beginning of an answer might be found in the religious concepts of awe and sacrifice. Part two examines various ways in which our incivility is reflected in, and reinforced by, our language and our culture and explains how a recovery of a sacrificial ethic might help the project of recivilizing ourselves. Part three explains the role of the family and religion in resolving the crisis—although not, perhaps, in the ways that the reader might expect. The book concludes with a summary of the basic rules of civility that I call (inspired by Alexis de Tocqueville) "The Etiquette of Democracy."

The reader will quickly note that there is no chapter devoted to either politics or the media—two of the favorite targets of incivility bashers. But as will quickly become apparent, both are parts of just about every story I tell. Politics matters because a democracy rests on self-governance; the mass media matter because their words and images so saturate our lives. In both cases, powerful institutions are providing all of us with models of public behavior and conversation; and behavior and conversation, as they were in the time of Erasmus and in the manners-mad nineteenth century, remain our only tools for distinguishing ourselves from other animals. And distinguishing ourselves from other animals—or, if you prefer, displaying our humanity—is what civility is all about.

2

· · · · · · · · · · · ·

Do Manners Matter?

IN MARCH 1997, amid great fanfare, members of our two great political parties converged on a conference center in Hershey, Pennsylvania, for what was billed as the Bipartisan Congressional Retreat. The retreat's stated purpose was to "seek a greater degree of civility, mutual respect and, when possible, bipartisanship among Members of the House of Representatives in order to foster an environment in which vigorous debate and mutual respect can coexist."[1] Representative Ray LaHood, an Illinois Republican who was one of the retreat's organizers, suggested that if members could "get to know one another" better, they would be able to work out their differences with greater civility.[2]

This instinct conforms to the teaching of both social science and common experience: we are less likely to be rude to those we know well.[3] Much of the nation's incivility crisis grows from our inability to get along—especially with political opponents. In short, the Bipartisan Congressional Retreat was so obviously a good idea that the tragedy is that some members scoffed instead and chose not to attend.* For example, Republican Joel Hefley of Colorado called it "[t]he dumbest idea I've ever heard," and Democrat David Obey of Wisconsin gibed, "You can go to Hershey 50 times and it's not going to make a difference." Both men invoked the other party's behavior to justify their dismissal of the retreat.[4] Stripped of verbal fillips, however, the objections came down to this: there is no need to be civil with those on the other side.

---

* I should here disclose that the retreat, which was funded by The Pew Charitable Trusts, was staffed by the Aspen Institute, of whose board I am a member.

This embarrassing idea suddenly has a good deal of political currency. In fact, in case you missed it, we are in the midst of an anticivility backlash. The onslaught of books explaining precisely why we are all so mean to each other and just how to fix it (see chapter 1) is suddenly being met by an army of articles contending that the whole civility thing is overblown, maybe even a distraction from more important societal business at hand.

Some critics have quietly cautioned that an overemphasis on civility-as-manners can obscure the importance of civility-as-community. This prudent position has lately been espoused, for example, by the political philosopher Michael Sandel[5] and the syndicated columnist Ellen Goodman.[6] Others, like the social critic Gertrude Himmelfarb, have warned of the costs of civility untempered by morality.[7] But others go much further, implying, and occasionally even stating, that the calls for civility are somehow sinister.

A few years ago, a very smart law professor, commenting on some trivial but bitter faculty dispute at one of the nation's finest schools, opined that we should make no effort to be polite to one another when we disagree—that our good manners simply mask the "real" issues. At the time, his view seemed rather eccentric, not to say uncivil. But today he might be more mainstream than we would like to think.

Take Benjamin DeMott's much-discussed 1996 essay in *The Nation*, revealingly titled "Seduced by Civility," in which he warns that too much civility might mask deep social conflict. Civility, says DeMott, is how people in power avoid criticism, or even turn it back on the critic. Civility, he tells us, is what slaveholders called for when abolitionists marched. The key, for DeMott, is accurate interpretation of behavior. Are people rude to each other? They are trying to send a message to those in authority. Do they refuse to participate in community? They are refusing to acknowledge the authority structures of the community. In fact, whatever people do that is uncivil, DeMott seems to think, should be construed as a form of dissent. We are not so much rude as disenfranchised. So he ends the piece with an italicized call to arms: *"And when you're in an argument with a thug, there are things much more important than civility."*[8] Evidently, as long as a single baby goes hungry, we really have no excuse for worrying about whether we are too rude to each other.[9]

And then there is the syndicated talk show host Michael Reagan, son of the former President, who announced not long after the congressional retreat that he was leaving the Republican Party because the revolution his father led had been allowed to die, "sacrificed on the altar of civility." It is not possible to make big changes, Reagan argued in an essay in *USA Today*, "without encountering resistance, which in turn hurts civility." Calls for civility, Reagan insisted, divert attention from the Republican abandonment of positions he thought vital to hold. What really mattered was not who was more civil, but who won the war: "After all, revolutions aren't made without ruffling feathers, and revolutionaries aren't renowned for their etiquette."[10] Benjamin DeMott could not have put it better.

Or consider the words of the columnist Maureen Dowd, who seems distressed by President Clinton's call for a more civil Washington. Clinton, speaking at the National Prayer Breakfast in February 1997, proposed that we "rid ourselves of this toxic atmosphere of cynicism." Dowd offered a sharp response in the *New York Times*: "The President does not grasp that disagreement, even intense and passionate disagreement, is a noble and necessary condition of democratic life." Perhaps recognizing that this sensible sentiment was not quite germane to the President's point, Dowd went further: "When political philosophies and political programs collide, civility can be a kind of hypocrisy."[11]

Let us consider Dowd's argument first. To the extent that she is asking our politicians not to be thin-skinned, she has a point. We should not try to run our politics without *any* insults or personal attacks. In a democracy, as the sociologist Charles P. Flynn points out in his book *Insult and Society*, gibes directed at political leaders actually serve important functions. For one thing, they symbolize our love of liberty: "Freedom to insult one's political opponents is an indispensable democratic privilege"—and one not available in many parts of the world. Thus, we may not always like to hear the attacks by one candidate on another, and we may believe that they distort healthy debate; but we should also be grateful to live in a country where no candidate is officially punished for insulting another.

Flynn also points to a second, equally important function served by insults directed at political leaders. Insults, he argues, "provide a check to those in power who may be tempted to think of themselves in grandiose terms, above the rest of humanity and hence not subject to insults."[12] His tantalizing example is Richard Nixon, who, when he did not like what the press was saying about him, simply stopped reading or listening. Nixon's embittered isolation is very old news, but, if Flynn is right, political leaders who want to avoid Nixon's fate may have learned the wrong lessons. It is not uncommon nowadays for politicians, when asked by reporters about one attack or another, to say something that amounts to "I never read that stuff." An understandable human response but, as Flynn points out, those who hide from other people's insults may in time come to believe themselves "above the rest of humanity."

Plainly, we neither want nor need such arrogant leaders, but we must not encourage gratuitous insult simply to drive the point home. That would be like going out and burning American flags simply because we have the constitutional right to do it, raising the level of social tension for no good reason. Dowd is dead right in proclaiming that democracy demands passionate disagreement, for a nation where everybody agrees is not a nation of civility but a nation withered of diversity, waiting to die.[13] She is dead wrong, however, in proposing that civility in pressing one's passionate cause is ever a form of hypocrisy. Civility, as we have already seen, is the set of sacrifices we make for the sake of our common journey with others, and out of love and respect for the very idea that there *are* others. When we are civil, we are not pretending to like those we actually despise; we are not pretending to hold any attitude toward them, except that we accept and value them as every bit our equals before God. The duty to love our neighbors is a precept of both the Christian and Jewish traditions, and the duty is not lessened because we happen to think our neighbor is wrong about a few things.

The fact that we Americans style ourselves a democracy, and call on the world to adopt our model, only makes the message more urgent. As the British historian Andrew St. George has pointed out, democracy itself "can be seen not only as a type of government but as a system of manners, a form of social life."[14] Our democratic commitments, whether to liberty, equality, due process, or perhaps simple respect for the election returns, may all be seen as rules of etiquette, behaviors that are necessary to allow us to travel in democratic peace with our fellow passengers. And we already saw in chapter 1 an important way in which our "form of social life" differentiates us from other animals: we humans, to call ourselves civilized, must have reasons for what we do, reasons apart from mere desire or impulse or even need. Alone of God's creation, we humans are able to apply the test of morality to our actions, and civility calls us to do so. For democracy without civility is like dieting without discipline: we may call ourselves careful eaters, but we know in our souls that we are gluttons.

Consider the mass protest wing of the civil rights movement. The true genius of Martin Luther King, Jr., was not in his ability to articulate the pain of an oppressed people—many other preachers did so, with as much passion and as much power—but in his ability to inspire those very people to be loving and civil in their dissent. This was the antithesis of hypocrisy: it was an act of high principle. The civil rights movement wanted to expand American democracy, not destroy it, and King understood that uncivil dialogue serves no democratic function. Democracy demands dialogue, and dialogue flows from disagreement. But we can, and maybe must, be relentlessly partisan without being actively uncivil.[15] Indeed, the more passionate our certainty that we are right, the more urgent our need to practice the art of civility—otherwise, we make dialogue impossible, and the possibility of dialogue is the reason democracy values disagreement in the first place. If civil rights marchers, threatened with fire hoses, police dogs, terrorist bombs, and assassins' bullets, could be civil in their dissent against a system willing and ready to destroy them, it is laughable to suggest that the rest of us, facing far lesser tribulations, lack that capacity. For those who believe in dialogue, then, hypocrisy lies in the pretense that we can discuss our differences seriously without the aid of civility.

CIVILITY, EFFICIENCY, AND
THE SEMIOTICS OF THE FORK

. . . .

Civility, I believe, is a precondition of democratic dialogue. That alone would be adequate reason to value it, and, in the next chapter, we will try to gain a richer understanding of what truly civil dialogue entails. But before embarking on that journey, we might pause to consider other ways in which civility adds value to the better society we are struggling together through our differences to build. Consider, for instance, what some in our market-crazy era would see as the most basic question of all: Is civility efficient?

Many scholars have answered this question in the affirmative, offering essentially functional accounts of the rules of etiquette, defending their development as a sort of survivalism. After all, some form of manners, some expectation of how we ought to behave, is seen in every culture. James Q. Wilson, in *The Moral Sense*, argues that rules of etiquette are valuable "as a way of signaling the existence of self-control."[16] Proper attention to politesse eases our social interactions (as laboratory experiments bear out[17]) and in that respect alone may be better than the alternatives, even to those who do not particularly like it. Thus, the philosopher Charles Taylor, in his elegant book *Sources of the Self,* has this to say: "I can see quite well how it helps things along to say 'please' and 'sorry' in the right places—and I know how to throw in functional equivalents where I can't say these words—even though I set no great value on the whole practice, even admire those brave enough to flout it."[18]

Or take the historian Arthur Schlesinger's amusing chronicle of etiquette in America, *Learning How to Behave*, published just after the Second World War. After tracing the rules of manners through two centuries, Schlesinger concluded with a sudden leap into the dangerous but optimistic present of 1946. Good manners, it turned out, were the key to reducing friction in an increasingly diverse America. Apart from the link forged by common language, Schlesinger wrote, the constantly mobile American population "carried no better letter of introduction than their adherence to common precepts of courtesy."[19]

Other historians have reached similar conclusions, but nobody has yet managed to refute Norbert Elias's witty explanation of the inefficiency of the fork.* Elias, a Swiss sociologist, published his masterwork, *The Civilizing Process*, in 1939.[20] Since the translation of its two volumes into English in 1978 and 1982, the book has become the standard reference for students of civility. Elias was the first to try to set the development of manners against larger trends in social history. In particular, he helped resolve the puzzle over why, in the seventeenth and eighteenth centuries, human beings who for millennia had urinated and defecated in the street or even at the dinner table, passed gas or burped or spit whenever the urge happened to strike, and eaten nearly everything with their fingers, suddenly began to worry about appearances. The answer to this question, Elias suggested, lay in recalling some of the other habits that people began to break at about the same time: killing on impulse, for example, or torturing and maiming over small disagreements. All of this, Elias argued, was part of a larger trend toward controlling the appetites of the body—a development that became necessary as power, particularly the right to use violence, was increasingly centered in the state. If the idea of the nation-state was to survive, individuals had to cooperate by restraining some of their impulses. The result was the evolution of a set of rules for the expression of everything from anger to sexual desire. Membership in the community—the letter of introduction, in Schlesinger's phrase—was symbolized by the willingness to abide by those rules, even when one's needs or wants led in a different direction.

Fair enough, if we want to know why dueling fell into disfavor and why bathrooms grew doors: but what about the fork? Erasmus of Rotterdam had tried as early as the sixteenth century to promote eating with the fork in a world that used knives and hands. But few listened, because eating with the fingers was easier. Even in the early nineteenth century, Americans still dismissed the fork as a foppish indulgence of the decadent Continental upper classes. As the historian John F. Kasson has pointed out, critics at first derided the practice—like "eating soup with a knitting needle," scoffed one—and yet, by 1884, we find a newspaper mocking presidential

---

* Wilson discusses Elias but does not quite follow him to his conclusion.

candidate Grover Cleveland as an uncivilized diehard who continued to eat with only hands and a knife.[21] (A furious Cleveland denied the charge.)

So why did the fork triumph? Here we see the Elias wit at work. He argues that the fork serves no obvious useful purpose, and that its apparent utility is misleading. It does not help us eat more efficiently: the hands alone, or the hands aided by a knife, are far better adapted to the task. It does not help us avoid disease: that problem vanished when people shifted from the common plate to individual servings. It does help us to keep our hands clean, but that explanation is insufficient, because some very messy foods— butter-slavered muffins, greasy fried chicken—are routinely eaten with the hands. Besides, the cleanliness explanation does not tell us why it is important to keep *our own* food off our hands when we eat. After all, we have napkins to wipe them on.

And that, says Elias, is the point. Had we no forks, we would have far dirtier napkins. We have the history of the fork backward—the napkin, not the food, is the key. The fork did not develop in order to keep our hands clean. The fork developed to keep our napkins clean. And why in the world would we worry about keeping our napkins clean, Elias asks, given that they exist (don't they?) to help us keep our hands and mouths clean?

The answer, Elias suggests, is that napkins do not exist to keep our hands and mouths clean. Napkins are symbolic, not functional. They exist to remind us that we are clean—the implication being that other people, other places are not. If our napkin is soiled, it is no different from "a kitchen rag"—and who would want to eat surrounded by kitchen rags? Once upon a time, nobody cared about such things, not until the onset of luxury (first in the upper classes, then in the middle classes) provided the opportunity to be free of the less pleasant aspects of ordinary life. Ultimately, says Elias, the development of our rules for eating seems best understood as part of an "increasingly strong tendency to remove the distasteful from the sight of society."[22] It is no coincidence that the fork became socially required just as dining rooms began to appear in the homes of the middle class.

Once eating was separated from food preparation, the one attractive, the other not, the need for symbols to separate the two became pressing.* Thus, our etiquette for everything from how to carve meat (we no longer bring the whole animal to the table) to keeping our napkins clean (we do not want the table to look like the kitchen) rests on the same set of psychic concerns as averting our eyes from beggars and zoning "adult" bookstores out of our neighborhoods: there is an unpleasant side of life we do not want to see. Our manners help us to mask it.

So it may be that my colleague who defended campus incivility was right, in his analysis if not in his conclusions. Good manners do provide insulation against hard truths: Meat *does* come from dead animals. There *are* beggars. We *do* disagree. So not only are our rules of etiquette often inefficient; they sometimes render pieces of the real world invisible. Is that always and necessarily an argument against them? To see why the answer is no, let us return for a moment to the civil rights movement—for as the reader will shortly see, the connection between the great (fundamental human rights) and the small (basic manners) is at the heart of a proper understanding of civility.

CIVILITY AND PURIFICATION

. . . .

If I am angry at you for some wrong you have done me, I may choose to lose my temper or to keep it. If I keep my temper, I very likely will not say everything that is on my mind, and what I do say, I will say with less passion. Consequently, by holding in my temper when it yearns to roam free, I am masking part of the world from your view: there are hard truths about my emotional state that I will not reveal. I am making a sacrifice, denying myself the satisfaction of anger. And in so doing, I may be making the world better, not worse.

Again, consider the nonviolent protests of the Civil Rights Movement. The leaders of the Southern Christian Leadership Conference (SCLC) knew that the protests would be met with violence, because they were challenging a violently oppressive system.

---

* This analysis suggests that in the current era, with busy families once more eating in the kitchen rather than the dining room, table manners should be falling by the wayside. Everybody seems to think they are. If everybody is right, then Elias's theory seems to be surviving its latest test.

But they also knew that success would be found not through incivility, but through the display of moral courage. They were willing to behave better than their oppressors. And they understood that in order to move a nation, the protests had first to spark a dialogue—for it is through dialogue and decision that democracy advances. So they trained the protesters to remain civil and even loving in the face of repression. This process of purification, as it was known, involved both prayer and repeated reminders that the Biblical injunction to love our neighbors is not a command to love only the nice ones. Purification helped the protesters to see God even in those who oppressed them and offered the confidence to be firm in the pursuit of justice without losing the conviction that means as well as ends are proper subjects of moral judgment.[23]

Purification also allowed the protesters to see their goal more clearly. Unlike the purveyors of today's selfish rhetoric of rights, who freely admit that they are in the fight for the benefit of their constituencies, King saw the struggle for basic freedoms as redemptive—not simply for the marchers, but for all America. The frankly stated purpose of the Southern Christian Leadership Conference was "to save the soul of the nation." King emphasized that nonviolent resistance was intended not to defeat the opponent, but to convert him—that the target of protest was the very soul of the opponent. The historian Albert J. Raboteau has summarized King's reasoning in terms that the student of civility should at once find familiar, and reassuring:

> Nonviolence . . . is based upon the belief that acceptance of suffering is redemptive, because suffering can transform both the sufferer and the oppressor; it is based upon loving others regardless of worth or merit; it is based upon the realization that all human beings are interrelated; and it is grounded in the confidence that justice will, in the end, triumph over injustice.[24]

But nonviolent protest is not passive. It is not meant to be ignored . . . or even ignorable. It is intended, according to King, to bring to the surface tensions that the system is designed to obscure. Here, then, is a point that Benjamin DeMott gets right: sometimes a group that has been left out has to make noise before it will be allowed in.[25] The boycott in Montgomery, the March on Washington, the Easter march in Birmingham, all were a kind of noise, a demand to be heard that interrupted the ordinary daily business of the white Americans who were the intended audience. But all the noise was civil. Had it not been, as King understood, the audience might have been less inclined to listen. The moment might then have been lost.

Consider once more Arthur Schlesinger's argument, back in 1946, that we should understand our adherence to standards of civility not only as a vital social glue, but as the "letter of introduction" that assures strangers that we are after all one community, linked by a shared set of practices and beliefs. Such confidence will seem to many a modern reader a little bit quaint, perhaps even naive. That we live in uncourteous times is both a truism and actually true.

Yet King understood the importance of making sure that the protesters carried their letters of introduction along with their placards and their Bibles. The goal of the movement, after all, was to ensure that black Americans could become full participants in the democracy, not to tear it apart. Today's many dissatisfied citizens, of all colors and all classes, could do well to remember the SCLC's example, to carry always the letter of introduction—the willingness to abide by standards of civility that demonstrate respect for their fellow citizens. No matter what the cause, we should take care to bring the letter with us to every rally, to include it in every letter to the editor, to speak it aloud on every talk show.

The Civil Rights Movement, of course, had one advantage that today's movements often do not: the religious convictions of the marchers, King often argued, gave them the courage and the power to remain civil, to remain focused, to shun immoral means in the quest for moral ends.[26] Does this mean that faith is necessary to civility? The question may seem a peculiar one in an era when so many prominent intellectuals have concluded that faith is the enemy of civility. For example, the literary theorist Stanley Fish has recently argued that it is the basic feature of religion not to believe in the marketplace of ideas, but to try to shut it down.[27] The feminist writer Wendy Kaminer, proudly trumpeting her atheism, concludes that religious people consistently "demonize" those who do not believe in God.[28] The silent subtext of such arguments is that we would be a good deal better off—or, at least, a good deal more civil—if religion would simply disappear.

This scary proposition is not only wrong, but dangerous and undemocratic, for reasons we will visit in detail in chapter 14. For the moment, let me stake out a contrarian position: No, faith is not strictly *necessary* to civility: there are plenty of people who lack faith in God who are civil, and there are plenty of people who profess faith in God who are not.[29] At the same time, as I explain in subsequent chapters, I think it likely that only a resurgence in all that is best about religious faith will rescue civility in America, for there is no truer or more profound vision of equality than equality before God. As Richard Mouw has argued, the very yearning for God that characterizes religion "also makes us bold to join others in the larger human quest for a healthy public space."[30]

A life without faith is a life without the most powerful language of sacrifice and aspiration the human race has ever known. "[W]hen God is forgotten," warned the Second Vatican Council, "the creature itself grows unintelligible."[31] In the absence of God, we cease to understand ourselves, our purposes, our connection to the transcendent. In the Western religious traditions, faith in God provides a *justification* for the equality that liberal philosophy assumes and cherishes but is often unable to defend.[32] (It is no accident that the abolitionist movement, which preached love of neighbor, began in the churches.) In the absence of that language of loving sacrifice, that connection to the transcendent, civility, like any other moral principle, has no firm rock on which to stand. Civility that rests on the shifting sands of secular morality might topple with the next stiff political wind.

This might explain why, just three weeks after the Bipartisan Congressional Retreat in Hershey, there was a shoving match on the floor of the House. The shover was Texas Republican Tom DeLay, the minority whip, who was angry about charges by Democrats that lobbyists who were major contributors had written legislation in his office. The shovee was Wisconsin Democrat David Obey—the same David Obey whom we met earlier in this chapter scoffing at the civility-building retreat as a waste of time. The incident evidently arose when DeLay lost his temper after Obey brandished in his face a news article detailing the allegations that DeLay moments before had denied.[33]

DeLay attended the retreat. Obey skipped it. But even though Obey was plainly the provocateur in the incident, DeLay allowed himself to be provoked. So both men were arguably in the wrong.* All of which goes to show that reconstructing civility will take considerable time and effort. Words alone will not suffice. Promises alone will not suffice. Press conferences alone will not suffice. Only a commitment to be as excellent at the task of being civil as we try to be at so many other important aspects of life will make the slightest crack in the wall of incivility that divides us.

CLASS STRUGGLE, REDUX

. . . .

Oh, and what about Benjamin DeMott's argument that incivility is simply a part of the class struggle, the oppressed crying out for attention? The premise of his argument is necessarily that civility benefits only the ruling classes, that incivility does no great harm to those on the bottom. (If this is not DeMott's premise, his entire essay becomes a non sequitur.) This is an empirical claim, and a dubious one. My intuition, unlike DeMott's, is that the indignities of incivility are visited mainly on ordinary folk. True, powerful politicians and the very wealthy may have to bear the occasional verbal barrage, but they possess ample resources to return fire. Most of us do not. An acquitted criminal suspect whose good reputation is ruined by an uncivil, money-grubbing press has no recourse. The rudeness of a shopkeeper can do violence to the already shaky self-worth of a restless inner-city teenager. And it is not the elderly rich who suffer from our society's growing disrespect for the wisdom and privileges of age. For decades, good manners have been characterized as the oil that lubricates our everyday interactions, making society bearable, and for all that it may be mundane, the explanation carries the solid ring of intuitive truth: life is tough, but incivility makes it tougher.

As for DeMott's ruling classes, I imagine them hiding in their limousines and weekend homes, hearing only Debussy and seeing only stock prices crawling across their computer screens. They are

---

* There was *some* civility in the course of the incident. Due to the arcana of House rules, the Democrats were not allowed to impugn DeLay's character directly. But they plainly did all they could to impugn it indirectly.

less affected than the rest of us by our growing incivility, because they possess the means to shield themselves from it. But they sometimes benefit from it and are often its agents. Once we understand the link between civility and morality, it becomes plain why DeMott's ruling classes should be delighted if the nation is growing less civil: The same hyper-individualism, the same reluctance to discipline our acts with morality, the same refusal to acknowledge the equality of others before God, the same social indifference that allows some of us to be rude, allows others of us to be ungenerous.

Indeed, the teaching of social science is that incivility is generally used by those in power in order to preserve their power. Although it is true that the modern concept of civility originated among the European upper classes, a lack of civility turns out to be a powerful tool for enforcing class structures and can create strong pressures to conform. Charles Flynn points to the use of insult and other tools of incivility to maintain social stratification in areas as diverse as the Middle East, India, and the old American South. Even in such societies as ours, modern nations that pride themselves on a robust egalitarian inclusion, rudeness serves this stratifying function— although, as Flynn explains, more democratic societies tend to be more subtle in their incivility. For example, Americans tend to use jokes to signal to low-status workers just how low their status is.[34]

Unfortunately, Flynn's arguments again accord with experience. College professors, for example, like to joke that the dean does those things that the janitor finds beneath his dignity. What lesson does the joke teach, and to whom? The ultimate object of this joke is never the dean, whose authority is understood; the object is the janitor, whose status ("dignity") is chosen as the point of comparison precisely because the chuckling audience will perceive that status as an undesirable one. Nor are jokes the only incivility that low-status workers suffer. Dismissal from reality is another: quite often, high-status workers simply refuse to acknowledge that low-status workers exist.[35] I am constantly amazed, and constantly depressed, by the number of my professedly egalitarian colleagues at Yale who do not seem to know the names of the people who clean their offices, despite encountering them several times a week for many years. I doubt that the custodial staff at Yale believes that civility is for the benefit of the well-to-do.

The idea that good manners are a plot of the ruling class may be ahistorical as well. Perhaps DeMott has been misled by the European experience. In Europe, with a well-defined class structure, rules of etiquette have often served a function of social exclusion. But in the United States, as the historian Andrew St. George notes, the rules of etiquette have been linked to an ideal of democratic inclusion.[36] In the nineteenth century, the burning desire of America's rising middle class to work out rules on how to treat others generated an explosion of helpful publications.[37] The books on manners that resulted were often of an almost radically egalitarian turn. Proper behavior was widely considered a sign of success: if you had good manners, you must have made it. Yet Americans believed in social mobility, and the message of the etiquette books, as the literary theorist Christopher Clausen has pointed out, was that anybody could follow the rules. And if anybody could follow the rules—if proper etiquette belonged to no particular class—then anybody could make it.[38] (In a peculiar reversal of political roles as the twentieth century draws to a close, it is said to be conservative to suggest that anybody can succeed, no matter what his or her starting place in life, which was the message of the radicals a century ago; and it is said to be liberal to argue that social circumstances hold some people back, the claim of class-conscious conservatives of the 1800s.)

Writers on etiquette were more conscious then than now that their message was at least quasi-moral, that the notion of proper and improper behavior implied a notion of right and wrong.[39] This idea, too, goes back to Erasmus of Rotterdam, who quite earnestly believed that adoption of his proposals on proper manners would lead Europe away from barbarism and toward civilization. So when Erasmus urged, for example, that the young be taught how to talk to prostitutes (and how not to), he wrote in a world in which prostitutes were a common part of the scenery: young people encountered them daily. His point was that boys had to learn to avoid their wiles, lest they fall into sin. He advocated eating with forks, but also pacifism and giving to the poor, and all for the same reason: the ability to discipline our desires, whether for food or violence or money, was all that separated us from evil.

How times have changed. We do not nowadays look to Miss Manners or Emily Post for guidance on our ethics; we want them to tell us only which fork to use and how to tell invited guests that the wedding is off. It may be, however, that Erasmus, along with the nineteenth-century writers on civility, knew a secret that we have forgotten, or at least suppressed. Perhaps good manners *are* a moral issue; perhaps how we treat other people *does* matter; and, if so, then following rules that require us to treat other people with genuine respect surely is morally superior to not following them. As Ellen Goodman has written, "'manners are about treating others as if they matter."⁴⁰ So perhaps civility, very far from being a sideshow in our judgments about right and wrong, should be very close to the main event. That is a possibility—no, a likelihood— that shall occupy us for most of the rest of this book.

Still, those who find DeMott's approach attractive might offer a last objection: It is morally wrong to deny a just claim because of the incivility with which the claim is pressed. This sentiment, even if true, is beside the point. Doing the right thing is a duty, but it is also a choice. Often it has a cost. Therefore, when we ask others to choose to do justice, we may also be asking them to choose to sacrifice for the sake of justice. The rich man would prefer to keep his money. The segregationist would prefer to go on segregating. We are asking them to yield their own preferences for a larger good. Once more, the civil rights movement provides both the example and the truth: Civil dialogue requires us to sacrifice the opportunity to display our own self-righteous anger, even when we have good reason to be angry. It requires us to see God in those who would rather not see us at all.

Indeed, the entire project of envisioning civility as a set of manners for democracy supposes a set of duties toward *all* our fellow citizens. The concept of duty, of course, supposes an obligation to do a thing we may not want to do; that is, the duties we owe each other do not depend on our desires. We need to learn anew a simple inequality: the question of how we *should* treat our fellow citizens is independent of the question of how we *feel like* treating them.

Throughout the book, I discuss the duties civility imposes. Here we see the first and most basic among them:

> *Our duty to be civil toward others does not depend on whether we like them or not.*

This may seem to be a burden. But if we are unwilling to make even these relatively small sacrifices in pressing our case—if we are unwilling to be civil—we can hardly expect others to make the larger sacrifices that justice so often demands.

HOW MANNERS CAN STILL MATTER

. . . .

To celebrate good manners, we need not, always, celebrate them in their traditional forms, but we do need to honor traditions sufficiently to search them for any deeper truths they may teach. Consider, for example, the old rules about men holding open doors for women and giving women their seats on a bus. Critics have scorned the rules as sexist. And, indeed, they do reinforce images of women as weak and in need of protection, suggesting woman-as-eternal-victim (which some say is true of today's arguments against pornography). But the student of civility should quickly see the deeper truth: holding open a door is a sign of respect, not of superiority. Why should we not all hold open doors for everyone else? As for giving up a seat on a bus, we can reject the image of women as needing seats more than men and still recognize that some people need seats more than others. And so we should still yield our seats to the infirm, to the elderly, to people of any age or sex who are weighed down with packages or carrying babies. Why? Because, at that moment, their comfort matters more than ours.*

We can follow this analysis—and should—with many of the traditional rules. Some have already been discarded, and with good reason. No great moral truth lies beneath the old requirement that gentlemen keep their heads covered in public—a practice, it is said, that the hatless President John F. Kennedy helped to kill—or the rule that a lady does not wear pants in public, a rule that survived, although it is easy to forget the fact, into the 1960s. But these rules have already died. One task of the student of civility, convinced that manners matter, is to discover which rules are worth saving or resurrecting, and in what form. The Victorians

---

* The reader may wonder whether this implies that the charitable impulse is itself a part of civility. As we shall see, the answer is yes.

taught, for instance, that it is important in conversation to listen attentively to what others say before taking our own turn to speak. That rule has been lost—especially on television!—but the student of civility should be part of the continuing efforts to revive it.

In the course of our investigation, we will consider rules of etiquette at the table but also in politics; rules for how we treat the members of our families, but also those with whom we work; rules of good manners on the roadway, but also on the information superhighway. The emphasis will be on the practical, on implementing civility in everyday life. Of these tiny, thoughtful sacrifices is an entire structure of civility ultimately constructed.

3

. . . .

The Death of the Golden Age

So where did all the civility go? And when? I have read all the
theories, the learned commentators who blame our incivility on
everything from the decline of religion to the rise of the television,
from our geographic mobility to the end of the Cold War.
Although many of these theories seem to me to hold bits and
pieces of the truth, they nevertheless are nibbling around the
edges. As I grope for a thicker, more filling plate of reasons, I keep
coming back to my long-standing hunch that it all began to go bad
around 1965, when, as somebody said, everything seemed to happen at once. That was the year that America, quite suddenly,
became postmodern. Many venerable American traditions—some
wonderful, some horrible—all withered at the same time. And
what has that to do with civility? Let us look and see.

LEVITTOWN, THE YANKEES, AND
OTHER SINGULAR FACTS

. . . .

The most salient fact about 1965 is that the New York Yankee baseball dynasty collapsed. This is a matter of no small significance. In
the preceding fifteen years—that is, since the start of the 1950s—
the Yankees had been to the World Series an astonishing thirteen
times. The team did it by being bigger and richer and smarter than
anybody else. The Yankees did not pay their players as much as
some teams did, and, as David Halberstam reports in his wonder-

38

ful book *October 1964*, they were not very nice to their players either, evidently believing that they were lucky to be Yankees. For example, they rarely allowed even their best pitchers to play often enough to win the twenty games a year expected of the top stars, especially when they were young. The Yankee view was that stardom was a reward for years of faithful service—and, besides, star players cost more money at salary negotiation time. The Yankees could get away with such shenanigans because they were . . . well, the Yankees.

And that was the point. Throughout the fifties and into the early sixties, the Yankees were solid, predictable, as thoroughly a part of the known and shared experience of being America as Ed Sullivan, the automobile, the Pledge of Allegiance, and the two-party system. America was like that, a singular experience, utterly known. A basic tenet of American life was that we were constantly celebrating our own uniqueness. The nation saw itself as special in the eyes of God, and that specialness explained its remarkable industrial expansion, its undefeated record in war (also a dynasty of a sort), and the enviable durability of its much-copied Constitution, then rushing toward its second centennial.

Part of this celebration of America was the deep belief that the nation could never place its moral foot wrong—not for more than a very short time. Racial segregation was accepted because it was the way America had always done business. There was one unique American race, and then there were other people, living here almost by accident, not yet entitled to all the benefits the nation offered to white people. There was a single American religion—an acutely nationalistic form of Protestant Christianity—and although Roman Catholics and Jews were welcome on the nation's shores, if their children attended the nation's public schools, they recited Protestant prayers. They learned Protestant values, described as American values, which was believed to be not a subterfuge but the simple truth. And if Catholic or Jewish parents chose to avoid this religious indoctrination by sending their children to private religious schools, they could not ask Protestant America for help—they had to scrape up the cash themselves. After all, America stood for separation of church and state.

America was also the world's greatest industrial power. The

nation produced almost everything it consumed, with plenty left over for export. Americans could build anything. President John Kennedy promised there would be a man on the moon before the end of the decade. After Kennedy was murdered, his successor, Lyndon Johnson, renewed the pledge, and Johnson's successor, Richard Nixon, kept it. General Electric in those days adopted a slogan awash in the confidence of the age: THE MERELY DIFFICULT WE DO AT ONCE. THE IMPOSSIBLE TAKES A LITTLE LONGER. Corporations, tamed a bit by the New Deal, were still on the side of the angels. Only a few Reds thought corporate power was bad, and the McCarthy era had reminded the nation that Communists were not genuine Americans, not really part of the singular experience. In 1953 President Eisenhower nominated Charles E. "Engine Charlie" Wilson, the head of General Motors, to serve as secretary of defense. Wilson was asked during his confirmation hearings what he would do were a situation to arise in which the national interest conflicted with the interest of GM shareholders. Engine Charlie sat there in his dark suit and white shirt and narrow tie and uttered the frequently misquoted words that would quickly become far more famous than he was: "I cannot conceive of one because for years I thought what was good for our country was good for General Motors, and vice versa. The difference did not exist."

Maybe he was even right. Because suddenly the automobile *was* America. The nation paved roads that had been dirt for a century and built an elaborate interstate highway system from scratch. Gasoline cost almost nothing and was sold, it seemed, on every corner; oil companies had to offer prizes to get people to stop in. Detroit turned out gigantic cars with chrome and fins and fantastically shaped headlights. The middle class aspired to Cadillacs and Lincolns. The automobile revealed a reckless side to the American character. Tens of thousands of people died every year on the exciting new roads. On weekends, teenagers borrowed the car to go to the drive-ins, where they watched the good guys win. Their rebellion consisted largely of listening to rock-and-roll on the radio that, in those days, picked up only AM stations, as bewildered parents shook their heads.

Yet there was still only one American experience. The culture was still built around the idea of single, unimpeachable moral and aesthetic truths. Politics was scarcely necessary because everything was so solid. A little-known evangelist named Jerry Falwell gave a sermon warning the faithful to avoid the contagion of politics. A little-known sociologist named Daniel Bell boldly declared the end of ideology. Everybody wanted the same things, and the market produced them. All over the country, real estate developers were aping the Levittown model: a planned community with shops and schools and churches in the middle and houses, row upon row of nearly identical houses, spreading in broad circles like ripples from that central commercial stone. The typical monthly mortgage payment was about sixty dollars. As the developer William Levitt explained, there was a simple ideology behind the Levittown idea: "No man who owns his own house and lot can be a Communist."

The planned community was a natural outgrowth of the nation's search for shared experience. So, of course, the aesthetics mattered: nobody would sell a house in a white neighborhood to a black family. (In Levittown, restrictive covenants forbade such unneighborly conduct as selling to members of the wrong race.) Norman Rockwell was the style of the day: America was white parents in church with their cherubic children. Television proved it. There were three television networks, and they were interchangeable: they hired different stars and announcers, they broadcast different shows, but they all promoted the same core of American values. All the programs were alike. Everybody was white. The father (who often went to a mystical place called "the office" during the day) never raised his voice. He was kindly but firm. The mother was never employed outside the home, but she wore a dress every day. The children never faced any crisis more complicated than the death of a favorite goldfish. Neighbors walked freely in and out of each other's houses. Doors were unlocked because there was no crime, not on television, except for the crime-fighting shows and the endless stream of Westerns, none of which betrayed a trace of moral ambiguity. The criminals were always wicked, and they were always caught or killed.

Everybody wanted to come to America. Then as now there were quotas on immigrants, but still they came by the hundreds of thousands, motivated by another singular American truth: this was the land of opportunity. Great fortunes could be made. Poverty was an irrelevant detail. Discrimination was an irrelevant detail. Besides, things were worse at home. And everybody who came to America seemed to wind up at the ballpark. The fans turned out in droves. They supported their teams, even the losing teams: for several years in New York, the miserable New York Mets outdrew the champion Yankees. The Mets were deemed lovable losers, and fans went to the park for the sheer fun of watching. But they had no illusion that their pathetic team would suddenly win. The same teams always seemed to be the champions. In the mid–1960s, each professional sport was dominated by a single team that seemed to win all the time: the Yankees in baseball, the Green Bay Packers in football, the Boston Celtics in basketball, the Montreal Canadiens in hockey. Even in sports, then, the American experience was of life as essentially predictable, marked by solid, eternal verities. The nation valued stability. Members of Congress served forever. Divorces were scandalous. People worked for the same corporation until they retired or died. The same was true of baseball players, at least the great stars: they usually spent their careers with the teams that first signed them. A player like Mickey Mantle or Willie Mays might stay with his team for two decades. Fans could form an almost personal bond with the team: it was the *players* they loved, win or lose.

And the citizens loved their undefeated national team, the military, too. Soldiers were heroes. There were parades and prayers on Memorial Day and Veterans Day. Candidates for office were expected to promise to be tough on communism, for the Cold War was another solid and eternal American truth. The nation took pride in owning more and better missiles and warheads than anybody else. President Kennedy brought the nation to the brink of war as he outbluffed the Soviet leader Nikita Khrushchev, who had tried to sneak atomic weapons into Cuba. The nation held its collective breath until Khrushchev blinked. But there were no campus protests. Young people loved Kennedy. They loved their schools as well. Observers found the campuses placid, the students serious. A survey at one university during the 1950s revealed that the top concern of students was finding a place to park their cars.[1]

People knew what was expected of them. There were duties and obligations and roles, and all of society's institutions worked together to enforce them. In the public schools, boys took wood shop and girls took home economics. Feminists did not exist. Homosexuals did not exist. Muslims did not exist. But John Wayne did. Wayne was more symbol than hero: men were raised to emulate him, to value being large and tough, kind to women and children, willing to kill in the cause of justice, although with regret.[2] The role of women was different. A federal court contemptuously dismissed a lawsuit challenging the all-male draft. The armed forces, wrote the judge, were allowed to "follow the teachings of history" and limit combat to men while women "keep the home fires burning."[3]

Then in the fall of 1964, an aging Yankee team lost the World Series to the St. Louis Cardinals. The following summer, the team lost more games than it won for the first time in recent memory, and the era of singular truths came to an end. The era had been battered in recent years anyway. In 1962 and 1963, the Supreme Court struck down spoken classroom prayers as unconstitutional, whether written by the state or chosen by the student.[4] It turned out that there was not just a single American religion. Nor, it became clear, a single American race. Grudgingly, a few Southern school districts were carrying out the Supreme Court's desegregation orders. Americans were growing tired of watching peaceful marchers beaten by police, bitten by their dogs, spat upon by the crowds. The Congress, prodded by President Johnson, religious leaders, and a chorus of editorial opinion, enacted the Civil Rights Act of 1964, banning discrimination on the basis of race in employment, in public accommodations, and in programs receiving federal funds. The St. Louis baseball team that ended Yankee dominance was led by its black stars—Bob Gibson, Bill White, Lou Brock, and Curt Flood—whereas the Yankees, whose racist personnel policies are painstakingly detailed by Mr. Halberstam, were one of the very last teams to integrate. Two years later, a team with five black starters won the college basketball championship, which had never happened before, by defeating another racist dynasty, Kentucky, which had won many championships but had never had a black player. The first black pilot entered the astronaut corps at around this time, and everybody knew that Johnson was awaiting the right moment to put his old friend Thurgood Marshall on the Supreme Court. And so another singularity of the

American experience, officially defined and protected racial privilege, began to disappear.

Then the Vietnam War suddenly widened. By 1968 an astonishing 525,000 American troops would be fighting there. The military draft was all at once controversial. This was a generation that had grown up with all the luxury that the amazing surplus of a mature industrial capitalist economy could provide. Now they were being asked to go off and die in a small country for an ideal that many did not think their country believed in. We were fighting for democracy in Asia, but we were not practicing it at home, not for Americans who happened to be black. So this same generation, raised amidst plenty, was the first in our history to be able to look at those with less and ask whether some fundamental flaw in the system might exist. Some became Marxists, because Marxism claimed to know what the flaw was. Some marched with Dr. King, because King insisted that the flaw could be fixed. Some went to Canada, because they ran out of ideas. Some wangled deferments, because their parents were rich.[5] But most of those who were called went off to fight, because that was what their country, with all its imperfections, asked them to do. So now there was plurality, there were multiple meanings, more than one way to understand America.

Young people were already restless. In 1964 a student named Mario Savio challenged a variety of restrictions at the University of California and sparked the Free Speech Movement, which changed the campuses forever (or at least for three decades). Students became aware of themselves as a force. They marched for peace and for civil rights. They discovered psychedelic drugs. They decided that convention was bad, tradition was the problem; they defied authority as repressive. They took over buildings. These students actually were a small minority of the young, but the press treated them as representative. They had their own vision, or visions. And some adults were on their side. Sympathetic professors canceled classes whenever students declared a strike. In New York City, Leonard Bernstein gave a party for the Black Panthers. Unknowingly, they set the stage for Richard Nixon, and even for Ronald Reagan, because, as the journalist E. J. Dionne has pointed out, Republicans have been running against the sixties ever since, even the ones who enjoyed the decade when it was happening.[6]

The Republican rise was unexpected. In the 1964 presidential election, Democrat Lyndon Johnson had brushed aside Republican Barry Goldwater with almost contemptuous ease, the Democrats held firm control of the Congress, and people began to wonder if the G.O.P. was dead. Johnson, strategist of the 1964 Civil Rights Act and apostle of the Great Society, ran as the candidate of peace, even though the war he kept expanding would drive him from office with what he considered his life's work of racial reconciliation yet undone. If Johnson was the candidate of change, Goldwater represented the status quo: Levittown, big business, and segregation. That was the way he was painted by the Democrats. Goldwater was a rich man. He knew nothing of poverty and hunger, unlike Johnson, who owned nothing, although his wife owned a chain of television stations. This was the campaign in which the Democrats invented the negative television ad, suggesting that Goldwater would start a nuclear war. People seemed to believe it, although the nuclear arms buildup began life as a Democratic program, not a Republican one. But truth was not the point. The message was all that mattered. There was no clarity. After decades of certainty, these were unclear times. Taxes were embarrassingly high, but the economy chugged along without a hitch. The Supreme Court decided that Southern cities could close swimming pools instead of integrating them.[7] But not schools.[8] In Stockholm, the Reverend Martin Luther King, Jr., was awarded the Nobel Peace Prize. In Washington, J. Edgar Hoover, director of the Federal Bureau of Investigation, decided that King was the most dangerous black man in America and began an illegal campaign to discredit him. Evidence was planted. Rules were broken. But elsewhere America was busily deciding that rules were repressive. Rules were the enemy. Public schools began to abandon the tracking systems they had used since the dawn of intelligence testing in the early years of the century. They abandoned explicit racial segregation. And corporal punishment. And dress codes.

Fairness was in vogue. Tests were not fair. Rules were not fair. Life was not fair. And America was not sure any longer that it could fix everything. In 1968 Lyndon Johnson decided not to seek reelection. Nobel Laureate King was assassinated, and the cities burned. Two months later, Robert Kennedy was assassinated, and the nation wept. As riots raged around its Chicago convention that summer, the Democratic Party nearly committed suicide. (It would go on to lose five of the next six presidential elections.) Two years later, National Guard troops opened fire on unarmed demonstrators at Kent State, killing four of them.

This was not the way our team, our winning, undefeated military team, was supposed to behave. Any more than Chicago was the way our police were supposed to behave. So now it was harder to find America. All at once people worried about inflation. Racial integration proved less popular than supporters had hoped. Violent crime suddenly surged. Social scientists offered explanations. Race riots flared. Social scientists offered more explanations. White families escaped to the suburbs, where they built beautiful new schools for their children, who then went off to the best colleges. But young people no longer wanted to learn the eternal verities. They were demanding changes on campus. Many of the changes involved sex. The students wanted coed housing and an end to parietal rules. They wanted colleges to distribute birth control pills. They wanted to revamp the curriculum: the old ways were *not* the best. Not on campus and not anyplace else. Sports stars were suddenly brash and talked back to their coaches. *Peyton Place* hit the best-seller list. Just a few years earlier, Betty Friedan had published *The Feminine Mystique*. Both sex and sexism were suddenly subjects about which it was polite to talk. Newspapers, the repository of reality conceived as a set of unchangeable words, ran into an unexpected wall, the popularity of television, which conceives reality as a series of ever-changing images crying out for commentary, and began a decline that has continued unimpeded to this day. Nothing seemed quite predictable any longer. America's confidence was shaken. An Apollo spacecraft burned on the launch pad with three astronauts inside. A federal judge named Royce Savage dismissed an antitrust case against Gulf Oil and resigned a couple of years later to become . . . general counsel of Gulf Oil.[9] The event was a perfect segue to the Great Society, which, momentarily triumphant, decreed that it was time to share at least a little of the nation's wealth: it was not right that a few people and corporations seemed to own everything. Not when so many were poor. The rest of the nation had an obligation to help.

The sports world replicated the Great Society model. One of the reasons the Yankee dynasty ended was that the other owners adopted rules making it harder for a few rich teams to hold on to all the good players. The rich had an obligation to help those less well off. This was the beginning of an idea that today dominates professional sports, the idea of parity, which was best captured in a line attributed to Pete Rozelle, who built the National Football League into the television powerhouse it is today: "On any given Sunday, any team can beat any other team." This is, actually, a rather postmodern idea, for it holds that life is not predictable. There is no singular experience. Anybody can lose, anybody can win. The verities vanish, and unambiguous truths are replaced by the vagaries of relativistic experience. Sports becomes literature: everything depends on context.

And the players! No longer vassals, they are nowadays bigger than their teams, but smaller than the heroes they were. They move around at will, signing with whomever bids the most money for their services. This doubtless adds to both the freedom and the income of players, but it also changes the very concept of *player*— not a long-time friend with whom a fan who has never met him can fantasize a personal relationship, but an employee, to be rewarded if his contributions merit or dismissed if he messes up too often. The solid, predictable, knowable associations of a player with a team and a city yield to a relativistic experience, altering in turn the nature (although evidently not the passion) of fan interest. There are no more lovable losers; fans no longer feel a personal connection to the players. Instead, the fans care only about the team as an entity, about the bottom line, which is to say, whether the team wins or loses. And if the team plays badly, this team of mercenary strangers, then the fans will boo.

And why not? This is what corporations do in the lean and tough post–1960s industrial order. Anonymous executives order anonymous cuts in an anonymous workforce to boost earnings, and the shareholders, like postmodern baseball fans, neither know nor care who the players are. They care only about winning. Fewer investors hold stock for the long run, convinced of the quality of the product, the commitment of the managers, the tested power of the brands; investors search instead for short-term financial gain. Under industrial capitalism, the workers were always fungible, treated as interchangeable machine parts, but with today's fluid capital markets, the firms themselves are fungible. If a stock performs badly, the investor can sell it and buy another. Investors who own shares of mutual funds may not even know what stocks their shares represent: like the new breed of sports fan who cannot keep up with the ever-changing cast of players and therefore just roots for the team, the modern investor has traded the very civil idea of relating to people for the very uncivil idea of relating to things.

THE DEATH OF TRADITION

So in sports, as in every other area of life, the American ideal of a shared experience began to vanish in the 1960s, and with it, the civility that shared experience can sustain. This was not entirely bad. No matter what we think we like about the past, we must not fall into the romantic trap of imagining that our forebears were necessarily our moral betters. The authors of the Constitution could not figure out how to do away with slavery (although some of them certainly wanted to). And as Garry Wills has pointed out, "[r]unning men out of town on a rail is at least as much an American tradition as declaring unalienable rights."[10]

The common claim that there was a "golden age" in which America was more civil than today is rather shaky. Even though the evaluation of such a claim is a matter more of taste than of fact, a handful of facts might be of assistance. True, there are aspects of our civility that are worse than they once were. For example, the collapse of even the minimal attention to mutual respect demanded by elementary rules of etiquette is very much a phenomenon of our century, as is the expectation that all our arguments will be nasty and the widespread inattention to fundamental questions of morality. But in other ways we are more civil. We no longer witness, for example, the spectacle of fistfights on the floor of the Senate, or of tarring and feathering unpopular speakers. We no longer burn Mormons alive or lynch Roman Catholics. We no longer countenance racial segregation or confine women unwillingly to the home.

So, were the good old days better? Were they worse? They were neither. They were both. Pick an era at random—perhaps the fifties, since much of our cultural and political nostalgia seems to focus on it. In the fifties, there was less crime. But there was more racism. There were fewer out-of-wedlock births. But battered women had nowhere to turn. There was less abuse of illegal drugs. But far more people smoked. Television was much cleaner. But many more Americans died in automobile accidents.*

In short, although some of what has changed, has changed for the worse, much of what has changed, has changed for the better. I suspect that what we remember, and miss, is not that the values of the age were better—some were, some were not—but the pervasiveness of those values. America, in its vision of itself, stood for something. There was, at least in form, an American creed, and the creed was an important moral resource. It was in this age that everything from the Pledge of Allegiance to the Comic Book Code Authority took on mystic significance. The words "under God" were added to the Pledge, to distinguish us from the "Godless Communists," and publishers, by adhering to the Comic Book Code, agreed to limit what their comics would depict, lest children be infected with un-American values. Such emblems as these signified the sharing of a moral vision. Americans (in their bold self-image anyway) were like the lovers in the old cliché, not gazing into each other's eyes but looking outward in the same direction. Not only were all institutions, public and private, expected to play their roles in the construction of the moral world, but a conversation about right and wrong did not immediately provoke the objection that somebody's fundamental freedoms were at risk.

The price for such consensus is often repression. If the fifties produced the Comic Book Code, it also produced the Un-American Activities Committee, which pressured the nation's citizens to engage in self-censorship . . . or to report those who did not. If the fifties produced the Civil Rights Movement, which expanded the boundaries

* Many observers also like to point with envy to the economy of the fifties, but the comparison is deceptive. There were actually fewer jobs (and higher unemployment), but there was probably more job security—at least if security is measured by the confidence of workers that they will still have their jobs tomorrow. In any case, the economy of the fifties was at least in part a historical accident: we were the only industrial power to survive World War II with our manufacturing base intact.

of the American dream, it also produced the Christian Nation Amendment to the Constitution, which, had it not died aborning, might have largely abolished religious freedom. So when we talk about the civility of the good old days, what we really must be yearning for is the moral consensus of the good old days—that is, a shared sense of morality, part of what helps us to be a nation at all.

Since Talcott Parsons, many sociologists have emphasized the role that shared values play in both creating and preserving a people *as* a people. Parsons, a follower of Émile Durkheim, largely introduced the concept of functionalism to American intellectual conversation. As Parsons's critics have long pointed out, however, he was probably too interested in the effect of norms of behavior and too little interested in where they come from; his greatest error, surely, was his seeming belief that norms somehow arise naturally, rather than being constructed. And yet, wherever norms may come from, Parsons was plainly right that they are needed. Shared moral norms generate the mutuality of respect (especially for those who follow the norms) that in turn allows civilization and, thus, civility. What we agree on then provides the background against which we are able to disagree, secure in the knowledge of the commonalities that bind us together. Our shared moral understanding gives us the confidence to be sure that those who oppose us politically are no more out to destroy the polity than we are. This is the point of John Courtney Murray's famous adage, that in order to disagree, we must first "share enough in common to have something to disagree about."[11] So when people say that we are less civil than we used to be, I think they are really saying that we are less morally united than we used to be . . . or than we would like to be. And moral disunity is the ultimate destroyer of any polity, even ours.

The Biblical story of the Tower of Babel (Genesis 11:1–9) captures the point dramatically. In the story, the reader will recall, God decides to punish the arrogance of humans who are trying to build a tower up to heaven, hoping to become like God. God responds by causing the builders to speak in different languages, so that it is impossible for them to communicate, and thus impossible for them to complete their work. What makes this tale one of incivility? An 1840 sermon on the subject of brotherly love by a certain Reverend I. R. Hall provides the answer. Hall offers us the following challenge:

[W]hat is the history of man from that hour up to the present time, but a history of strife and selfishness and continual quarreling among those who were of the same common origin and the same blood, and were designed therefore by their gracious Creator to dwell together in unity?

After God "confounded" their languages, so that they could not speak to each other,

disunion seemed to be complete. Speaking different languages, and dwelling in different countries, men soon learned to forget that they were all originally children of the same father, and therefore brethren to each other, or that they had any common bond of union.[12]

For the student of civility, the point of Hall's sermon—and of the Babel story—is not the problem of language in the ordinary sense of whether we all happen to speak English or not. (A common language is, however, an important component of successful common life.) Rather, the "disunion" results because of our inability to speak a common moral language, a difficulty that Murray's adage anticipated but cannot resolve for us. Surely one of the reasons our public moral debates are so shrill and inconclusive is precisely that we lack the rhetorical skills to reason together about morality—because we share no common starting point. It is hardly surprising, then, that we have "learned to forget that [we] were all originally children of the same father." Or that we have forgotten why discovering what we share matters.

To be sure, it may be that the claim that we ever had a strong commonality is itself partly an illusion. John Kasson, the leading American historian of civility, argues that even at the start of the twentieth century, "[t]he 'American Way of Life' became defined as one, not of vital political commitments, but of abundant consumer choices."[13] On the other hand, it may be, as the historian Mary P. Ryan contends, that our very lack of agreement during the nineteenth century was a mark of the thriving of our democracy, now deadened by the idea that consensus matters.[14] In other words, it may be (again thinking of John Courtney Murray) that what we agreed about was our disagreement. And yet, whether or not

America possessed actual consensus, it fought hard in the years after World War II for the illusion of consensus: in that brief historical moment, the nation knew, simply knew, that it was firmly on the side of the angels.

And small wonder. The yearning for certainty is a fundamental characteristic of the human. That is why we form monogamous relationships when most of the animal kingdom does not.[15] That is why we are so tribal in our instincts, wanting to belong to a group—a sorority, a regular poker game, a tenured faculty, a gang—that offers support and sure knowledge of our place in the world.[16] That is why we exalt science: we want not to suspect what is true, but to *know*. That is also why we believe in government under law: knowing what is allowed and what is not makes life predictable. And it may also be one reason why the tug of religion, the instinct for God, seems to grab nearly everybody in the end: God offers clarity and purpose in the midst of chaos.[17] And it may also be why the dominance of a single sports franchise—the Yankees, the Celtics—never seemed to hurt the other teams at the box office. Not, at least, in the era of shared experience.

Furthermore, we must not exaggerate the breadth of our disagreements, even now. Consensus on values still exists, at least if we measure consensus by what values an overwhelming majority of adults—say, 90 percent—believe children should learn in school. We do indeed lack consensus on a number of divisive social issues, but we should not confuse those divisions with differences over what matters: both supporters and opponents of classroom prayer, for instance, would doubtless describe themselves as defenders of religious freedom. Moreover, the mass media, stormily in love with controversy, tend to emphasize the most extreme voices, a focus that makes us appear more divided than we really are. So when the subject is abortion, for example, television features only the most committed (and narrowly focused) activists, never the voices of the great middle.[18]

Admittedly, the ideal of a singular America was always in some sense an illusion, masking as much about the country as it purported to reveal. Yet the illusion of a set of shared meanings possessed tremendous sustaining power, holding the nation together through one Great Depression and two Great Wars. Perhaps it needed to be shattered—but not, I think, with such thorough fury. Even those on the outside mainly wanted not to destroy the illusion but to be comforted by it. The Civil Rights Movement, for example, was quite explicitly premised on making the American dream a reality for more people; the aspiration had a multiracial appeal because America wanted so desperately for the dream to be true. As long as the illusion stood, even as aspiration, reformers and reactionaries alike could devote their energies to making it real, even as they disagreed on how; thus did the illusion provide a shared reality.

As the sixties swept into the seventies, leaving behind the wreckage of the illusion, there was nothing available to put in its place: no shared meanings, no shared commitments, none of the social glue that makes a people a people. Nobody had thought that far ahead. Americans were like homeowners who find a huge crack in the basement floor of their new home and, in their fury at the previous owners for not revealing this flaw, decide not to strengthen the foundation but to demolish the house. Only afterward, when they calm down and survey the mess, does it occur to them that they now have no place to live.

If we are to rebuild a truly sacrificial civility, we will have to rebuild its shattered components: generosity when there is cost, and trust when there is risk. But we are building on weakened soil. We live in an era when both generosity and trust come hard . . . very hard. And so we live life as though there are no limits to our freedom. Having abandoned the illusion of commonality, we have adopted an even more dangerous illusion: that social norms are not important and thus we can do as we like. The fact that some of the old norms were repressive seemed to prove that all norms were repressive.

There is a well-known line from *The Brothers Karamazov*: "If God does not exist, everything is permitted." The American analogue is evidently something like this: "If the singular meaning was an illusion, everything is allowed." Which is how wearing droopy pants and refusing to share one's wealth with the poor come to be described as basic rights rather than selfish desires. We have adopted almost as a creed the proposition of Dostoevsky's soulmate Friedrich Nietzsche that we are self-created, that we must put aside the "moralistic drivel" that limits us. We should, argued Nietzsche, pursue our proper goal in life, which is to become what we already are. Despite the careful glosses of Nietzsche's defenders, the idea in practice amounts to little more than following our instincts . . . and thus risking retreat, as Erasmus might say, into barbarism. Erasmus argued that we must discipline desire for the sake of civilized community, but our bold new illusion insists that there is no community. There is no common meaning. We have no obligations to our fellow passengers because we have no fellow passengers. We have only fellow strangers, and we owe them nothing we choose not to give.

4

· · · · · · · · · · · · ·

Welcoming the Stranger

T HERE IS—or recently was—a shameful bit of software floating
around the Internet. Known as AOL4FREE, the program evidently
helped users to break the law by setting up America OnLine
accounts without the inconvenience of paying for them. Then, in
the late spring of 1997, the United States Department of Energy distributed an alert about a fake version of AOL4FREE. This fake
theft program looked like the real theft program but was actually a
deadly computer virus. Any user who tried to run it received a surprise. Rather than establishing an illegal America OnLine account,
the program would erase the entire contents of the user's hard drive.

There is a certain existential irony in the image of a federal
agency issuing a warning that a program somebody uses because he
thinks it is designed to abet fraud may actually be a fraudulent
copy of a program designed to abet fraud and may do harm to the
would-be defrauder. But I suppose this is less unusual than it
seems. After all, government agencies publish studies all the time
on the harm that is caused by illegal drugs, in what is presumably
an effort at deterrence. And the attorney general of one of our
largest states, it is said, once pursued a consumer fraud action
against an individual who offered "grass by mail" at low prices—
grass that turned out to be the kind mowed from the lawn, not the
kind hidden under the mattress. So perhaps the warning was not
as bizarre as it first appeared.

Nevertheless, my own initial reaction to the warning was, "Serves
them right!" That is, I quickly decided that anybody who would try
to steal computer time deserved to lose a hard drive or two. And

although I soon recognized that this rather uncivil and certainly un-Christian response was a little bit like saying that people who decline to feed parking meters deserve to have their cars vandalized, a part of me clings to it still. My dislike for theft is, I confess, visceral.

My more sober reaction, the same reaction I have to the problem of computer viruses generally, was, "Why would anybody do such a thing?" Because lots of people undeniably do. From the creation of the first computer virus, apparently in 1983, to the present day, more than seven thousand different types of viruses have been created—recently at the rate of two or three new ones per day.[1] Although some viruses are relatively benign, others can cause losses ranging into the millions of dollars. Viruses are metaphorically violent—a typical name of one of the many virus-making kits easily available on the Internet is Nightmare Joker—and, in what cannot be an accident, many of the most vicious target only the products of Microsoft. (I also find it rather interesting that *every* identified virus writer has turned out to be male.)[2]

Nobody seems to know exactly why people create viruses, although experts talk confidently about pathological levels of loneliness, alienation, rejection, anger, and frustration, all the usual causes of vandalism, as well as, for that matter, suicide. "I don't have any real-life friends," moans one nineteen-year-old virus creator.[3] And, for the student of civility, that is the moral of the story. The virus writer never seeks recognition. Viruses are sent out to attack people the writer does not know. The virus writer who thinks the activity a big joke (as some evidently do) is able to play it with aplomb in part because the victims are strangers.

And here, indeed, is a point on which most students of civility seem to agree. A big part of our incivility crisis stems from the sad fact that we do not know each other or even want to try; and, not knowing each other, we seem to think that how we treat each other does not matter. For the virus writer, whose alienation from others may be extreme, this is particularly true: the same anonymity behind which the virus's creator hides also cloaks the virus's victims. To the virus writer, whether motivated by anger, perverse pleasure, or ideology, the infection of other people's computers is an end in itself. The people who pay the costs may not seem real . . . assuming he thinks of them at all.

The creation of a virus to harm a complete stranger perfectly exemplifies much that is uncivil in our turbulent age. An important part of civility, as we have already seen, is simple good manners as a signal of respect for others and for the community. Another important part, which has lately occasioned a substantial literature, is about reconstruction of our social institutions. But civility is, fundamentally, an ethic for relating to the stranger. Indeed, much of civility is premised on the notion that the concept of stranger actually exists—that everybody will not in fact come to know, still less grow close to, everybody else. Yet we live in a society in which each of us encounters strangers every day, by the dozens, the hundreds, even the thousands. Civility is about how we treat each and every one of them. So civility is not the same as affection, and when we try to treat the two of them as the same, we end up making matters worse.

I am annoyed when I go into a store and introduce myself, by my full name, to a sales clerk, only to be immediately called by my first name alone. First names are commonly used among close friends, but it is only recently that they have trickled down into ordinary encounters. It may be that I am especially sensitive on this issue. Black Americans fought hard and long for the right to be called by "Mr." and "Mrs." (and, lately, "Ms.") rather than by first names—only to discover, just as the battle is won, that an increasing number of white Americans think these politely formal sobriquets should be discarded.

I was raised to think—and I still think—that the use of a stranger's first name requires an invitation. It is a form of social intimacy, not an entitlement. Using a more formal manner in addressing those we have just met is more than common courtesy—it is a signal of respect. But, of course, respect for our fellow passengers is fast disintegrating. So I suppose I should not be surprised when I see a receptionist at a doctor's office, a young woman scarcely out of high school, call patients three times her age, whom she evidently has never met before, by their first names. No doubt the receptionist imagines that she is being politely informal, but what she is really doing is forcing on strangers an intimacy they should not be required to share. I suspect that the receptionist's thoughtless effort at familiarity offends some of the patients, actually making them less, not more, comfortable. We can be civil without being familiar, and recovering the skill of doing so is vital if we are to relate to strangers; otherwise, we run the risk of disappointment and even anger when these strangers do not reciprocate, a bitter sensation of rejection.

The social scientists agree. The psychologist Richard Sennett has argued that the desire for some form of intimacy in all our relationships is the enemy of civility, that we cannot relate to each other as a polity unless we rediscover the value of "bonds of association and mutual commitment . . . between people who are not joined by ties of family or intimate association."[4] Similarly, the sociologist Benton Johnson, following the work of John Murray Cuddihy, has pointed to the ways that civility and "niceness" ease our relationships with strangers: "They make it possible to jostle someone by mistake in the elevator and avoid a flare-up. They enable customers and clerks, diners and waiters, clients and attorneys to conclude transactions with each other quickly and with a minimum of friction."[5]

Johnson's point is that none of these busily jostling and transacting people know each other. He goes on to quote Cuddihy's argument that civility allows us "to live with unknown others without transforming them into either brothers or enemies"[6]—that is, we need neither love them nor hate them in order to be civil toward them. Civility, in short, is a virtue that equips us for everyday life with strangers, our daily democratic train ride with people we do not like or do not even know. Thus, we see the second rule of civility:

> *Civility requires that we sacrifice for strangers, not just for people we happen to know.*

This is, in its way, rather a radical notion. Many of us have trouble being as civil as we should even toward those we love or with whom we are otherwise close: our family members, coworkers, neighbors, or friends. (See chapter 13.) But at least we believe that we *should* treat them well, however short of our aspirations we may fall. Dealing with strangers is harder, and we seem to be losing many of the tools that once enabled us to relate to them. The clerk in the convenience store, the beggar in the street, the passenger in the next seat: How are we to relate to these strangers? Certainly simple politeness—*Please, Thank you, Sir (Ma'am), Excuse me*—would be a good start.

When I was growing up, a frequent admonition, at home and school alike, was, "Say the magic word!" This phrase, always spoken with enormous gentleness, was a reminder to preface a request with *Please* and to acknowledge a kindness with *Thank you*. If we failed to say the magic words, we did not receive whatever we were asking for, a discipline that helps a child learn quite quickly. There is no simpler piece of the civility puzzle, not only because the magic words are a part of our letter of introduction to the rest of the world, but also because using them is a symbol of respect for others. Yet the magic words have become rarer to the ear because, it seems, they have become harder to pronounce.

The psychiatrist Robert Coles, in his thoughtful book *The Moral Intelligence of Children*, argues that we should be quite proud of the many five- and six-year-olds who arrive at school already understanding and using the magic words. In these young people, writes Coles, "[c]ivilization has taken root."[7] Coles is right that we should recognize how considerable an accomplishment this degree of civility is in these tiny human beings so newly arrived on the earth. The troubling aspect is how many of these polite little children grow into sullen adolescents and mean-spirited adults, the magic words, like the rest of the magic of childhood, forgotten. Because nowadays the magic words are in a decline. Cashiers, cab drivers, the people for whom we hold open doors—all of them seem to have lost the art. We may smile and greet those we know well, but (in our cities at least) a sunny greeting offered to a stranger in the street may invite in response an angry glare or averted eyes.

So how are we to relate to these strangers? The simple answer is that we are to be civil toward them, which means that we should accord them respect and even (although it may seem unfashionable) that we should be polite. We may certainly, in our civility, make *offers* of friendship. But we must not insist on friendship as the price of civility. If it turns out that the many strangers we meet each day do not, after all, desire close relationships with us, we should not repay them with incivility. The respect that we owe them does not diminish. Indeed, as we shall see, an important component of civility involves respecting the privacy of others, what used to be called the right to be left alone, accepting that parts of their lives are no part of our business. Another component, however, involves not insisting on our own right to be left alone when, by connecting with others, we can improve the community . . . and therein lies a story. In fact, therein lie two stories. By considering them, we can better understand what the relentless focus on the functionality of civility tends to miss—that treating each other with civility is a moral imperative.

STORY #1:
A DARK, SKINNY STRANGER
IN CLEVELAND PARK

. . . .

In the summer of 1966, my parents moved with their five children to a large house near the corner of 35th and Macomb Streets in Cleveland Park, a neighborhood in the middle of Northwest Washington, D.C., and, in those days, a lily-white enclave. My father, trained as a lawyer, was working for the federal government, and this was an area of the city where many lawyers and government officials lived. There were senators, there were lobbyists, there were undersecretaries of this and that. My first impression was of block upon block of grim, forbidding old homes, each of which seemed to feature a massive dog and spoiled children in the uniforms of various private schools. My two brothers and two sisters and I sat on the front steps, missing our playmates, as the movers carried in our furniture. Cars passed what was now our house, slowing for a look, as did people on foot. We waited for somebody to say hello, to welcome us. Nobody did.

We children had no previous experience of white neighborhoods. But we had heard unpleasant rumors. The gang of boys I used to hang out with in Southwest Washington traded tall tales of places where white people did evil things to us, mostly in the South, where none of us had ever lived, nor wanted to. Now and then, perhaps on a Saturday afternoon, we would take a walk to see the evil empire. We would walk up Fourth Street, beneath the highway and the railroad tracks that separated our neighborhood from the federal areas of the city, past the red-brick police station, a half-mile or so up to the Mall. Then, nudging each other with nervous excitement, we would turn west and continue our march. We wanted to see. We would pass with barely a glance the museums that on any other day would keep us occupied for hours. We would circle around the Washington Monument, whose pointed top with twin windows on each side, some of the older boys said, reminded them of a Ku Klux Klan hood, an image that scared me a little, although at eleven years old, raised in the North by protective parents, I was none too sure what the Ku Klux Klan was. We would walk along the Reflecting Pool and continue past the Lincoln Memorial, which, then as now, seemed under constant repair. At last we would reach the shores of the Potomac River which, in those days, exuded the fetid odors of sewage and industrial waste. And we would stand on the bank, a tiny band of dark skinny children, still growing into full awareness of our race; we would stand there and gaze across the river at the shores of the forbidden land. Mostly what we saw was trees. Sometimes we could pick out a house, perhaps a mansion, including one named for Robert E. Lee. We knew nothing of General Lee except that he had something to do with slavery. On the wrong side. That was enough. We looked, but from our safe distance. There were bridges, but we never crossed them. We had somehow picked up the idea that to go there for more than a short time meant death. Or maybe worse. Emboldened by the river running before us like a moat, we stood our ground and kept looking. A few of the boys claimed to have visited the evil empire, but the rest of us laughed uneasily to show our doubts. We stood, we gazed, we told bad jokes. We poked each other and pointed.

"That's Virginia," we would say, shuddering.

Times have changed. Virginia has changed. I have changed. Today I love the state, its beauty, its people, even its complicated sense of history. But in 1966, sitting on the front step of our grand new house in our grand new lonely white neighborhood of Washington, I felt as if we had moved to the fearsome Virginia of the sixties, which, in my child's mind, captured all the horror of what I knew of how white people treated black people. I watched the strange new people passing us and wordlessly watching back, and I knew we were not welcome here. I knew we would not be liked here. I knew we would have no friends here. I knew we should not have moved here. I knew . . .

And all at once, a white woman arriving home from work at the house across the street from ours turned and smiled with obvious delight and waved and called out, "Welcome!" in a booming, confident voice I would come to love. She bustled into her house, only to emerge, minutes later, with a huge tray of cream cheese and jelly sandwiches, which she carried to our porch and offered around with her ready smile, simultaneously feeding and greeting the children of a family she had never met—and a black family at that—with nothing to gain for herself except perhaps the knowledge that she had done the right thing. We were strangers, black strangers, and she went out of her way to make us feel welcome. This woman's name was Sara Kestenbaum, and she died much too soon, but she remains, in my experience, one of the great exemplars of all that is best about civility.

Sara Kestenbaum's special contribution to civility back in 1966 was to create for us a sense of belonging where none had existed before. And she did so even though she had never seen any of us in her life. She managed, in the course of a single day, to turn us from strangers into friends, a remarkable gift that few share. (My wife is one of the few.) But we must never require friendship as the price of civility, and the great majority of us who lack that gift nevertheless hold the same obligation of civility.

This story illustrates what I mean when I say that civility is the set of sacrifices we make for the sake of our fellow passengers. Sara Kestenbaum was generous to us, giving of herself with no benefit to herself, and she demonstrated not merely a welcome that nobody else offered, but a faith in us, a trust that we were people to whom one could and should be generous. And so we have the beginning of a definition of the sacrificial civility we have been discussing:

> *Civility has two parts: generosity, even when it is costly,*
> *and trust, even when there is risk.*

Saying hello to a stranger on the street or driving with a bit more care are acts of generosity. Conceding the basic goodwill of my fellow citizens, even when I disagree with them, is an act of trust. By greeting us as she did, in the midst of a white neighborhood and a racially charged era, Sara was generous when nobody forced her to be, and trusting when there was no reason to be. Of such risks is true civility constructed.

INTERMEZZO: CIVILITY AND THE CITY

· · · · · · · · · · · · ·

Historians and sociologists of civility might have predicted that our new neighbors would be unfriendly, even had the racial issue not been present. The city, in a peculiar way, holds within its history the collapse of one form of civility, based on norms learned from small, known communities, and the development of another, based on norms learned from larger, anonymous ones. Although this is not the place to do the history in great detail—others have done it, and excellently[8]—it will be useful to hit the high points.

Most of us have heard the old bromide that people who live in cities are not as polite as people in the country. New Yorkers, we think, epitomize rudeness, whereas folks in the South, say, are just as friendly as they can be. The bromide, however, turns out not to be a bromide: more and more experimental evidence confirms it. Something seems to happen to the psyche, to the personality, maybe even to the soul, when people live together in vast numbers. We find ourselves avoiding each other if only to keep from tripping over each other. We demand what has come to be called our "space."

In his classic text *The Individual in the Social World*, the psychologist Stanley Milgram warns against overstating the case for urban incivility: "In some instances it is not simply that, in the city, traditional courtesies are violated; rather, the cities develop new norms of noninvolvement." Thus, when visitors arrive from rural areas with very different rules of conduct and complain that they seem to have landed in a foreign country, they are, in a sense, absolutely right. The city, like any other community, creates its own standards of behavior, along with its own pressures to obey them. The only trouble is, the standards are often morally inferior to the ones they replace. Milgram continues:

These [new norms] are so well defined and so deeply a part of city life that *they* constitute the norms people are reluctant to violate. Men are actually embarrassed to give up a seat on the subway to an old woman; they mumble "I was getting off anyway," instead of making the gesture in a straightforward and gracious way.[9]

Instinct says that Milgram is right. So do experiments—for example, observing whether passersby will help a disabled man who falls to the ground. For half a century, every scholar who has examined the question has found city dwellers far less likely to be helpful or polite than those who live in rural areas—and the bigger the city, the ruder its citizens.[10] Probably they do not see themselves as rude: they are only conforming their conduct to the expectations of their urban world. And why do city dwellers develop these norms—what might be called norms of rudeness rather than norms of civility? Because, says Milgram, "everyone realizes that, in situations of high population density, people cannot implicate themselves in each others' affairs, for to do so would create conditions of continual distraction which would frustrate purposeful action."[11] In words, if people in cities are nice to each other, they will be too busy with each other's problems to get anything done.

Yet this explanation is obviously incomplete. In the city of Milgram's vision, strangers are cold to each other because it is too costly to behave any other way. Social historians, however, have linked the rise of the national concern over matters of etiquette in the nineteenth century to the rise of the great industrial city precisely because the bold new cities were places where, for the first time, it was possible to live and work entirely among strangers.

Prior to the development of the great cities, most people lived in the same community for their entire lives, surrounded by an extended family (perhaps a large one) and a thick network of other relationships that helped to nurture and enforce norms of behavior. The new industrial cities created enormous freedom: people moved to the cities and lived there alone, or with their nuclear families, but without the significant community ties that simultaneously offered moral guidance and limited their choices. People were mobile: they went where the jobs were. But this new freedom, as the historian John Diggins has pointed out, created problems of its own: "The more free the individual felt himself to be, the more isolated and lonely he actually became until he craved to forsake his solitude in order to surrender his self to the new invisible authority of society itself."[12] With the advance of capitalism, then, the nation moved from the idea of local norms of behavior, created and nurtured by the community (often the religious community), to the idea of citywide or even national norms. Now the norms were generated not by people one knew but by a larger, anonymous, untouchable entity. "Society" replaced "community."

One beneficiary of the change was the publishing industry. As the new citizens—now literally citizens, residents of cities—struggled to work out how to relate to the strangers by whom they were surrounded, the demand for authoritative rules exploded. Suddenly, everybody wanted to know how to behave, how to get along with strangers. Responding to the manners craze, publishers coughed up a flood of books on etiquette, most of them quite thin, producing, as one observer has noted, "weak opinion strongly held."[13]

Unlike the Europeans, who held that good manners were the property of the upper classes, Americans nourished the conceit that anybody could learn etiquette. Many of the books were inexpensive. One of the most popular was Irwin Beadle's popular 1859 volume, *Dime Book of Popular Etiquette*, the price of which was stated in the title. There were books about how to act when traveling on the railroads, books about behavior on the street or in the theater, books aimed at women, books aimed at men.* Special books were written to guide foreign immigrants to America—and rural immigrants to the cities.[14] And people who never read books on anything else worked on their manners: "[M]ost etiquette manuals were sold to people who would never have thought of entering a bookstore," mainly by direct mail.[15] There were books for all ages, for all regions, from all angles, and they shared a common theme: If you want to be somebody in America, you must learn to mind your manners.

---

* As the sociologist Lyn Lofland has shown, the books for women have survived in a peculiar way: the rules that once were intended to guide women on the streets of the cities have become the rules that everyone follows in urban areas. Nineteenth-century women were urged to avoid eye contact, to avoid allowing their bodies to brush passersby, to ignore offensive sights and sounds—which nowadays describes the behavior of most of us when we walk the streets of the city.

One result of this urban fad was that the fledgling public schools (most of them in those days still called common schools) began to include the study of manners in the curriculum. Part of the reason was nativism, a fear that the new immigrants did not know how Americans were expected to behave. But a larger part was probably status anxiety, a fear that if children did not learn proper etiquette, they would not amount to anything. In an eerie foreshadowing of today's debates over character education, journalists warned that the family could not do it alone: the schools had to help. And so a new subject—"morals and deportment"— was born.[16] Now that society rather than community set the standards, children needed a way to find out what the standards were.

Which leads us to our second story.

STORY #2:
THE CASE OF THE DROOPING PANTS
. . . .

When I was a child, attending grade school in Washington, D.C., we took classroom time to study manners. Not only the magic words we have already discussed ("please" and "thank you") but more complicated etiquette questions, like how to answer the telephone ("Carter residence, Stephen speaking") and how to set the table (we were quizzed on whether knife blades point in or out). We were taught to address adults with a title ("Sir" or "Ma'am") or by surname ("Mrs. White"). And somehow nobody—no children, no parents— objected to what nowadays would surely be viewed as indoctrination.

Today instruction of this sort is so rare that when a school tries to teach manners to children, it makes the news. So when the magazine *U.S. News & World Report* ran a story in 1996 about the decline of civility, it opened with what it must have considered the man-bites-dog vignette—an account of a classroom where young people were taught to be polite.[17] Ironically, this newsworthy curriculum evidently teaches a good deal less about etiquette than we learned back at Margaret M. Amidon Elementary School in the sixties, but that is still a good deal more than children learn in most places. Deportment classes are long gone. Now and then the schools teach some norms of conduct, but almost always about sex, and never the most important ones: *Do not engage in harassment* and *Always use a condom* seem to be the outer limits of their moral capacity. The idea that sex, as a unique human activity, might require a unique morality, different from the general moral rules against physical harm to others and harm to the self, is not one that public schools are prepared to entertain.

Respect for rules of conduct has been lost in the deafening and essentially empty rights-talk of our age.[18] Following a rule of good manners may mean doing something you do not want to do, and the weird rhetoric of our self-indulgent age resists the idea that we have such things as obligations to others. We suffer from what James Q. Wilson has described as the elevation of self-expression over self-control.[19] So when a black student at a Connecticut high school was disciplined in 1996 for wearing pants that drooped (exposing his underwear), not only did he claim a right to wear what he liked, but some community leaders hinted at racism, on the theory that many young African American males dress this way. (The fact that the style is copied from prison garb, which lacks a belt, evidently makes no impression on these particular defenders of the race.)

When I was a child, had my school sought to discipline me, my parents would have assumed the school had good reason. And they probably would have punished me further at home. Unlike many of today's parents, they would not have begun by challenging the teacher or principal who thought I had done wrong. To the student of civility, the relevant difference between that era and the present is the collapse of trust, particularly trust in strangers and in institutions. My parents would have trusted the school's judgment—and thus trusted the school to punish me appropriately—but trust of that kind has largely dissolved. Trust (along with generosity) is at the heart of civility. But cynicism has replaced the healthier emotion of trust. Cynicism is the enemy of civility: it suggests a deep distrust of the motives of our fellow passengers, a distrust that ruins any project that rests, as civility does, on trusting others even when there is risk. And so, because we no longer trust each other, we place our trust in the vague and conversation-stifling language of "rights" instead.[20]

Consider again the boy with the droopy pants. To talk about wearing a particular set of clothes as a "right" is demeaning to the bloody struggles for such basic rights as the vote and an unsegregated education. But the illusion that all desires are rights continues its insidious spread. At about the same time, a fired waitress at a restaurant not far from Yale, where I teach, announced a "right" to pierce her face with as many studs and rings as she wishes. And, not long ago, a television program featured an interview with a woman who insisted on the "right" to be as fat as she likes. Rights that are purchased at relatively low cost stand a fair chance of being abused, simply because there is no history behind them, and thus little pressure to use them responsibly—in short, because nobody knows why the right exists. But even a right that possesses a grimly instructive history—a right like freedom of speech—may fall subject to abuse when we forget where it came from.

This proposition helps explain the facts, if not the outcome, of *Cohen v. California*,[21] a 1971 decision in which the Supreme Court overturned the conviction of a young man who wore on his jacket the benign legend F—— THE DRAFT. The case arose as the public language grew vulgar.[22] The nineteenth and early twentieth centuries offered a tradition of public insults that were witty, pointed, occasionally cruel, but not obscene or particularly offensive. Politicians and other public figures competed to demonstrate their cleverness in repartee. (One of my favorites is Benjamin Disraeli's explanation of the difference between a misfortune and a calamity: "If Gladstone fell into the Thames, that would be a misfortune. And if anyone pulled him out, that would be a calamity.") Nowadays the tradition of barbed wit has given way to a witless barbarism, our lazier conversational habit of reaching for the first bit of profanity that comes to mind. The restraint and forethought that are necessary to be clever, even in insult, are what a sacrificial civility demands. When we are lazy about our words, we are telling those at whom our vulgarity is directed that they are so far beneath us that they are not worth the effort of stopping to think how best to insult them; we prefer, animal-like, to make the first sound that comes to mind.

In *Cohen v. California*, the justices were unfortunately correct that what the dissenters called "Cohen's absurd and immature antic" was protected by the freedom of speech. But it is important to add that when the framers of the Constitution envisioned the rough-and-tumble world of public argument, they almost certainly imagined heated disagreements against a background of broadly shared values; certainly that was the model offered by John Locke, by then a kind of political folk hero. It is unlikely that the framers imagined a world in which I might feel (morally) free to say the first thing that came into my head.[23] I do think *Cohen* was rightly decided, but the danger deserves emphasis: When offensiveness becomes a constitutional right, it is a right without any tradition behind it, and consequently we have no norms to govern its use.

Consider once more the fired waitress. I do not deny that the piercing of one's body conveys, in many cultures, information of great significance.[24] But in America, we have no tradition to serve as guide. No elder stands behind our young to say, "Folks have fought and died for your right to pierce your face, so do it right"; no community exists that can model for a young person the responsible use of the "right"; for the right, even if called self-expression, comes from no source other than desire. If we fail to distinguish desire from right, we will not understand that rights are sensible and wise only within particular contexts that give them meaning. The Constitution protects a variety of rights, but our moral norms provide the discipline in their exercise. Sometimes what the moral norm of civility demands is that we restrain our self-expression for the sake of our community. That is why Isaac Peebles in the nineteenth century thought it was wrong for passengers to sing during a train ride; and why it is wrong to race our cars through the streets, stereos cranked high enough to be sure that everyone we pass has the opportunity to enjoy the music we happen to like; and why it was wrong for Cohen to wear his jacket; and why it is wrong for racists to burn crosses (another harmful act of self-expression that the courts have protected under the First Amendment). And it is why a waitress who encounters the dining public each day in her work must consider the interest of that public as she mulls the proper form of self-expression.

Consequently, our celebration of Howard Stern, Don Imus, and other heroes of "shock radio" (as it is sometimes called) might be evidence of a certain loss of moral focus. The proposition that all speech must be protected should not be confused with the very different proposition that all speech must be celebrated. When radio station WABC in New York dismissed a popular talk show host, Bob Grant, who refused to stop making racist remarks on the air, some of his colleagues complained that he was being censored. (He was no more being censored than the producer of a television program that is canceled because of low ratings: in both cases, the content is the problem.) Lost in the brouhaha was the simple fact that Grant's comments and conduct were reprehensible, and that his abuse of our precious freedoms was nothing to be celebrated.

I am not arguing that we should rule the offensive illegal, which is why the courts are correct to strike down efforts to regulate speech that some people do not like, and even most speech that hurts; the advantages of yielding to the government so much power over what we say have never been shown to outweigh the dangers. Yet we should recognize the terrible damage that free speech can do if people are unwilling to adhere to the basic precept of civility, that we must sometimes rein in our own impulses— including our impulses to speak hurtful words—for the sake of those who are making the democratic journey with us. The Proverb tells us, "Death and life are in the power of the tongue" (Proverbs 18:21). The implication is that the choice of how to use the tongue, for good or for evil, is ours.

Words are magic. We conjure with them. We send messages, we paint images. With words we report the news, profess undying love, and preserve our religious traditions. Words at their best are the tools of morality, of progress, of hope. But words at their worst can wound. And wounds fester. Consequently, the way we use words matters. This explains why many traditional rules of etiquette, from Erasmus's handbook in the sixteenth century to the explosion of guides to good manners during the Victorian era, were designed to govern how words—these marvelous, dangerous words—should be used. Even the controversial limits on sexual harassment and "hate speech" that have sprouted in our era, limits that often carry the force of law, are really just more rules of civility, more efforts, in a morally bereft age, to encourage us to discipline our desires.

Throughout the book, I will offer examples of dialogue that is civil and dialogue that is uncivil, but my point is not to tell us how to speak. My point is to argue that how we speak is simply one point on a continuum of right and wrong ways to treat one another. And how we treat one another is what civility is about.

WELCOMING THE STRANGER

. . . .

All of which brings us back to the problem of the stranger . . . or, less formally, the problem of the five black children sitting unhappily on the front step, waiting for one of their new white neighbors to acknowledge our presence.

We were not waiting for them to love us. We were only waiting for them to greet us. Yet if Sennett and Johnson are right (and I am sure they are), we require civility precisely to mediate our relationship with those we do not love. Our community, after all, is not limited to those to whom we are closest. Nowadays, whether we speak of our neighborhood, our town, our state, or our nation, our fellow passengers are mostly strangers. But our duty to be both respectful and kind does not disappear simply because they are people we do not know. Thus, we can see another rule of civility— one of the simplest and most straightforward—a simple duty of kindness:

> *Civility creates not merely a negative duty not to do harm,*
> *but an affirmative duty to do good.*

In the Jewish tradition, this duty is captured in the requirement of *chesed*—the doing of acts of kindness—which is in turn derived from the understanding that human beings are made in the image of God. This understanding imposes a duty to do as God would do.[25] Perhaps this teaching is part of what motivated Sara Kestenbaum, our welcoming neighbor back in 1966, whose family was deeply religious. Civility itself may be seen as a part of *chesed*: it does indeed require kindnesses toward our fellow citizens, including the ones who are strangers, and even when it is hard. When we are polite rather than rude, warm rather than cold, when we try to see God in others, we are doing acts of kindness. In all of these

71

acts, we welcome the stranger, not because of any benefit we think will come to us, but because we come to believe that welcoming the stranger is right.

Remember what we have observed about desire: civility often demands its discipline. No matter what civility might counsel, we are always free not to be kind to each other, but it is almost always morally wrong to exercise that freedom. (I speak, of course, of self-restraint, not restraint through law.) We are free to remain impolite, and efforts to legislate otherwise have ended up looking a bit silly. The state of Washington has tried to forbid untruthful political advertisements, to no noticeable effect. A town in New Jersey has tried to ban cursing, to the predictable and unfortunate fury of civil libertarians . . . and to no noticeable effect. Even anti-noise ordinances, once the glory of many a small town, have fallen into desuetude. If we are to reconstruct civility, especially in a nation that prides itself on being free, we will have to do it through better habits, not better laws.

This raises some rather basic questions. It is one thing to carry sandwiches to new neighbors; that is, after all, an old and honored American tradition, even if it is still too often ignored when the new neighbors are the wrong color. But what does it mean, for example, to say we must be civil in this strong sense toward a homeless beggar who confronts us on the street? Are we to give him the money he seeks? Buy him a hot meal? Perhaps turn over to him all that we have? The admittedly unsatisfying answer is that civility by itself cannot provide the proper standard of charitable giving. Each of us must decide that for ourselves—in accordance, however, with strong norms of sacrifice for others. But civility, as we have used the term, does suggest that the one thing we cannot do about the beggar is ignore him. If we owe to our fellow passengers an obligation of respect, then to pass by the beggar as though he does not exist is to pretend that he is not a passenger at all—indeed, that he is other than human. We owe the beggar the same boon of greeting or conversation that we would bestow on anybody else we happen to meet.

At the same time, we must not force others to be our friends. We owe to everyone we meet the simple life space in which to carry on an intimate existence of which we know nothing. We owe to every stranger the chance to remain a stranger, whether the stranger is a seatmate on an airplane who is more interested in that book in her lap than in conversation, or a coworker who has no desire to share with us the slightest details of his love life. So civility requires respect for the privacy of others.

And then there is the matter of politics. The reader may well wonder how campaigning for office might be different if opposing candidates treated each other with the respect that comes of knowing they share equally in God's creation. Politics would not be less partisan—there are genuine differences to be aired—but it would undoubtedly be more polite. Opponents might decide that they could do business together. They would not sling mud (even though, as we have already seen, it seems to work). They would not lie about themselves or each other.

And if this all sounds like a pipe dream, that is but further evidence, if any is needed, of how far our politics and our day-to-day lives diverge from any civil ideal. It might seem to require an awesome feat of imagination to persuade ourselves that we should try to feel this sense of awe, this need to give thanks, each time we meet another human being. But nothing less—and certainly no merely instrumental conception of civility—is likely to get us back to where Isaac Peebles suggested we should be. Peebles, whose book *Politeness on Railroads* we discussed in chapter 1, calls upon us to respect the comfort of our companions along the way, even when it means less comfort for ourselves. The idea of civility as sacrifice is one that he would readily have understood, and one that we, even in this postmodern age when so much seems up for grabs, should understand and applaud. If it is a dream, I think it is an achievable one. But we have already gone as far as secular morality by itself can take us. I doubt that we can reconstruct civility in America without a revival of religion as a force in both our public and our private lives, because religion can give believers the power to resist the dangerous, self-seeking moral understandings that are coming to dominate our social life. Believers, in turn, can show by the power of their example the better way to live.

The creation of computer viruses—the subject that opened this chapter—is, in a peculiar way, an exercise in secular morality run rampant: it requires thinking of oneself to the exclusion of others, and somehow persuading oneself that a course of action is not a whim but a right. As to the claim that virus-making is harmful (all that data lost, all those hard drives damaged), many a virus writer will say, with evidently straight face, that this virtual information is not property, that it should be free for anybody to borrow, manipulate, or destroy. Or that the act is a protest against the domination of the human spirit by technology. Or a helpful means of indicating where computer security is weak—the defense offered by Fred Cohen, creator of the first computer virus.

Listening to these arguments, one is put in mind of the basketball player Dennis Rodman's justification for intentionally bumping his head into that of a referee (an act that led to a hefty fine and suspension): "I was making a statement that I was free and independent and not like everybody else."[26] Like the virus maker's protest against intellectual property, it sounds vaguely like a liberal principle but is really nothing but an incoherent justification for the uncivilized self-indulgence that the student of civility abhors.*

Our secular moral conversation—sometimes, not accurately, referred to as liberalism—tends to answer such protests as these by stating the conclusion as a premise, suggesting, for example, that computer viruses do real harm because the damage they cause is measurable in dollars. This form of argument, often clothed as the "harm principle," is actually a surrender to the ideology of the market. It calls upon nothing admirable in the human spirit and, indeed, proposes that until we know how much money an action has cost, we cannot know if it is immoral or not. It is reminiscent of the argument that chattel slavery is bad only if human beings who are enslaved turn out to be less efficient workers than human beings able to sell their labor freely.[27] Unfortunately, there is little in secular ethics to refute such claims.

But civility—civility as a moral proposition—begins with the assumption that humans matter, that we owe each other respect, and that treating each other well is a moral duty. As we have seen, civility so understood often requires us to put aside our own interests and desires for the benefit of others—which, as Erasmus

---

* One can hardly answer by saying that digital information is property just because most people think it is. A purely majoritarian theory of property rights (or rights of any other kind) would play havoc with the ideal of constitutional law.

understood, is what civilization is all about. Nothing in contemporary secular conversation calls us to give up anything truly valuable for anybody else. No politician would dare run for office asking us to sacrifice for others. Only religion offers a sacred language of sacrifice-selflessness-awe that enables believers to treat their fellow citizens as . . . fellow passengers. But even if religion is the engine of civility, it has too few serious practitioners, which is why those who are truly moved by it to love their fellow human beings are so special. I learned that truth in 1966, and, to this day, I can close my eyes and feel on my tongue the smooth, slick sweetness of the cream cheese and jelly sandwiches that I gobbled on that summer afternoon when I discovered how a single act of genuine and unassuming civility can change a life forever.

5

· · · · · · · · · · · · ·

The Embarrassment of Free Will

Nobody, of course, forced Sara Kestenbaum to carry those sandwiches across the street. She chose freely to do it—and could have chosen just as freely not to do it. The choice she made was a moral and welcoming one. Perhaps religion impelled her to do it, or perhaps a more personal sense of right and wrong, or an instinctive warmth of personality; most likely, some combination of the three was involved. And yet, in the end, she made a voluntary decision. She did the right thing because she chose to.

We Americans sometimes like the idea of choice, the idea that our lives are in a sense self-created, spent in the exercise, or nonexercise, of our many precious freedoms. Indeed, we have for a very long time defined our republic largely in terms of the marvelous range of choices it presents for us. We are a nation of consumers, and our unprecented wealth has emboldened us to imagine that we, unlike the less fortunate folk who dwell in other lands, are entitled to possess whatever we can afford. The luxury of discretionary spending has become the very definition of freedom. The reason that supporters of abortion rights like to cast their position as "pro-choice" is precisely that the term appeals to this broad and deep American notion that freedom is good and restrictions on freedom are bad. The same appeal explains why cigarette makers battle restrictions with a defense of the right of *choice*—the choice whether to smoke—and why, before its unfortunate recent flirtation with scientism (see chapter 11), the gay rights movement popularized the term "lifestyle choice."

Do not misunderstand the point. In principle, choices are a

good. Freedom is a good, especially in our private lives. But we are sometimes overwhelmed by our choices: just let a layperson go into a computer store—or an automobile showroom—and ask about options. This phenomenon, which has led to the resurrection of the phrase "tyranny of choice," makes marketers cringe, because they know that sometimes the range of possibilities confuses and intimidates customers.[1] Philosophers and theologians have derided the idea that we should work constantly to expand our range of choices, believing, correctly, that choice without wisdom leads to moral disaster. And all of us have seen the damage that unfettered choice can do: we see it in the ridiculous divorce rate, in the inexcusable gap between rich and poor, in the continuing appeal of the "militias" and other extremist organizations, and in the frighteningly high number of children born to unmarried women.

Civility is possible only if members of a community bind themselves to obey a set of rules of behavior not because the law requires it but because they understand the virtue of sacrificing their own desires—their own freedom to choose—for the good of the larger community of which they are a part. If this sounds like following the rules just because they are the rules, perhaps it is. That does not mean that no rules are objectionable, for even a widely accepted rule can be wicked and thus not entitled to obedience. In the thoughtful exercise of our personal freedom, we might choose to defy standards to which others defer, yet, if the community is to survive, "I don't feel like it" must not be taken as a sufficient objection. If we are less civil than we should be, one reason is surely that we have confused injustice and inconvenience. So let us try to unpack them.

THE FREEDOM PROBLEM

. . . .

We Americans have earned a rather sour distinction. American children turn out to be more likely than any other children in the world to believe that falling out of love is reason enough to end a marriage.[2] We adults have somehow taught our young people that the relationship of husband and wife—marriage vow or no marriage vow—is no different from the relationship of boyfriend and girlfriend. We have convinced our kids that the spouse is disposable, like any other consumer product: If you do not like the one you have, by all means trade your spouse in and choose another!

Once upon a time, marriage was viewed as a commitment, a word that suggests some higher level of responsibility than an ordinary promise. It is in the nature of commitment that we curtail other options. Marriage is, fundamentally, a commitment not to make different choices later on: not to cheat, not to be unloving, not to leave. One reason to surround marriage with so much ceremony is precisely to remind the parties that the relationship they are entering is unlike any other. So when the divorce rate approaches 50 percent of the marriage rate—as it did, briefly, in the early 1990s—it is fair to say that many people are not taking their commitments as seriously as they should. (And goodness knows what the incivility with which we conduct our divorces is teaching our children about how to treat those we once loved and love no longer.) For the student of civility, a trend like this one is a reason to worry—to worry that our freedom to choose is getting out of hand.

It is both the ideology and the conceit of Americans that we live in a free country, by which we mean a country that allows its people to be free. That is in itself a marvelous proposition, in its way unique in the history of the world. Despite the almost pathological tendency of Americans to complain about our lives, no people has ever been as free, whether one's measure of freedom is the degree of political and personal liberty or the breadth of choice in consumer goods. The only trouble is that we are in the process of forgetting what it means to be free. We are forgetting what the philosophers of the Enlightenment well understood: the freedom that humans possess is not the freedom to do what we like, but the freedom to do what is right. This act of collective amnesia is putting at risk our claim of civilization.

In one sense, choice is but the handmaiden of free will: if freedom truly exists, it is coherent only if options exist. I have the freedom to fly or not to fly in an airplane. We call it freedom because both choices are available. If I am barred from entering the plane (for example, because I do not have a ticket), then I no longer have the freedom to make that choice. Similarly, I have no freedom to choose to fly by flapping my wings: the option does not exist.

And yet we use the word *freedom* too often and think about it too little. Much as I despair at their passion in an unjust cause, I think the Montana "Freemen" are aptly named in our uncivil era. The Freemen, an antigovernment offshoot of the same movement that includes the Constitutionalists, Posse Comitatus, and a variety of other groups that deny the authority of the federal and (sometimes) state governments, spent much of 1996 surrounded by federal agents at an armed compound. Why are they aptly named? Because the Freemen represent the apotheosis of the dangerous side of the American idea of freedom: freedom from commitment, freedom from responsibility, freedom from sacrifice, freedom from community. The Freemen, in other words, seek to be free of precisely those aspects of life that create the possibility of civilization. They are, in a sense, the ultra-Americans, epitomizing an ethic (or perhaps an aesthetic) that says you need not do what you would rather not do. Their strange vision of a life lived without any connection to others is a threat to civility and, ultimately, to the project of human civilization.

But so is the laissez-faire economic vision of some on the right, like the wealthy California software entrepreneur who explained in the mid-1990s that he did not give money to charity because if the poor were supposed to have money, they would—as though morality and destiny are somehow the same thing.

And so is the laissez-faire social vision of some on the left, like the (acting) head of Planned Parenthood, who in 1995 expressed the remarkable opinion that there are no bad reasons for having abortions—as though the fact of becoming pregnant places one beyond the ordinary moral condition of requiring a justification for an act.[3]

Indeed, it is the unhappy moral burden of our politics that nobody seems to be concerned with the limits to freedom. Liberals refuse to accept the idea that sexual freedom has limits or, for that matter, consequences; pregnancy itself, the start of a new life, is treated as no more than a temporary inconvenience.[4] Conservatives refuse to accept the idea that there are any limits on how much money one should have, or what one should do with it. As the theologian Stanley Hauerwas has pointed out, the contemporary liberal emphasis on the radical autonomy of the individual to make choices about sex has made it impossible for liberals to articulate a persuasive program to restrict the autonomy of the wealthy to make choices about money.[5] The price of John's freedom to sleep with whomever he likes whenever he likes is evidently Jane's freedom to do with her wealth whatever she likes whenever she likes. And all because we no longer remember what freedom is for.

Freedom, although the academy likes to forget the fact, is a distinctly Western notion, and, in a sense, a strongly Christian notion.[6] In Christianity, freedom has played two roles: it describes a self liberated from the oppression of the material world, and it also describes the ability of the free self to accept or reject God without any coercion. But Christianity has never pretended that because the self is free, all choices are equally good. Even Enlightenment thinkers like Locke were quite clear that human freedom mattered in large part because it was better that people choose freely to do what is right than that they be coerced into doing what is right. The ability of people to choose wrongly, then, was a cost, not a virtue, of freedom.

Consequently, to remember the meaning of freedom is to remember that there are good choices and bad choices, even within the realm of choices that we may legally make. And there are good reasons or bad reasons for doing anything we may choose to do, even the most private of activities. When we forget these simple propositions, we become twice uncivil: once, for our insistence on a form of freedom that is wholly separate from morality; and, second, for the inevitable meanness with which we defend this uncivilized freedom. But if we are mean-spirited and closed-minded, we cannot hold the public dialogues on which successful democracy rests. And if we believe that freedom is separate from morality, we cannot construct the shared moral commitments on which every successful society is built.

Communitarians such as the legal scholar Mary Ann Glendon and the sociologist Amitai Etzioni have long argued that our society has tilted too far in exalting the individual's autonomy over responsibilities to the community.[7] This is certainly true, although the hard part of the analysis is finding where to strike the balance. Still, they are correct to suggest that a linguistic habit of turning every dispute into a battle over rights is powerfully antithetical to civility, because if everything we do is protected by a claim of right, there is no longer any purpose for dialogue. When drooping pants and pierced eyelids are described as rights (as we saw in the previous chapter), we are confusing right with desire. A right is a needed bulwark against oppression, but not every rule is oppressive simply because I do not want to follow it. I am speaking here not of legal rules, but of the norms of behavior, the rules of conduct, that a community imposes on its members. If my desire not to follow a norm constituted a sufficient justification to declare a right to ignore it, there would be no point to having rules. Yet norms have a point.

Communities are in large measure defined by their norms—the expectations that they place on their members—even when the norms do not have the force of law. Social scientists know this, but it is important that the rest of us understand it as well. Consider a simple example. Suppose that I purchase a house in a neighborhood where the very friendly people all loan each other tools and where everybody keeps beautiful gardens and neatly trimmed lawns. If I let my grass grow wild and allow the weeds to run rampant in my garden, I am not living up to the expectations of my neighbors. They probably cannot take legal action against me, but through implicit and perhaps explicit criticism, they would place upon me enormous pressure to conform to the neighborhood's norm of lawn care. To say that I have a "right" to keep my garden as I like is only a distraction: if such a right exists, what my neighbors believe is that I should not exercise it. If I insist on exercising it anyway, I am demonstrating that I am not interested in membership under the community's rules. So I can hardly complain when one of them refuses to loan me a snow-blower. After all, I am the one who decided first to be unneighborly.

Arthur Schlesinger, in *Learning How to Behave*, refers to good manners as the "letter of introduction" we carry with us as we meet new people. But what does it mean to have good manners? Schlesinger cannot be referring to some abstract, universal, and idealized set of manners; following them could not serve as our letter of introduction, because the new people we meet might not recognize them. So he must be referring to following rules that others will recognize as we travel. Consequently, when he writes of displaying our good manners to gain acceptance, he must mean following the rules of the community. Nationally accepted standards of behavior imply a national community. And why not? As we saw in chapter 1, democracy itself may be viewed as a set of manners. Those who love democracy should love its rules.

For Schlesinger, the rules play an identifying function. In this, he follows the understanding of sociology: by conforming to a set of what seem to be highly formalistic, more or less arbitrary rules, the polite individual signals the intention to follow other rules and norms—in short, to be a reliable member of the community that considers those norms important. If I work in an office where men customarily wear ties, by putting on a tie of my own I signal my desire to belong, because I wish to follow the rules. Again, I signal reliability. I signal that I will not upset the steady flow of office routine. Now, suppose I do not wear a tie. Perhaps I have some objection to the practice. When I appear, tieless, at the office, I do not offer the signal that my coworkers are looking for. It may be that I am still reliable. It may be that I still wish to follow the other rules. It may be that I will not disrupt the office routine. But I have denied my coworkers a quick and easy way to discern my intentions—I have denied them the signal they seek. Now obtaining information about what sort of coworker I will be takes more time and energy, on both their part and mine. So, not unreasonably, I will be an object of suspicion, and perhaps even irritation, until, through some other means, I establish my bona fides.

Let us put aside for the moment any search for the reasons the community might value a particular set of norms of behavior. For the moment, it is enough that we understand this to be a fact: the community has norms. When they prove stable over time, they become traditions. By complying with these traditional norms, I signal my desire to be accepted as a member of the community. These signals matter. So does my refusal to send them. Consider once more the question of the fork, which we visited briefly in chapter 2. Perhaps, in the abstract, I do not care about the etiquette of forks. But I might choose to care for the sake of sending the proper signals. Put simply, by choosing the proper fork, I propose that I am interested in the respect of, and ultimately membership in, the community that cares about which fork its members use.

The mother who, seeing that her daughter's fiancé does not know which fork to use for which course, discourages the marriage on the ground that the young man intended is "beneath" her daughter, is actually reading the message that the young man's ignorance signals: he will not, the mother thinks, fit comfortably into her community. Of course, most of us would nowadays be uneasy with the mother's conclusion, which is based entirely on what transpires at the dinner table: the mother may know no more about the young man than what she has seen on this single evening. If we think that the mother is misbehaving, however, the reason must be our rejection of the values or the boundaries of the community in question; it cannot be that we think the use of etiquette signals inherently wrong. Why not? Consider instead a mother whose daughter's intended uses the proper fork but spouts foul, graphically sexual invective throughout the meal. Here, too, the mother who reads the signals would (one hopes) try to get her daughter to reject the suitor—and most of us would agree with her, even though she possesses no evidence of the young man's character but the content of the dinner table conversation.

In both cases, the alarmed mother is evaluating the suitor based on his rejection of a norm the family considers important. In both cases, we might say, the suitor is carrying the wrong letter of introduction, or perhaps no letter at all. The only difference between the two cases is the content of the rule that has been breached. Plainly, we as autonomous citizens are free to make the judgment that the norm against spouting invective is a good one and the norm against using the wrong fork is a bad one, but we are now evaluating the norms themselves; there is no issue of a "right" to disobey the fork-norm.

I may decide, of course, that the community's obsession about forks is foolish, and thus that my integrity does not allow me to follow the rules, but in that case there is no basis on which to demand membership. There is no point in trumpeting my integrity while complaining about my exclusion. Integrity without risk, as the philosopher Lynne McFall has pointed out, is not integrity at all.[8] To say, "I will follow the rules I like, and you will abandon the ones I dislike," is not integrity but self-absorption. As an autonomous citizen of a liberal democracy, I am free, always, to reject the community's core norms of civility. But, if I choose to do so, I have little basis for complaint if the community rejects me in turn. The cost of including me as a full member—the cost of *trusting* me—is simply too high.

Sometimes the costs are quantifiable. For example, the woman we met in chapter 4 who claimed a "right" to be as fat as she likes may be forced to pay more for health insurance as a result of her weight. In other words, she cannot require other members of the community to bear the costs (the risk that additional health care dollars will be needed to care for obesity-related illnesses she might develop) of her exercise of the right, any more than a man who exercises his "right" to smoke can demand that an insurer not treat his lifestyle as an additional risk factor.

More often, the costs are harder to calculate, but that does not mean the costs do not exist. During my Boy Scout days, I was once marked down after a uniform inspection because one of my arm patches was off center by perhaps half an inch. Why should this matter? Because one of the most important functions of Scouting is to teach young people self-discipline, and thus to deny the proposition that some rules are too trivial to matter. To allow me to get away with a seemingly small infraction of the rules could easily have sent a signal to other Scouts that this discipline issue was not so serious after all.

I am not suggesting that personal freedom is unimportant; on the contrary, in a liberal democracy, personal freedom is fundamental. But so is the sense of owing duties to others that leads us to impose limits on our own freedom, not because it is required by law but because it is required by morality—the morality of trying to build a civil community together. And no American soldier, I suspect, ever died for the proposition that none of us should care about another.

To be sure, nobody should live a life governed entirely by norms or the expectations of others: conformity can itself be stifling, and even oppressive. We are, after all, individuals, with our individual needs and wants. American culture has always celebrated a degree of nonconformity, often revering those who refuse to follow the rules that bind others: the Emerson or the Thoreau in literature, the Henry Ford or the Steven Jobs in commerce, the Adam Clayton Powell or the Mayor Curley in politics. We often admire people who suffer the laughter or scorn of others for their differences and emerge triumphant in the end. But I think we admire them in part for the same reason we admire saints: we know that they are needed, and we also know that society could not survive if everybody were like that. The world needs its Mother Teresas, but it needs its Douglas MacArthurs too.

COMMUNITY AND "MORAL LIBERTY"

. . . .

A society that is free must allow the broadest possible scope for personal choice, but a society that is civil must recognize that the exercise of free choice must always be bounded by morality. This is not to say that immoral choices ought to be illegal. Rather, we as individuals have the responsibility to exercise moral judgment about the choices that we make. Otherwise, we are no better than animals. Jean-Jacques Rousseau captured this point in *The Social Contract*: "[T]he mere impulse of appetite is slavery, while obedience to a law which we prescribe to ourselves is liberty." The liberty of self-control Rousseau called "moral liberty"; it was, he argued, part of what we gained when we left the state of nature and entered civil society.

A part of that moral liberty—if society is to survive—must be the discipline to resist the modern urge to ignore the rules whenever we happen to find them inconvenient. When we find the norms of our community immoral, we should have the moral strength to defy them: conformity for its own sake shows no moral judgment. But neither does nonconformity for its own sake. If we lack serious moral arguments against particular norms or traditions, we should try to adhere to them if at all possible; otherwise, the signal that we send is that we fundamentally disbelieve in the virtue of community.

In our evaluation of the fork-norm, for example, we may think the norm is silly or outdated. But I doubt that it is possible to make a serious case that the norm is immoral. In fact, if we think back to our discussion in chapter 2 of the work of Norbert Elias, we should recognize that the fork-norm is at least descended from a rule carrying an important moral message: human beings are different from animals and can discipline the desires of the body, even the desire to eat. Perhaps, as Erasmus argued, using a fork is morally superior to not using one—at least in our culture. So even if the rules about proper fork choice have grown complicated (or, for most of us, unimportant), those who give them weight are not indulging in an act of folly. They are seeking a signal of willingness to learn *and to obey* the complicated rules that their community has developed to separate its members from others.

Norms that develop over time to inform the character and the actions of members of the community are the community's traditions. The historian Jaroslav Pelikan has cautioned that it is important to distinguish *tradition* from *traditionalism*. Tradition, in Pelikan's view, celebrates the "living faith of the dead"; traditionalism, as he defines it, is the "dead faith of the living."[9] A reverence for tradition, then, calls on us to respect and extend the faith of those who preceded us. We need not, however, surrender our own critical faculties. On the contrary, if we wish to avoid the trap of traditionalism, we must not make the error of assuming that every voice from the past has matters precisely right. We must honor those past voices, but must allow them only to guide, not to rule. This task is not as paradoxical as it may appear; it simply requires the exercise of moral judgment.

The student of civility must not, however, allow the exercise of moral judgment to turn a community's traditions into arguments, or, worse, into mere suggestions. The sociologist Samuel Fleischacker has proposed that we think of tradition as "the sum total of what is *not* argued" as a community teaches its young.[10] This is a sensible approach, as a simple example demonstrates. In chapter 4, I mentioned the words *Please* and *Thank you*, which, when I was growing up, were known as the magic words. Like most parents, my wife and I have tried to train our children to say them too. Although the question of *why* we say the magic words is one of some intellectual weight, I as a parent would not propose to my children that they follow the tradition only if they decide that it is valid. It is not that I want to raise them without an ability to evaluate what they are taught, but I do not want the freedom to evaluate traditions to trump automatically the responsibility to respect them. I want my children to possess the moral liberty that will enable them to follow rules rather than instinct unless there is a good reason to make a different choice.

Edmund Burke criticized the French Revolution on the ground that it seemed bent on overturning traditions for no reason but that they were traditions. Since the 1960s, when a number of genuinely immoral traditions were swept away, America has too often behaved as though what was bad about them was the fact that they were traditions—whereas what was bad about them was the fact that they were wicked traditions. Postmodernism's principal and rather bleak contribution to American public culture has been to create a suspicion about rules and norms themselves. The QUESTION AUTHORITY bumper stickers that proliferated on college campuses in the 1980s exemplified this skeptical stance. The mistake is not in encouraging people to be thoughtful—the massacre at My Lai, even now, should speak for itself—the mistake is in supposing that questioning authority is an end in itself.

One cannot build a community of any kind by encouraging everybody to invent their own norms as needed, and then to abandon them according to whim. The very idea of democracy rests on the broad popular acceptance of a set of democratic norms—the best examples are liberty and equality, but there are more—and our national community is built around them. Should we all feel free to discard them as we wish, we would no longer be a democratic community. To be sure, we should always resist the application of norms that we consider immoral (a subject to which we will return), but we should not conclude that a norm is immoral simply because we think it silly or find it inconvenient.

Thus, we see another rule of civility:

> *Civility requires a commitment to live a common moral life, so we should try to follow the norms of the community if the norms are not actually immoral.*

This proposition leads to one of the most interesting, and most debated, questions in social science: How are norms that are not laws enforced? We do not, yet, know as much on the subject as we should. Still, it seems safe to say that the short answer is that most norms must be self-enforcing—that is, must be obeyed even when the likelihood of punishment is small—in order to exist as norms in the first place. The skeptical assertion that both norms and laws are obeyed chiefly because of a fear of the consequences of disobedience has been largely refuted by empirical research suggesting that norms and laws alike are obeyed in large part because of a strongly held super-norm that counsels obedience to constituted authority.[11] This research has a commonsense moral appeal: a society in which people follow the rules because of a constant worry about getting caught is what most of us consider a police state.

Nevertheless, norms are sometimes violated. When they have the force of law, that violation may entail legal punishment. Most norms, however, are not laws, and they are enforced, if at all, through community pressure.[12] Those who violate them are made to feel that their status as members may be at risk, or they may actually be expelled from the community. Examples abound. Lisa Bernstein's pioneering work has shown how the diamond trade is based on norms, not formal laws—and yet, she concludes, it works.[13] My Yale colleague Robert Ellickson has done the same for the relations among cattle ranchers.[14] In both cases, members of the relevant community have worked out elaborate systems of expectations that allow them to carry on their businesses efficiently and at a relatively high level of morality, systems that continue to work as long as those who refuse to follow the rules are quickly brought into line by the pressure of others.*

Even without studying the scholarship, we find examples in everyday life. In the example we saw earlier in the chapter, one neighbor may hint to another that the grass is getting a little high. A boss may suggest that an employee wear something more appropriate to the office tomorrow. A pastor may warn a parishioner that a course of conduct runs contrary to the denomination's understanding of God's law. In each case, the pressure, if successful, rests in part on the status anxiety of the pressured—in short, the need to belong to the group.

---

* If too many members of the community defect, the system collapses. But this is just further evidence that a community is able to define itself by its norms only as long as the norms themselves are obeyed by community members.

Sometimes there may seem to be no entity adequate to the task of exerting social pressure. This may lead to the conclusion that a law is necessary. But there will be times when no law is remotely possible. Consider one of the examples from chapter 3—negative campaigning by politicians. Once upon a time, as we have seen, attacks on political opponents were barbed yet subtle. The historian John F. Kasson has linked this practice to a strong nineteenth-century norm against verbal attacks on gentlemen by other gentlemen.[15] (The norm was most likely adopted because of a shared interest in protecting the upper class.) Those days, of course, are well behind us. The decline of class distinctions, at least in our public life, has largely eradicated the ability to enforce any such norms, as the celebration of a Dennis Rodman or a Rush Limbaugh makes apparent.

Surveys show that American voters detest the personal attacks that have become so common a feature of the political season. Nobody seems to know what to do about them, however, because attack ads evidently work. The student of civility should find the way they work instructive. Social scientists tell us that negative advertising rarely persuades voters to change their minds, but it does seem to reinforce the preferences of voters who are leaning toward supporting the candidate running the ads. Soft support becomes firm support.[16] Or, in terms of civil dialogue, people who might have been open to persuasion cease to be.

Anything that interferes with dialogue is bad for civility. But what is there to do? A few states have actually enacted laws in an effort to limit negative campaigns—and have generated only litigation.[17] The Congress has been presented with a number of bills with the same intention in recent years, but none has ever come to a vote. So laws are impossible, and norms (if there are any) are evidently unenforceable. And we would not want, I take it, a federal agency to review campaign materials. Yet there is in America an entity with the power to regulate the content of political advertising, able to punish a candidate who is too negative, and reward a candidate who conducts the campaign with honor and integrity. That entity, from whose judgment there is no appeal, is *us*—the American voters. We simply must be courageous enough and self-sacrificing enough—in short, civil enough—to do it. (Chapter 8 includes some tips on just how.)

Community enforcement of moral norms is not easy work. Treating people as outsiders makes them feel bad—a cardinal sin in a nation that nowadays often seems to worship feeling good. So standing fast in support of a moral norm, even one that is widely shared, requires a degree of moral courage, because there will often be criticism, and it will rarely be civil in tone.

This brings us back to the high school student disciplined for his falling pants, whose story I told in the previous chapter. No doubt he could be cast as a resister against the norm that requires pants to stay up rather than sagging low enough to expose the buttocks. No doubt obedience to that norm would make it more difficult for him to signal whatever it is that his falling pants are meant to signal. But the fact that he does not wish to follow the norm is no evidence of the immorality of the norm. His inability to abide by a sensible compromise on the standard of dress that has evolved over time is evidence instead of his unwillingness to discipline his desires. That so many young people today, across a broad range of issues, show the same unwillingness is a sign not of our society's freedom but of its incivility. We do not value our young people enough to teach them that the satisfaction of their immediate desires is no proper measure of the morality of a course of conduct. And so our children, black and white, rich and poor, are growing up deprived of a sense of civility, the willingness to sacrifice for others, that forms the foundation for a sense of morality.

SHARED SACRIFICE AND SHARED MEANING

. . . .

And what has all this to do with democracy, the subject that opened the chapter? I suspect that most Americans, if asked to define democracy, would probably say something about voting. But most nations of the world have elections of some kind or other, and even though the number is growing, not all of those nations are true democracies. Back in the 1950s and 1960s, political theorists investigated American "exceptionalism"; they wanted to know why our democracy worked when so many others did not.[18] Although our relativistic times make it hard to imagine the debates, the questions still hover: Are we as a nation different? Is our system better? If we are, and if it is, the distinction must be that despite our bickering and incivility, we as a people share a commitment to realize in our national life a set of common values. Those commonalities, not the accident of our borders, are what make us a nation.

In America, the commitment to realize shared values stems in large part from the nation's common religious inheritance.[19] But the commitment has also been created by experience: in particular, the nation most of us know and love today has been molded by the shared experiences of what has come to be called the World War II generation. Despite its name, that generation had two formative experiences—the Great Depression and the Great War. The experiences were shared because everybody risked something, everybody sacrificed. And that shared experience forged a moral consensus that has survived to the present day, providing the springboard for everything from the civil rights movement and the Great Society to the contemporary rhetoric of returning government to a level where people feel it is touchable.

Earlier generations also suffered through common experiences of the sort that create nations: the Civil War, for example. The baby boom generation seems to be only the second in our history to move into positions of power without ever having shared a national experience of sacrifice of the sort that molds not only character but the nation's sense of itself and what it values. The first such generation, the post–Civil War babies who began to run the country just after the turn of the century, ultimately gave us the Red Scares, the great trusts that paralyzed the economy, the uncertain victory in the First World War, the self-indulgence of the Roaring Twenties, and the Depression itself.

Okay, I am oversimplifying. Nevertheless, I do fear that the current generation's lack of the experience of shared sacrifices that helps create genuine shared meaning places the nation at some risk. The reckless and nasty attacks on Bill Clinton for not having served in the military actually masked an important point that deserves public discussion. It is true that Clinton's generation (which is also mine) missed military service. It sometimes seems as though everybody did—not just Bill Clinton, but Pat Buchanan, Newt

Gingrich, Phil Gramm, much of the current Washington crowd.[20] The larger problem, however, is not that my generation missed Vietnam, but that we missed *the* war, World War II, the formative event of the modern nation. That was not our fault: we were born too late. But if we allow that accident of birth to persuade us that we share too little in common to be civil to one another, we will be destroying what earlier generations fought to preserve.

Not long ago, I had lunch with the mayor of a large American city, who told me with a kind of despair about the new breed of politician, for whom all policy disagreements are reasons for personal animosity. The mayor, a black man, was a veteran of the Civil Rights Movement and remembered it fondly as a time when it was possible for those who disagreed to work together. But the new politicians, he complained, have no sense of the need to do business with those on the other side of the aisle—because they missed World War II, he explained. Not because they missed fighting in it—they even missed being children in it. They are a part of the generation, he proposed, that has accomplished little for America, in part because America has given them everything and asked them for nothing. The new breed, he concluded, is a bunch of spoiled children.

Although a Democrat, the mayor had no political ax to grind: he condemned both parties equally. Not because they disagree. Not because they are partisan (which is what parties, literally, are supposed to be). But because neither party has a program that calls Americans to sacrifice for others for the sake of belonging to something greater than themselves. And there is sad truth in the mayor's lament. Civility as we have been using the term is not central to either party's platform. Republicans tend to promise tax cuts, and Democrats tend to promise rights and entitlements, but both parties are really doing the same thing: appealing to our selfish side, to our desire to have.

We saw in the previous chapter that a sacrificial civility has two components: generosity when there is cost, and trust when there is risk. American politics is not about either. Conservatives refuse to call voters to be generous (for example, by supporting programs that might cost money), and liberals refuse to call voters to be trusting (for example, by looking to legislatures rather than courts in the effort to turn our desires into rights). Neither party is willing to ask us to give. Neither party calls us to duty and obligation—to ask not what our country can do for us, but what we can do for our country. One wonders whether it is even possible to ask Americans to sacrifice when we lack the shared experiences from which commitments of that kind are drawn.

Consider once more the example of marriage, which we discussed earlier in the chapter. In earlier generations, married couples understood what was expected of them and knew that the commitment did not end simply because one of them grew bored or fell in love with somebody else. This shared understanding did indeed leave some husbands and wives in unhappy marriages, but it also avoided the costs of our current, looser attitude: the evidence of the destruction that divorce does to children is overwhelming.[21] Furthermore, although we do not yet have enough information to be sure, there is good reason to think that divorce is also terribly damaging to spouses whose expectations are shattered. And then there is the larger, less measurable damage that divorce does to the stability, the settledness of the society itself: family should be a bedrock on which the rest of the culture can rest.

So what is to be done? One proposal that is growing in popularity is the idea of allowing couples to choose "covenant marriage," in which divorce would be harder to obtain. A covenant marriage would evidently be what all marriages were thought to be a generation ago, when the force of religious belief and community expectation did the work of holding marriages together. So it is sad that we even have to think about it. But think about it we must, if family is to survive. Unfortunately, the American Civil Liberties Union, an important organization with a terrible habit of shooting itself in the foot, at once opposed the proposal, on the ground that it would trap people in unhappy marriages. What some call an infringement of liberty, others call a genuine commitment. It would be nice if the ACLU understood that freedom includes the freedom to commit ourselves to less freedom. Our commitments matter, and we should be guided by them except when there is a strong reason not to be.[22] "I don't feel like it" is not a strong reason. We as a nation once understood this, before the idea that all our desires should be satisfied began running roughshod over everything else.

The absence of a shared moral understanding, developed through shared experience of sacrifice, leads us to the kind of radical individualism that causes ordinary social interaction to become both stressful and dispensable. We travel through life alone, with no fellow passengers: the automobile, not the train, remains our metaphor. Avoiding this fate will require us to adhere to rule 5: to try to live a common moral life. That life does not require us to be indistinguishable from one another, to share the same views on every issue, to never disagree. It need not lead to a stifling of the glorious diversity that is one of America's gifts. It does ask us to look behind that diversity to understand what we share in common before we begin our search for the ways in which we are different. And it requires a commitment to be guided, at times, by the moral opinions of others, even when we think they are wrong—one of the sacrifices we make for the sake of our fellow passengers. If we lose that commitment, whether it is forgotten in the hurly-burly of contemporary life or left behind in our mad rush toward self-fulfillment, we also lose the connections to one another that bind us into a single nation. Without those connections, we are left to face each other armed with nothing but mutual suspicion, skepticism, fear, and hostility—in short, the deep instinct for self—the tools with which, prior to civilization, an earlier generation of human beings doubtless faced all strangers. Which is to say, we act like animals.

Avoiding this fate is a matter of choice—the choice to be civil. Exercising that choice requires what we might call, with appropriate apologies to Nietzsche, the will to democracy: not the desire, as Nietzsche would have it in his will to power, to twist the world into one in which we can become what we already are, but the desire to sustain democracy by discovering (or developing) the basic values that make us a people. If the rising generation has missed the chance at shared sacrifice, we must not miss the chance at shared conversation, to discover and also to shape the common meanings that bind us together.

The alternative is to continue our destructive tendency to engage in behavior aimed only at satisfying our own (or perhaps our family's or our employer's) wants and needs. In our rush to self-fulfillment, we forget the crucial civilizing insight of the

Enlightenment—that human freedom is good because it is better to do right voluntarily than to be coerced into doing it. As we have seen, that act of collective amnesia opens the entirety of our social life to the pollution of politics and the market. That pollution in turn damages democracy, perhaps beyond repair. Living in a nation that encourages us to do what we like rather than what we should, it is small wonder that we are so uncivil (and also so uncivilized). And once we are persuaded that we have no background values in common, it is a very small step to being persuaded that we are not a people at all.

6

. . . .

Sacrifice and Neighbor-Love

Y ES, FINE, you might still ask—but so what? Why should we worry about how we treat strangers who do not love us and whom we do not love? In particular, why should we care enough to sacrifice for them? Why should we be generous, or trusting, or even respectful?

The answer I have offered is that a sacrificial civility is a moral obligation. But very little in contemporary political theory teaches us much about the discipline of our desires for the sake of others. Conservatism teaches us to worship our property, liberalism teaches us to worship our rights. Both teach us to worship ourselves, but neither one teaches us to yield our own desires for the sake of others. So where do we go to learn the language of sacrifice? In a nation where both discourse and behavior are dominated by the political ethic of *victory-at-any-cost* and the market ethic of *getting-mine*, where do we learn to put aside our own desires and even needs for the sake of the larger good? By now, the answer should be obvious, even if controversial: We go to our churches, our synagogues, our mosques, and our temples. In short, we go to God.

CIVILITY AND NEIGHBOR-LOVE

. . . .

Just before her death in March of 1815, a Mrs. Martha Williams of Providence, Rhode Island, asked that at her funeral the minister discourse on one of the most famous passages in the Christian Bible, John 14:12, in which Jesus commands the apostles to "love one another as I have loved you." Her request was answered in the form of a sermon by one Luther Willson, pastor of the Congregational Church in Brooklyn, whose remarks, entitled *The Character and Effects of Christian Love*, have fortunately survived. I say fortunately because Willson, without even using the words, offers a forceful and clear explanation of the link between the virtue of civility and the willingness to yield our self-interest for the interest of others.

Christian love, Willson explains, is not about self-seeking but about "conscious responsibility to the God of Love."[1] And what form does this love take? It is, says Willson, "an elevated and practical principle" that has a straightforward effect on the man (he uses gendered pronouns) who practices it: "His heart expands with a generous desire, a feeling solicitude for the comfort and welfare of the human race." This in turn leads the person who is practicing Christian love to a willingness to sacrifice:

> He enters into the views and feelings of the happiest and most miserable of our species, and makes *their* interest, *their* joys and sorrows his *own*. Gladly would he make the greatest sacrifices to alleviate the wants and distresses of the unfortunate, could he but expect that his sacrifices and wishes would be successful.[2]

One need not be a Christian—or be religious at all—to be moved by this passage and to understand its point. Giving to others is a positive good; it improves society. Every religion, every secular moral philosophy, agrees on this. We admire those who give to others because we know how difficult it is—especially when we are asked to give to those whom we do not know well, or at all. Most of us, when we do make sacrifices, probably find it easier to sacrifice for those we care about than for the stranger. Yet the ethic of neighbor-love that has sustained both Christianity and Judaism has long called on believers to sacrifice for those we do not know.

According to a story in the *B'tuv Yerushalayim*, Rabbi Yehoshua Leib Diskin once warned a fellow rabbi against joining a friendship club, the members of which pledged to help each other. Said Rabbi Diskin, "Such a group is not a manifestation of loving one's fellow man. It is a manifestation of love for one's self." Why? Because the members were helping one another only to guarantee that they, too, would be helped in time of trouble. This, argued Diskin, "is against the Torah's commandment to love everyone, even those who are not members of the group."[3] In a similar vein, the Lutheran theologian Deitrich Bonhoeffer warned that having close, special friends is a threat to the Christian requirement that we love all equally.[4]

This is a fascinating, if challenging, idea—but, once we think about it, the logic is impeccable. If we (whether secular or religious) believe in the duty to treat all human beings with equal respect, it becomes difficult to explain why we should treat those we know well or with whom we are on intimate terms with a special respect that we do not accord others. The Biblical command is that we love our *neighbors*. Many translators substitute words like *others* or *our fellow men* or *other people* for *neighbors*, in order to avoid possible confusion with the modern understanding of *neighbor* as someone who lives near us in a geographical sense. Diskin and Bonhoeffer (and many other commentators) want us to avoid a more profound version of the same error: supposing that we can place limits, for our own convenience, on the unconditional duty of love. But we cannot. The Biblical command is neither to love those who are close to us nor to love those who treat us well. The command of love is universal.

The unexceptionable moral rule Diskin and Bonhoeffer demand of us may seem a bit inhuman. Which of us does not have family and friends for whom we make special sacrifices? Does not the nature of family actually *demand* special sacrifices? Yes, and yes again. But Diskin did not say it is against the Torah to have friends—only that it is wrong to favor one's friends above others. As for Bonhoeffer, his special concern was for the mischief that might occur when those who are under holy orders—priests, monks, nuns—enter into relationships that distract them from their more general duty of Christian love.

The point, then, is more subtle than it seems, but it harks back to our first rule of civility: our duty to be civil toward others does not depend on how much we like them. Civility is not related to liking at all; that is why I call it a duty. Worded this way, the principle does not deny that we have special relationships, like marriage, that may entail special duties. But the duties flow from the relationship itself, not from our feelings about the relationship. So, for example, our duty to cherish the sacred bond of marriage does not depend on whether we are happy with the particular marriage arrangement in which we find ourselves.[5] Similarly, our duty to love our neighbor—in civility terms, to sacrifice for the stranger—does not depend on whether our neighbor is somebody we happen to like.

I am not denying that we should love our families and friends. I am not denying that it is natural and human to favor them above others. (I know I do it.) I am not denying that God basically made us for family life. (That is why those who take Holy Orders that include celibacy are making so sublime a sacrifice for the Lord.) I am only pointing out that a very honored strand of the Judeo-Christian tradition warns that it is possible to love family and friends in a way that makes it difficult to love others. And this is what civility counsels us to avoid.

In the years before the Civil War, the Biblical command to love our neighbors was the favorite text of abolitionist preachers, and no wonder: it possesses a power and a simplicity that sweep away the strained and eerie readings of Scripture that are needed to argue for a God who mandates inequality. Listen to the words of the great evangelist and abolitionist preacher Charles G. Finney on the subject of slavery and love of neighbor in an 1860 sermon at Oberlin:

> We see how we are to treat those who are oppressed and in slavery. We are to put ourselves in their position and inquire what we should ask them to do for us, in their circumstances. Suppose my family and I were in slavery. Election time is approaching. Have I a right to expect my friends in Ohio to cast their votes so as to bear directly upon my liberation? I should be very prone to think that no one ought to cast his vote against my liberty for the mere sake of money or office. Even politicians can see how shameful and how outrageously wrong it is to hold any person as a slave.[6]

Finney, like Willson, asks us to love our neighbors by making their sorrows our own—which we do, says Finney, by trying to decide what we would want them to do for us were our positions reversed. Some eight decades earlier, pro-independence preachers had offered a similar analysis, accusing the British of not acting toward the colonies in the way required by love of neighbor.[7]

The preachers of the eighteenth and nineteenth centuries well understood the continuum of neighbor-love, on which good manners certainly formed one pole. The link between the war on slavery and the war on incivility was explicit. In 1787 the evangelist William Wilberforce penned the following words in his diary: "God Almighty has set before me two great objects, the suppression of the slave trade and the reformation of manners."[8] And the connection makes perfect sense: enslaving other human beings is simply an extreme form of the lack of respect for their createdness that allows us to be rude. In both cases, we violate the requirement to love our neighbors.

This commandment of love, common in some form to all the world's great religions, captures the greatest beauty and the greatest difficulty of the life lived in faith. We look at our neighbors, and we see people who hate or lie or kill or cheat or in other ways do enormous damage—and then we turn to God and are told that we should love them. This must seem a tremendous burden, but it is a burden that we must take up if we are to reconstruct civility and strengthen it against all the many threats it faces.

In both Christianity and Judaism, the ability of the human to love other imperfect humans is a symbol of God's love for His creation. That is the significance of Jesus' calling on his followers to love one another as he has loved them. The idea that we are called upon to love because God loves is more solid, more satisfactory, than the competing secular moral ideal of compassion, which, for all its fine intentions, often sounds like the famous words of Mammy Yokum: "Good is better than evil because it's nicer." And yet, whether our motivation for treating our neighbor well is religious devotion, secular moral understanding, or even the simple self-interest that we discussed (and found wanting) in chapter 2, the one thing that remains crystal clear is that loving the neighbor is hard work.

Consider a subsidiary of the command to love our neighbors, the Golden Rule, perhaps best known in the West in its formulation from the King James Version of the Bible: "Do unto others as you would have them do unto you." The Golden Rule is the simplest of commands, and maybe the hardest one to follow. The psychiatrist Robert Coles has written movingly of the effects on our children when we adults—too often!—ignore this central principle of moral life.[9] Instead, we tend to follow the principle that game theorists call tit-for-tat: we treat others, at best, however they treat us. At worst, as when we drive, we treat others as though they are not even there.

If we have trouble following a simple principle that is almost a matter of self-interest, treating others as we would like them to treat us, it is small wonder that we have trouble following a more difficult command to treat others with love. The command to love our neighbors does not demand of us the psychologically impossible—that we actually feel an emotional intimacy with every person we meet—but it does require us to *act* with love toward others. This rule demands of us a hard discipline that may seem ill suited to our self-indulgent age. If we decide to treat others well merely in order to provide a social lubricant, we quickly begin to make enough exceptions to swallow the rule: this one does not deserve respect because he is so rude, that one because of her political views, a third one because of some deep, dark secret that is suddenly a part of the public knowledge. All we really want to know about manners is what is in it for us. This is surely the reason for Arthur Schlesinger's warning, first quoted back in chapter 1, about the disentangling of ethics and etiquette: taking them apart tends to weaken both.

I suspect it will be possible to treat each other with love only if we are able to conceive doing so as a moral obligation that is absolute, something we owe others because of their personhood, bearing no relation to whether we like them or not. My wife puts it this way: every encounter with another human being should inspire in us a powerful sense of awe. Why? Because that other human being, whatever his or her strengths, weaknesses, and simple complexities, is also a part of God's creation. We should be struck with awe at the fact that we are face to face with a part of God's work. It is one of those propositions that, once stated, seems like a truth we should have seen all along—but somehow it takes someone of uncommon wisdom to point it out.

To enter into the presence of another human being, then, is to enter into the presence of God in a new and different way. We are admonished in the psalm to come into His presence with thanksgiving (Psalms 95:2), not with suspicion, self-seeking, or disrespect. The great theologians Karl Barth and Martin Buber both arrived at this point along their different paths: our obligation is to see God in everyone, not merely as possibility, but as reality. So whenever we mistreat others, we are abusing our relationship with God. And awe alone does not capture what we owe. We should encounter others with a sense of gratitude, for here is a fresh and different corner of God's creation—or, for the secular-minded, a new and different human being. We should be grateful to be traveling where we have not been before.

So the rule, a hard one, is this:

> *We must come into the presence of our fellow human beings with a sense of awe and gratitude.*

Consequently, we can see that the obligation of civility entails more than charitable acts; it entails a habit of the mind, perhaps an orientation of the soul, toward the other, the one who is outside of us and may seem very different from us, and yet is part of us through our equal share in God's creation.

In secular terms, we would be required to treat all our fellow citizens as full equals, signaling our respect for them whether we happen to like them or not. Those who doubt that human beings are created in God's image (or who doubt the existence of God) can nevertheless recognize in *Homo sapiens* an organizational complexity that places humans at the apex of nature's creation; the nearly impossible chain of coincidences needed to bring about the human organism is reason enough for awe. (I have often thought it takes a far greater leap of faith to believe humans to be the product of blind natural selection than to believe them the product of Divine Will.) We must believe—and behave as though we believe—that our possession of more money or more education or even what we deem to be more moral truth than somebody else does not alter in the slightest degree the respect that we owe. This helps explain why Benjamin DeMott was so terribly wrong in his argument discussed in chapter 2: even a thug shares equally in

God's creation, and so even a thug is entitled to the respect that we owe our neighbors. (Which is not to say that civility forbids us ever to fight back.) That is what the marchers of the civil rights era knew, and what most of us today seem to have forgotten. But we can learn again both to believe that way and to behave that way if we can conjure the awe that our fellow humans are due and manage the sacrifices that awe demands.[10]

THE GOSPEL OF SACRIFICE

· · · · · · · · · · · · ·

Sacrifice. Few things are harder for us mortals than giving up something we would rather keep. Thus, the more people are willing to give up for others, the greater the likelihood that we will celebrate them in our mythology of virtue.* So we acclaim Francis of Assisi, who distributed to the poor all he owned before beginning his ministry; we are occasionally astonished by Nathan Hale, who, according to the traditional story, faced execution regretting only that he had but one life to give for his country; we cheer for the great philanthropists, especially the anonymous ones, like the man discovered by the press in early 1997 who was thought to be a billionaire, except that it turned out he had given nearly all of it away, in secret; and, of course, we accept without question the heroic character of anyone who dies defending our nation or trying to rescue a drowning child.

These much-admired sacrifices involve the surrender of something we can readily understand as large and important: the entirety of one's worldly goods, the totality of one's life. The project of constructing civility will also require all of us to surrender some of our desires, although mostly smaller ones: things we want to do, things we want to possess, things we want to be, and, of course, things we want to say. For civility *is* sacrifice. This is the simple and beautiful truth that eludes the legions of journalists and politicians and national commissions who have spent recent

---

* I am using the word *mythology* not in its colloquial sense of denoting a story that is false but in its technical sense of denoting a story, even a true one, that helps us to define ourselves.

years bemoaning our inability to treat each other with dignity and respect. Civility, as Luther Willson understood, is founded upon our willingness to make the interests, joys, and sorrows of others our own. And the measure of our commitment to the construction of civility is how much we are willing to give up to achieve it.

What forms of sacrifice does civility demand of us? Some of the answers are (or should be) obvious. As we saw in chapter 2, keeping my temper when I would rather lose it is a rather basic sacrifice I might make for civility. So is being respectful to those with whom I strongly disagree: it is easier, and feels more natural, to be rude and dismissive. And then there is the other side of civility, the call to acts of community. The call may require something as small as attending a P.T.A. meeting or leading a Cub Scout troop when we would rather be watching television, or as large as going off to fight for our country when we would rather be safe at home. But in every case, the model is the same. There is the thing that I should do to show my love for others, and there is the thing that I would rather do, out of a desire for my own pleasure and comfort.

Religion, by calling for sacrifice, acts on the human mind and spirit, teaching values that are different from the materialism that characterizes both politics and the market and that has lately battered every sphere of social life. The religious individual and the nonreligious individual necessarily see the world differently, if only because religion orients the mind in directions that the secular world might find startling. "Why am I here?" and "What do I owe in return for my creation?" are questions not meaningful or important in a world of atomistic, advantage-seeking individuals, but to most religions, especially in the Western tradition, they are of first importance.

Consider Jürgen Habermas's view that religion, although once quite important to human progress, is a stultifying force in a modern world that now emphasizes autonomy.[11] The same argument, albeit in less conciliatory form, finds its way into much of contemporary philosophy, which tends to view religion as an obstacle in the construction of the liberal state.[12] One difficulty with this argument is that it assumes the superiority of the culture that values the individual over the culture that values community or tradition.[13] This assumption itself violates the autonomy of people who disagree with it, but that is a very moot point. More important, religion's value in a democracy is precisely that it focuses believers on questions (and answers) different from those of the dominant culture. It is this aspect of religion, which the theologian David Tracy calls its subversive nature, that makes it threatening to the existing order and makes it a force for change. Religion's subversive nature is always scary to those who benefit from the status quo, but it is glorious and powerful for those who seek change.

Although theorists who write about the subversive nature of religion tend to be liberals—Tracy himself sometimes leans toward what has come to be called "liberation theology"—it would be an error to suppose that religion's challenge to the status quo is invariably helpful to the left. Any dominant idea might be subject to religious resistance. In contemporary America, religious forces may seek to subvert established understandings about the glories of capitalism or the desirability of nuclear weapons, but those forces may also seek to overturn the status quo on abortion. The morality of religious resistance is potentially quite complex, even, sometimes, within the same religion. One thinks, for example, of the 1997 comment by a spokeswoman for the United States Conference of Catholic Bishops, who said her group wished that President Clinton had vetoed rather than signed the welfare reform bill and signed rather than vetoed the partial-birth abortion ban. (Most liberals seemed to think he should veto both; conservatives seemed to think he should sign both.)

The subversive nature of religion is also the reason we need more of it now. As we have seen, our social life, the space where we live in common, is being overwhelmed by the values of politics and the market, which emphasize not community but individuality and thus encourage us to be self-seeking. My reference here is not to greed; as the political scientist Andrew Hacker has pointed out, there is a difference between being greedy and simply accepting what comes your way in a prosperous age.[14] What politics and the market teach is the elevation of the self, and the desires of the self, above all else. By instructing the faithful that there is something of first and greatest importance that lies beyond the satisfaction of desire, the religions at their best provide exactly the moral armament that is needed to resist the domination of social life by self-seeking, and thus to rescue civility.

Think for a moment about another well-known story in the Christian Bible: Christ's response to the rich youth seeking salvation. This passage, too, may be read as an instruction in sacrificial civility.

The story is quickly told. When Jesus is preaching in Judea, a rich young man shows up and asks how he can achieve salvation. Jesus tells him to keep the Commandments. The man says, "I have kept all these; what do I still lack?" Jesus responds: "If you wish to be perfect, go, sell your possessions, and give the money to the poor, and you will have treasure in heaven; then come, follow me." The Gospel writer adds the sad denouement: "When the young man heard this word, he went away grieving, for he had many possessions." Jesus then turns to his disciples and utters these famous words: "[I]t is easier for a camel to go through the eye of a needle than for someone who is rich to enter the kingdom of God" (Matthew 19:20–30; see also Mark 10:17–31).

The tale is often cited, correctly, for the proposition that it is not easy for the rich to find salvation. But to read it at so literal a level is to miss the principal point. Christ's admonition is not about wealth as such, but about sacrifice. Consider: Why is it so difficult for the rich man to enter the kingdom of heaven? Because money is itself evil? If so, it may be that everybody should be poor and, indeed, that possession of any amount of money may be corrupting. This position does in fact have behind it a strong and thoughtful theological tradition, although it must be added that the Biblical text contains examples—some of them in Jesus' own parables—of wealthy men who do what is right. A better understanding is that the rich man has trouble achieving salvation because he loves his money so much. Indeed, he loves his money so much that it may serve to distract him from his duties to God. So when Jesus calls on the rich man to surrender his possessions, the reason is not to engage in some redistribution of wealth, for his concern at that moment seems to be not the poor but the puzzled and desperate man who stands before him. Jesus' words are more a warning of what is likely than a concrete rule for living; he is trying to get the wealthy young man to see that his money is too central to his life, that it is drawing his eyes away from God. The rich man is, in effect, worshiping his wealth, and should share it with the poor before it is too late. His refusal to share is evidence of what he most deeply values: he cannot give to the poor because he cannot bear to part with his money, and he cannot bear to part with his money because he loves his money more than he loves God. Properly understood, then, the story is about idolatry.

But the story would work as well with anything else that we value so highly that we will not give it up to turn our eyes toward God. The admonition is not principally about charity, but about giving up what we value most, for God's sake. In modern terms, Jesus might as well be saying to a big-city machine politician, "Give your temporal power to the next in line," or to a star baseball player, "Give your superior batting average to a weak-hitting teammate." He might even be saying to a committed political activist, "Take your cherished political convictions, put them aside, and follow me"—for a beloved political ideal, no less than a beloved fortune, can serve as a distraction from following God. The sacrifice comes in yielding what we value most.[15]

The story, then, is about the sacrifice that is at the heart of our relations with God. Once we accept our equality before God, our being made in the image of God, the story is also about the sacrifice that is at the heart of our relationship with others, and therefore is really about civility. Civility, the reader will remember, demands a willingness to sacrifice for the sake of our fellow passengers—to do less of what we want and more of what we should—and the story of the rich man illustrates its workings: Jesus' words call on us to ask what things we value so much that they interfere with our ability to recognize the face of God in others.

What are some of the things that interfere? One obvious villain is racial prejudice, for it is the nature and purpose of racism to interfere with our ability to see God in others. Racism proposes that the stranger (the racial stranger) counts for less than the familiar. The need to overcome this difficulty is, for the student of civility, the strongest argument against segregation. For decades, supporters of school integration have argued that white children who attend racially integrated schools have less hardened racial attitudes than those who attend all-white schools. The claim possesses a commonsense appeal, because of what we have already seen: it is far easier to treat well those we know well.[16] Racism blinds us to who others are; it treats the stranger as so radically different that it is not possible to feel the "generous desire, a feeling solicitude," that Willson said should characterize our relations with all others.

But this blindness may grow equally from many other commitments and desires that complicate our lives. One person is rich in money. The next is rich in political convictions. The rich man may be unable to find awe when facing the poor one, but that is no more sinful, and no more uncivil, than the committed activist unable to find awe when facing those of very different political commitments. In short, anything about which we feel so strongly that we are unwilling to cast it aside in order to see the face of God in others is a part of the structure of incivility that is so warping our world.

The modern American way is to treat such sacrifices as costs, as limits on freedom. Both Christian and Jewish ethics, however, insist that such sacrifices can be liberating. Thus, the marriage vow that is kept to the end of life is not the surrender of possible future pleasures, but liberation from possible future betrayals. Giving to the poor is not the surrender of the opportunity to spend one's own money, but liberation from a life of greed and self-seeking. And dying in a war for the nation's defense is not the surrender of years of future enjoyment, but liberation from the knowledge that one could have helped and did nothing. When we pay for the privilege of doing what is right, we are saving ourselves from sin.

WHAT CIVILITY ISN'T

· · · · · · · · · · · · ·

Sometimes, listening to today's preachers, I worry that the concept of love of neighbor has become confused with the very different concept of making the neighbor feel good. So it is useful to pause for a moment and reflect, not on the definition of civility, but on some of the concepts that falsely masquerade as civility. We have already seen that disagreement, even passionate disagreement, is not the same as incivility; the flip side is that agreement, even consensus, is not the same as civility. Democracy needs dialogue, and dialogue requires disagreement. Indeed, we show greater love for our neighbors by telling them when we think they are wrong than by lying to them, pretending we think they are right. We should thrash out our disagreements as sharply as may seem necessary, as long as we do so, always, in a civil manner.

Similarly, criticism, even sharp criticism, is not uncivil. If I read a paper by a student and say, "This is not a very good job," the student may be unhappy, but hurt feelings are no index of incivility. I show no respect for the student by lying, and I do not do my job as a teacher if I fail to point out error. Nor is this lesson limited to the teaching profession. A boss who does not correct an errant employee should not be a boss. There are even Talmudic stories suggesting that love of our fellows *requires* that we criticize them when it is appropriate to do so.[17]

Civility involves the discipline of our passions for the sake of living a common life with others—as Luther Willson put it, making their interests our own. But we do not make the interests of others our own when we think only about how to make them feel good. This is why the self-esteem movement in education is, in the end, deeply uncivil. If we propose to reward students without demanding achievement, we are neither showing them the respect to which they are entitled nor offering them a sense of the world's hard truth—that rewards, with rare exception, are earned, not granted as gifts. When we emphasize self-esteem, we fail to focus the attention of the students on self-discipline, which is at the heart of living a common life. So it is scarcely surprising that the DARE program—an anti-drug effort centered on raising the self-esteem of students—has turned out to be a well-intentioned failure. There were never any data supporting the proposition that young people who are told how great they are, are less likely to use drugs, but there have always been data to suggest that young people who achieve positively, whether in the classroom, in sports, or in community activities, are less likely to use drugs. DARE resulted from a confusion: the belief that it is the glow of feeling good, rather than the glow of feeling good because one has accomplished something, that reduces the chances of drug abuse.

Breaking the connection between achievement and self-esteem

proposes that there is value in feeling good for its own sake—or, more to the point, that nobody should feel bad. The unwillingness to cause unhappiness in others helps bring about everything from the grade inflation rampant on our campuses to the seeming epidemic of spoiled children.[18] It encourages others to lead lives according to desire, which is at the heart of incivility. As we have seen, the refusal to discipline our impulses is ultimately at the heart of everything from the negative way we conduct our political campaigns to the selfish and dangerous way we drive our cars.

But our driving habits are only a symbol of a much deeper refusal to make many of the sacrifices that leading a civil life—civilité—demands. Probably the greatest sacrifice that all of us must make, but also the most important one, is to try to live our own lives in a way that models civility. We must do this for the benefit of our children, who look to our actions, not our words, for guidance on how to live. Lots of organizations call on adults to mentor children, but mentoring without moral content will not solve the problem. The syndicated columnist Cynthia Tucker argues that all children are entitled to "old fuddy-duddies" in their lives: people who stand up for such traditional norms as the idea that the mother and father of the same child should be married to each other.[19] In our morally uncertain era, standing up for moral traditions that require people to do things they may not want to do is not as easy as it once was, but that very lack of ease makes it all the more important for each of us to try.

This leads to the final confusion about the nature of civility. Although impoliteness is almost always uncivil, politeness alone is no mark of civility. A concentration camp guard possessing the most exquisite good manners is a concentration camp guard nonetheless. His willingness to say, "Would you mind stepping into the gas chamber, sir?" is a mark only of horror. This suggests that there are some ideas (although the number is small) so repugnant to civilization that those who propose them or work to achieve them are necessarily uncivil, no matter how cultured or well-mannered they may appear.

What might these ideas be? In brief, they are proposals that we hate our neighbors rather than love them. Racism—the will, or even the desire, to do harm to others because of their skin color—is perhaps America's quintessential example of an uncivil idea. In my book *Integrity*, I suggest beginning our list with three ideas that we can agree (I hope) represent true evil: racial hatred; violence based on difference; and violence resulting from a closed mind. Genocide, I argue, is the greatest evil of all, combining as it does all three.[20] All of us could probably offer lists of our own. What is important as we list the ideas that constitute neighbor-hatred rather than neighbor-love is to take care that we not simply list all the political ideas with which we disagree. For perhaps the easiest way to spot an uncivil fanatic is to look for the person who admits no possibility of being wrong on any issue. Such a person lives a life that itself represents contempt, rather than love, for the neighbor. Democracy, morality, and simple humanity all demand more of us.

. . . .

Let us close part one with a review of five reasons for a democracy to value the sacrificial civility we have been discussing:

1. By encouraging us to see even those with whom we disagree as full equals before God, civility enables us to hold the respectful dialogues without which democratic decision-making is impossible.

2. Civility reminds us that in a democracy all our actions must meet the test of morality, and that our ability to discipline ourselves to do what is right rather than what we desire is what distinguishes us from animals.

3. That self-discipline, in turn, enables us to resist the tendency of the values of politics and the market to swallow all of social life.

4. Our adherence to standards of civil behavior serves, in Arthur Schlesinger's term, as our letter of introduction to our fellow citizens, thus helping us to build community.

5. By treating each other with the respectful civility that our shared createdness requires, we help make bearable the many indignities and frictions of everyday life.

In part two, we will consider various aspects of our language and culture that contribute to, or are damaged by, our incivility crisis. Before considering politics, technology, religion, and other troubled spheres of our national culture, we will start by investigating the remarkable and depressing violence that has taken hold of the English language. The emphasis throughout will be on reminding ourselves that civility calls us to sacrifice, and that sacrifice involves doing those things we would rather not, or not doing those things we wish we could. But these we should consider small prices to pay: after all, our very humanity is at stake.

II

Incivility's

. . . .

Instruments

7

The Demon on the Other Side

I ADMIT IT: I am in love with democracy. I have even run for office a few times, with what the professionals call mixed results. As an eighth-grader, I ran for secretary of the student council, and won. As a junior in college, I ran for editor of the campus paper, and lost. Along the way, I served as president of my junior high school's stamp club and, in high school, of the chess club and the Diplomats Club (our debate society), as well as editor of the paper—although, if memory serves, I was awarded most of these posts because nobody else wanted them. (I am not sure the stamp club even had any other members.) Nevertheless, I want here to certify that in each of these contests, whether I won or lost, I ran a clean campaign. Even in my closest electoral battle, the eighth-grade student council contest that was decided by the absentee ballots cast by upperclassmen who were off on a field trip the day of the vote, I kept to the same high standard: I was never nasty. Not only did I not attack my opponent, I never even mentioned my opponent. To do so would have been wrong . . . but, more important to the thirteen-year-old I then was, it would have been against the rules.

What rules? The school's rules. For we had actual discipline in the public schools in those days, and along with the discipline came censorship of nearly everything. The old doctrine of in loco parentis—that the school authorities acted in the place of parents, with much of the same discretion—was firmly in place. Quite apart from the classes on morals and deportment that appeared at the end of the nineteenth century, the schools of my youth, like the families of my youth, had rules restricting what kids could say, how kids could dress, when kids could talk (never between classes), even how kids could stand—posture—for the courts, fortunately, had not yet discovered this unmined field of First Amendment law. We studied how to speak to adults, how to answer the phone, how to set the table, and there were right and wrong ways to do each. They were quite unlike the schools of the present day, where it sometimes seems the only censorship is of religious expression.[1]

I will confess my biases: I think we were better off with schools that enforced such rules. But whether or not you agree, my junior high school had stern rules that I sometimes wish we adults were able to enforce against each other. Like the rule that we must not, on pain of disqualification, allow our posters to litter the floor. Or the rule that we could spend only a tiny amount of money on our campaigns. (I forget the dollar amount, but I do remember the requirement that every poster be hand-lettered.) The rule that is relevant here is the rule against personal attacks in our campaigns for office. The rule was enforced through the very mechanism the First Amendment does not in other contexts allow: all our speeches had to be cleared by the school before they could be delivered.

And so it was at Alice Deal Junior High School, in Washington, D.C., in the spring of 1968, when, along with the other candidates, I faced the need to address the school assembly, explaining why I deserved the votes of my fellow students. Before I could do so, however, my speech had to pass the muster of the formidable Mrs. Tiptree. (I have changed her name.) Mrs. Tiptree taught math. She was one of those brilliant but terrifying teachers that most of us can probably remember from eighth grade. I turned in my draft with a flutter in my heart. Mrs. Tiptree did not much like what she read. She called me out into the hall during a math class, and, in whispers, we went over my speech right there. She required revisions for grammar and word usage and nearly ordered me to delete my single sophomoric joke, but relented. However, she had no need to force me to remove any personal attacks, because I did not include any.

Why did I refrain from personal attack? As an adult, I have read the literature on insult. So I know psychologists say that nasty personal comments circumvent the higher parts of the brain, stirring to action something more atavistic. I know sociologists argue that a verbal attack is a form of definition of a group, marking the target as an outsider, and so is intended to alienate. I know postmoderns insist that offensive, harassing words are a culturally permitted form of violence. And I know theologians condemn gratuitous insult as a sin against God's gift of speech. All of these strike me as fancy ways of saying that insulting people is wrong. But none of them influenced my decision not to attack my opponent.

No, I did not attack my opponent because attacks were not permitted. Thank my parents if you like, but I was what used to be called a goody two-shoes, a kid who believed in obeying the rules just because they were the rules. I think my opponent was too, for she also followed the rules and did not attack me. My friends told me stories, however, about how my opponent's boyfriend was conducting against me what passed in eighth grade in the 1960s for negative advertising, whispering widely that I should not be elected secretary because I was a boy and it was, in fairness, a girl's job—a quiet and frustrating campaign that my single sexist joke, which Mrs. Tiptree so nearly deleted, was intended to deflate.

So there you see the innocence of an earlier age, both in years and in era: a negative whispering campaign accusing me of being a boy, speeches that the authorities read in advance for content, a ban on attacks on the other side, and candidates who followed the rules because they were there. I miss the ease of that time, the shared values, the respect for the rules. We could not, I suppose, apply the same rules to politics. It would be a bad idea, and an unconstitutional one, to allow some government agency to screen candidates' speeches and advertising. (For the most part, they don't even want an agency to screen their fund-raising.) And yet, the student of civility must recognize that the nastiness of our political fights is a threat to our beloved democracy. This chapter and the next consider what, if anything, might be done.

AH, DEMOCRACY!

· · · · · · · · · · · · ·

In 1996 New Jersey voters were treated to a United States Senate race so vicious that journalists (who tend to have very short historical memories) quickly tagged it as one of the worst in history. It wasn't, of course, not even close. Oh, it had its little horrors. Republican Dick Zimmer (who lost) implied that Democrat Bob Torricelli (who won) was taking campaign donations from the Mafia and perhaps from Iranian terrorists as well. Torricelli in turn falsely stated that Zimmer, who has three sisters who survived breast cancer, had opposed government funding of mammograms. Zimmer was probably the nastier of the two (if only by a hair), and neither candidate covered himself with glory—but one of the worst campaigns in history? Well, actually, no.

Thomas Jefferson, to take a prominent example, actually paid journalists to attack his opponent. Or, rather, he promised to pay them. When Jefferson (who was never wealthy) reneged, one of the same journalists turned around and savaged Jefferson himself for a purported affair with a slave, Sally Hemings (which is how that particular story, true or not, first came to public attention). Grover Cleveland was dogged throughout his first run for the presidency by rumors of an illegitimate child. There was even a ditty, recited regularly by his critics: "Ma, ma, where's my pa? Gone to the White House, ha, ha, ha." (The rumors, as Cleveland eventually admitted, were true.) A vicious whispering campaign accused Warren Harding of being a black man passing for white—or, more precisely in our race-foolish nation, the claim was that Harding's father was a black man passing for white. (Historians doubt it, but Harding never denied it.) The list could go on and on, but the point is clear: there has never been an era in American politics that was not marked by personal attacks. At times the attacks have been more subtle and clever than today; at times they have been the merest whispers; but they have never been absent.

How far back does the practice go? Even George Washington, revered as the father of our country, a man whose personal prestige probably did more than any legal document to hold the nation together in its early years, was not immune. He was dogged for years by allegations of financial improprieties, including a claim that he swindled Lord Fairfax out of a good chunk of the Shenandoah Valley. The most outrageous of the attacks on Washington was the claim that among the many out-of-wedlock children he was supposed to have fathered was a man who grew up to be a member of his own cabinet: Alexander Hamilton. (No reputable historian thinks it is true.)

To be sure, negative political *advertising* may be on the rise. Not so very long ago, a television commercial slinging mud at one's opponent was considered the last, desperate throw by a candidate who had fallen far behind. But this practice seems to have changed drastically in 1988.[2] That year the Republicans, having worked the matter through with focus groups of "Reagan Democrats" whose votes they needed to keep, rejected the conventional wisdom that negative campaigning always boomerangs in the end, following instead the counsel of the late Lee Atwater, who advised them to lead off campaigns with attack ads and never relent. (Nobody is innocent here: the Democrats quickly emulated the practice and have also never relented.)

But even the television attack ad is not really quite as new as some critics suggest. Lyndon Johnson was the pioneer, with the infamous "daisy girl" spot of 1964, in which a little girl picking flowers fades into a mushroom cloud. The message of the ad was that LBJ's opponent, Barry Goldwater—whose name was never mentioned in the spot—might, if elected, set off thermonuclear war. (In fairness to Johnson, it was Goldwater who started the argument when he advocated the use of tactical nuclear arms in Vietnam.) In 1980 Jimmy Carter and Ronald Reagan dueled with attack ads, albeit relatively mild ones by today's standards, including Carter's desperate effort to duplicate the "daisy girl" success by suggesting that Reagan thought nuclear proliferation was nobody's business. Four years later, Reagan's strategists heralded the modern era by clobbering Walter Mondale with the subtle yet powerful (and misleading) "bear-loose-in-the-woods" message. And besides, the politicians of the nineteenth century, who knew their way around an innuendo-filled pamphlet, would undoubtedly have made dastardly use of television had the medium been available.

Very well, our campaigns have always been nasty. And although one scholar credits "ad watches" by journalists for a supposed decline in negative political advertising in 1992,[3] they are nasty still. It is easy to count the costs. Public dialogue is debased, so we voters, who supposedly are sovereign, have more and more trouble figuring out who stands for what. Public cynicism rises, because a campaign in which each candidate smears the other does not produce a winner who smells like a rose. And when candidates treat each other so badly, it is folly to suppose that they will readily kiss and make up when the election is over. This was the very point made by the opponents of the congressional civility retreat whom we encountered in chapter 2: the other side has treated us so badly, they whined, that it is not reasonable to expect us to treat them civilly. And the effects filter out beyond politics: in a dreadfully insightful bit of self-analysis, three of four Americans say that the nastiness of our political campaigns is one reason that "people are less civil now."[4]

Why then do we behave this way? And why do we reward our political candidates for behaving this way? The answer is that we do not fully believe that everybody is entitled to the same measure of respect. The vision of civility as sacrifice is, in our politics, not so much rejected as ignored. If you disagree with me, our politics teaches, the reason can only be that you are some sort of monster, and therefore you deserve whatever you get. This is not an ethic that welcomes the stranger, that searches for the face of God even in those whose views we do not like. It is the ethics of the kindergarten, where small disagreements often explode into major tantrums. So let us consider how a reconstruction of civility might help us to behave like adults.

OPPONENTS AND ENEMIES

. . . .

Bob Dole, when he accepted the 1996 Republican presidential nomination, cautioned his supporters that President Clinton and Vice President Gore were "opponents, not enemies." And the victorious President Clinton, in his second inaugural address, called for an end to the "bickering and extreme partisanship" that seem to characterize official Washington. Sadly, various pundits rushed to assure one another that no end was in sight, because neither the Democrats nor the Republicans actually have much to lose by being uncivil. In fact, although the data suggest that voters are unhappy with the tone of political campaigns, the same data show that few candidates are ever punished for being nasty.[5] And many candidates believe they have no choice but to be nasty if they want to win.

In that same 1996 political year, the Democratic and Republican nominees for a hotly contested congressional seat in Iowa agreed not to run any negative advertisements; in particular, they promised that any charges one of them made against the other would be offered from the mouth of the candidate himself. And the agreement held up all the way until October, when it collapsed, tragically but predictably, after the first attack ad ran and the candidate whose side ran it immediately swore that he had nothing to do with it—precisely the behavior the public agreement was supposed to avoid. The other candidate went negative in return, and that was the end of that.

A few months before the 1996 election, I sat on a panel in Chicago with Ed Rollins, the prominent Republican political consultant, who explained the job he is paid well to perform in eight tragic words: "to diminish the reputation of the other side." This does not sound like a job that involves being awed by the presence of the stranger. So why, the student of civility might ask, would anybody spend his career performing such a task? The simple answer is that it works; that is, the consultant's skill at diminishing the other side is immense and valuable, so the candidate who employs it enhances the likelihood that he or she will prevail.*

If this is so, then the candidate who refuses to employ the skills of a consultant to diminish the other side has less chance of winning. The candidate who is unwilling to change a position for the sake of an extra vote or two, who plays all his cards face up on the table, who refuses to sling mud when mud is slung by his opponent, who refuses, when necessary, to be uncivil, would simply fall by the wayside, a victim of electoral Darwinism. Demanding civility thus asks the candidate to give up something quite substantial—in some sense, the reason for making the race in the first place. Defeated candidates for elective office often say in their concession speeches that they ran to get their issues to center stage. And yet, as the losers stand before the cameras, thanking their

---

* My point is not a partisan one. I have no doubt that well-paid Democratic political consultants feel exactly the same way.

long-suffering spouses and tireless volunteers, one cannot help thinking that they would just as soon be the winning candidate, listening happily to their defeated opponents talk about how issues are what really matter. In short, candidates run not to spark interesting conversation, but to win. For a politician, losing is the ultimate sacrifice.

We voters seem to feel the same way: nothing is worse than losing. This implies that an uncivil victory is better than a civil loss. If we voters did not believe this, we might decide that the only way to rid ourselves of negative campaigning is by a willingness to sacrifice the chance to win on our other ideals. For example, we might vote against A (who shares our politics) and in favor of B (who does not) in order to penalize A for the sleazy nastiness of his campaign. This entails a significant sacrifice, but if we are not willing to punish candidates when they run their races in uncivil (and often immoral) ways, it is laughable to think they might stop unilaterally just because we complain about it. Indeed, our refusal to vote against candidates who run sleazy campaigns is simply evidence that we do not, in fact, value civility in politics quite as highly as we tell pollsters we do.

The point of the example is that voting for B rather than A entails a considerable sacrifice: you must put aside an issue that is of great importance to you. The sacrifice is, in fact, the very same one that we ask of candidates when we beg them not to run negative campaigns: the sacrifice is to risk loss on election day for the sake of practicing civility. But if we are not willing to make such sacrifices in our voting, it becomes absurd to argue that our politicians should make such sacrifices in their campaigns.

THE DEMONS EMERGE

. . . .

The classic effort to escape the power of this example is to respond that if B holds the wrong position on whatever issue may be of the moment—abortion, for instance, or classroom prayer—then B cannot possibly be a person of the rectitude that I have described. In other words, all truly moral people agree on the issue; there is no reasonable alternative. Those on the other side then become monsters, and demonizing them is not incivility, it is simply description. This is the essence, for example, of the anticivility polemics by Benjamin DeMott and Michael Reagan that I mentioned in chapter 2.

We are all familiar with this move, and most of us commit it from time to time. (I know I do.) We do it when we dismiss those who disagree with us as extremists, or radicals, or nuts, because all of these are words that tend to silence by drawing a circle around a sensible middle (where we right-thinkers dwell) and a lunatic fringe (where our enemies babble and scheme). And so we are able to say that those on the other side of the argument do not actually deserve to be treated with civility, because they are themselves profoundly uncivil in their desire to subvert . . . well, to subvert what makes America great.

In the abortion battle, for example, the tiny minorities who hold absolutist positions on either side of the issue routinely portray their opponents as the fanatics. The language has grown so mind-numbingly familiar that we forget how rough it is. Thus, we have on one side the baby-killers who are perpetrating America's own Holocaust, and, on the other, the religious zealots who oppress women and murder their doctors. This demagogic style gets plenty of coverage from lazy journalists who prefer to report what people say about each other instead of the issues, but it adds little light to the debate. How could it? Labeling as wicked those who do not agree with us is nothing but a transparent excuse for avoiding debate. And yet, transparent or not, we do it all the time.

This inability to be struck with awe when facing an opponent is hardly limited to our public political fights. Stephen Bates, in his fine but tragic 1993 book *Battleground*, describes the way that publishers of grade-school textbooks often sort criticism by the politics of the critic. The tendency, according to Bates's well-documented account, is to view the demands for changes by conservative groups as censorship to be resisted, but to view similar demands by liberal groups as constructive advice to be taken into account.[6] So, once again, the groups we like are in the mainstream, the groups we hate are the extremists, and the space for conversation scarcely exists.

How much damage does name-calling do? It turns out to

depend on the name that one is called. A well-known study of 186 college students in the 1970s confirmed the intuition that the nastier the name, the more aggressive the response. In particular, although there are some sex differences in what counts as an insult, harsh words that went to the heart of self-worth (for example, "He's a real loser," or, "I wouldn't trust him") were considered much more aggressive than more constructive or descriptive criticisms ("He's probably moody sometimes," or, "He seems to be unsure of himself").[7] Much recent work has confirmed and even expanded these findings. So it turns out that the kind of public nastiness in which we seem to rejoice—the kind in which we toss the most personal epithets we can think of—is precisely the worst kind in a democracy, because it sparks anger rather than dialogue.

Moreover, the politics of personal attack shows more than disrespect for the opponent. It also shows a disrespect for the voters. The evident belief, by candidates and their staffs, that we, the voters, are so malleable, so ready to be deceived, no doubt helps to feed the alienation from politics that the pundits decry and the polls confirm. Like the opinion-poll politics we will discuss in the next chapter, attack politics manifests contempt rather than love for the voters who are the candidate's fellow citizens. And when we allow ourselves to be swayed—in effect, relying on the candidates for our information about their opponents—we help create a terrible but powerful negative synergy in which politicians demean us through their manipulations and nastiness, and we encourage them by responding to the manipulations even when we know we should not.

Nowhere in our politics does this destructive habit appear as clearly as in Senate hearings on the confirmation of nominees for the Supreme Court, where we try to dispose of judges we dislike by labeling their views as outside the mainstream. A common misconception, fueled by a spate of books of dubious worth, is that this trend began with the left's hysterical and vicious assault on Robert Bork in 1987. But it actually began with hysteria and viciousness on the right. In the 1950s, following the Supreme Court's decision in *Brown v. Board of Education*,[8] the Senate's diehard segregationists, of whom there were many, controlled the Judiciary Committee. From that platform, they launched a decade-long campaign aimed at demonstrating that only an un-

American extremist could possibly agree with the ruling that racially separate schools were inherently unequal.[9] As with the Bork battle, the political purpose was to make disagreement tantamount to outsider status, to show that the nominee was not one of us—in effect, that he did not know which fork to use.

Indeed, it seems not widely known that, until *Brown*, the Senate almost never held confirmation hearings for Supreme Court nominees. The idea of calling the nominee to Capitol Hill to answer questions was invented by the segregationists. If today's hearings appear to be invitations to incivility, it is because confirmation hearings were designed to be precisely that. When opponents of *Brown* found that they could not obtain commitments from the nominees to vote to reverse it—potential justices, as we see every few years, have this maddening habit of standing on principle and refusing to discuss how they might vote—they turned the hearings into circuses, smearing the more liberal nominees with everything from manufactured allegations of Communist sympathies (William Brennan) to blatantly racist accusations of incompetence (Thurgood Marshall).[10] This feckless recklessness was, once more, evidence of such passionate commitment to a cause that the ability to see God in others disappeared.

Robert Bork, of course, was treated no better. Opponents took his scholarly speculation out of context to make it seem like a settled moral position; they misled the public about the content of judicial opinions Bork had written; attributed to him views that he had never expressed or had expressly denied; and, in general, successfully painted his then-moderate conservatism (which Bork himself preferred to call "classical liberalism") as malevolent and even monstrous.[11] Once more, the cause (mainly preserving abortion rights—the rest, from what I can tell, was a smokescreen) had been deemed so important that mere civility was swept aside.

This, of course, is the very point made by Ed Rollins when he described his job as diminishing the reputation of his candidate's opponent. If you want to win, you must not be civil, especially if the other side will not be civil in return. Every politician, upon being accused of going negative, answers that the other side did it first. Game theorists call this tit-for-tat and insist that it is often the only non-losing strategy, but, to the student of civility, it is, again, the ethics of the kindergarten. Civility, unlike so much in modern America, is not merely or even mostly about winning: civility is about sacrifice, and one of the things that might need to be sacrificed is victory. Simply put, civility entails risk of loss . . . in service of the great ideal of loving our neighbors.

Unfortunately, hardly anybody seems to believe this, which is why our protestations about negative campaigning carry a hollow ring, like a dream of traveling to Europe mixed with a refusal to put aside any money for the trip. Politics, the misleading old saying goes, is the only game for adults. If you are not willing to do all that you can to win, it seems, you should not be in public life at all. So if victory requires demonizing your opponents—or, as Ed Rollins put it, diminishing their reputations—well, then, may the best mud-slinger win.

ATTACK POLITICS AND
THE DEATH OF SOCIAL LIFE

This brings us back to the problem of negative politics that opened the chapter. I am hardly the first to note that our political campaigns have always been uncivil. Yet the vitriol of our politics is a far greater threat to democracy than it was fifty or a hundred years ago. What has changed in America, making these political battles more dangerous and thus helping to create our incivility crisis, is not the tenor of our politics. What has changed is *everything else*.

When election time comes, politicians have always been as small-minded, as narrowly focused, and as willing to exchange verbal blows as they are now. An electoral democracy, in true Darwinian fashion, selects for candidates who will do what is necessary to win. (Those who will not, lose, and thus disappear.) But viciousness in partisan politics, I would suggest, poses no significant threat to the republic as long as three conditions hold:

- First, the political battles themselves must take place against the background of a shared understanding of what America most fundamentally means.

- Second, politics itself (in the sense of struggles for political power) must represent only a small part of the life of the nation.
- Third, the rest of the nation's life must feature institutions that provide their members with the moral weapons to struggle against the incursion of politics into the rest of life and to resist the urge to behave like . . . well, like politicians.

Unfortunately, all three conditions are breaking down.

The first condition matters because as long as the politicians themselves share a broad set of values, they are able to do business with each other behind the public veil of animosity. That is why, during the nineteenth century, presidents so often asked political opponents to join their cabinets. That is why the late Thurgood Marshall (for whom it was my great privilege to serve as a law clerk from the summer of 1980 through the summer of 1981) was able to make backroom deals, in his civil rights days, with politicians who, in public, used ardently segregationist rhetoric. "You could do business with him," he used to say of one Dixiecrat or another, which was, from Marshall, high praise. He meant that whatever the man might say to his supporters, when the doors were closed, they could sit down and come to an agreement—and both sides would keep it.

That first condition, that our leaders must share a background moral vision, a paradigm they will not challenge, also explains why the nation faces grave antidemocratic danger whenever a genuine radical who can give no quarter to opponents grows briefly dominant—Senator Joseph McCarthy in the 1950s, for instance, or, to a lesser extent, some of the angry young politicians on both sides of the aisle in today's Washington. Fortunately, as long as we, the sovereign people of the United States, share a background moral vision, no radical is likely to remain dominant for very long.

The trouble, as we saw in chapter 3, is that the background vision seems to be breaking down. The story of my eighth-grade student council speech that opened the chapter is a story of a time when the nation was more confident in its consensus and, in consequence, more willing to trust school authorities to perform such tasks as censoring student speeches. Although the polls continue to tell us that Americans share many common values, I nevertheless have the sense that some vital consensus has been lost, and, with it, much of the trust that is crucial to making civility work.

I miss particularly the idea that traditions play an important role in helping us decide how to behave. I very much doubt that the formidable Mrs. Tiptree stopped to consider whether the rules she was charged with enforcing actually met some standard of deontological morality (a tongue-twisting philosophical term for morality not measured by the outcome) or even whether the benefits would outweigh the costs. She followed the rules, and expected us to do the same, because the rules were there. The loss of that ability to approach rules and traditions with respect for their creators, rather than with contempt for their restrictions on our desires, is perhaps the most overlooked factor in our incivility crisis. But as traditions collapse around us, the nastiness of our politics is likely to do more damage, because we have less to hang on to, less to remind us that, at bottom, we are indeed a single people.

The second condition, that politics must be only one sphere in a rich and complex social life, proposes the importance of somehow cabining the reach of partisan politics, shutting it out of some areas of life. Political vitriol affects us less directly if it occurs in only one of the several spheres in which we exist. To oversimplify a bit, if we have other places to go, other things to do, we can, for a time, escape the political wars.

For example, even if our politicians snipe viciously at one another, we should be able to fold the newspaper and forget them as we drop by our social club or community center. We should be able to focus our minds and souls on great and transcendent issues as we sit prayerfully in our place of worship. We should be able to concentrate on understanding the great wisdom of the ages as we sit thoughtfully in the college classroom. We should have a broad set of places to go in which we live lives where the political wars play no part.

But the other spheres of social life are dying—or, if they survive, they are coming to mimic, or even to be engulfed by, the model of political vitriol. The universities, the churches, the public schools, the few remaining social clubs, even the family, so sacred and cherished in American ideology and iconography, all have become battlegrounds of the same political style (and over many of the same issues) that we see in our partisan political fights. Here television rightly comes in for a significant share of blame, for it is television that has largely destroyed the barriers between different spheres of social life.

The television "talk show" has been bashed sufficiently that there is hardly a need to say anything about it. I think that Roderick Hart, in his book *Seducing America*, captures the aspect of these programs that should most worry the student of civility who understands what Erasmus was trying to achieve. Erasmus wanted us to learn to discipline our instincts for the sake of our humanity. But too much of the conversation on television, Hart notes, reflects a very different ethic: "The emotions displayed on *The McLaughlin Report* and *The Capital Gang*—the shouting, the name calling, the exotic spontancity—are truly primitive. They are pagan emotions, the sort that worried the Roman church in the Middle Ages and that eventually spawned the Enlightenment."[12]

In the terms we have been using, these programs are not so much uncivil as uncivilized. They do indeed hark back to an earlier, more primitive era, one in which people killed and maimed (and defecated and urinated) as the urge struck. They reject any notion of self-control. Such shows seem to suppose that proper argument consists of saying the first and worst thing that comes to mind, rejecting any notion that either forethought or discipline matters in rhetoric. Here again, one thinks of Rousseau: the style of these programs exalts yielding to passion over moral liberty.

I have occasionally appeared on television talk shows, to "discuss" various issues of the day. What immediately strikes me, whether as viewer or participant, is how difficult it is to construct an argument within the time-conscious frame of the medium. Even on the best and most serious of the programs, all participants know how little time exists, and so each rushes to make his or her points, even at the risk of speaking over others. Consequently, no true engagement is possible: there is no conversation. On this point, Hart quotes the social theorist Peter Sloterdijk: "[T]he Enlightenment has never been able to form an effective alliance with the mass media." That is, the media fundamentally disbelieve in—or rather, are unable to squeeze profit from—the possibility of humans reasoning together to find truth. Why? In part because of the limited time available, and in part "because the language of television is so naturally cynical, at least where politics is concerned."[13]

Cynicism, as we have seen, is civility's foe. The cynicism of the media is also reflected in news judgment, less in the emphasis on scandal (although that is a problem too) than in the emphasis on controversy. There is little coverage of issues; there is coverage instead of what people say about issues—that is, "both sides" must have the chance to speak, as though listening to the most extreme and outlandish sound bites is the path to discovering the truth. Through its growing emphasis on controversy in deciding what is and is not news, television implicitly suggests that the venomous attack is the way to get attention (and thus perhaps to win). Naturally, the politicians themselves share a part of the blame, but television provides the nasty politician with positive reinforcement: he says something outrageous or vicious, he gets free television time, and, in true Skinnerian fashion, he learns to repeat his behavior.

Honest politicians admit this. In 1989 Republican attacks on his ethics forced the resignation of House Speaker Jim Wright, a Democrat. The criticism of Wright, it should be said, was entirely deserved, although the tone, including Republican Bill Frenzel's weird comparison of Wright to Adolf Hitler, left much to be desired. Once Wright stepped down, exhausted Democrats, led by the new speaker, Tom Foley, called for calm, but Representative Newt Gingrich, at that time the House Republican whip, promised to continue the "war." Why? Because "We finally have the public's attention."[14] Democrats roiled, but Gingrich was only doing what the television age requires: staging political theater in the knowledge that the medium will giddily carry the message into every home in the nation. Never mind that young people will watch, and learn, and emulate.

That is why the third condition is the most important: that the other institutions with which we interact must provide us with the moral tools to resist the urge to allow politics to impose its cardinal rule—*winning at all costs*—on the rest of social life. This rule is already immoral in any sensible ethical system; not even utilitarians seriously try any longer to defend the proposition that the end justifies the means. We might be better off with politicians *not* committed to winning at all costs, but, as we have seen, the system quickly discards them, for the simple reason that they will not win.

Nevertheless, the images of political incivility would matter less if young people were taught something different in the rest of their lives. So if we are increasingly uncivil, one reason must surely be the weakness or collapse of the institutions that should inculcate the moral norms that would help us to behave better . . . better, that is, than our politicians do. And better than the values of politics require. The emphasis in politics on winning is really a part of the more general human impulse to get what we want. What politicians want is to win. And if winning requires that the candidate on the other side be a monster . . . well, then, the candidate on the other side is a monster.

8

....

The Varieties of (Not) Listening

WE COULD avoid some measure of incivility if we simply agreed with each other all the time. But quite apart from being plain boring, a nation where we all agreed would wither and ultimately die. Civil dialogue over differences is democracy's true engine: we must disagree in order to debate, and we must debate in order to decide, and we must decide in order to move. And it all works, as James Madison noted in *Federalist No. 10*, only if we begin by understanding the necessity of disagreeing: "As long as the reason of man continues fallible, and he is at liberty to exercise it, different opinions will be formed."

Civility does not require consensus on everything. Civility and disagreement can both thrive at the same time. That is why it may be a mistake to appeal too often, as President Clinton has tried to do, to the political center: it is not clear that there always is a political center, or that we should want one. As Hendrik Hertzberg of *The New Yorker* has written, "The center that Clinton touts is a mathematical resultant, not a functioning consensus."[1] I do not mean that Clinton (or any President) would be well advised to move hard to the left or the right. I mean only that we must be careful about suggesting that consensus on every issue is possible or even desirable. Politics in a vibrant, successful democracy requires disagreement and debate; civility simply provides the guidelines within which that debate should occur. Which leads us to another rule:

Civility assumes that we will disagree; it requires us not to mask our differences but to resolve them respectfully.

Sadly, we are losing the skill for respectful debate—if, indeed, we ever truly had it. Instead, we are awash in undebatable propositions. I refer here not to the dying controversy over "political correctness" but to a more general problem: everybody tries to find ways to put their own cherished positions beyond debate. One way of doing so is to try to enact our political preferences as constitutional law, as liberals have done, successfully but incompletely, with the abortion right (although lately with little else). Another is to identify them with patriotism, as conservatives have done, successfully, with the proposition that expansion of foreign markets for American products is invariably a positive good. In this chapter, I will consider these and other uncivil tools through which we avoid debate with those who disagree with us.

THE LOGIC AND THE RISK OF BOUNDED DISCOURSE

. . . .

We employ, all of us, a rhetoric of silencing, trying to deter opposition, perhaps so that we will not have to spend energy refuting it. A few decades ago, the vocabulary of silencing featured "un-American," which became a catchall for many forms of liberal dissent from the moderately conservative post–World War II consensus, as well as a part of the name of an often malevolent committee of the House of Representatives. More recently, we saw the left briefly accede to the idea that anybody troubled by affirmative action was racist, and the right, for a while, to the idea that nobody but those memorably dismissed as "feminazis" cared about sexual harassment in the workplace. Fortunately, most of this labeling turns out to be a passing fad. But even today, in a bit of a paradox, the more certain we are of our rightness, the less interested we seem to be in debate.

Pick any divisive issue: gay rights, for example, where the nation has recently fought pitched rhetorical battles over everything from marriage to military service. The strongest advocates of gay rights are sure that those who disagree with them are necessarily homophobic—gay-hating—and the strongest opponents are sure that those who disagree with them are necessarily ungodly. In both cases, the certainty that one side is right makes the other side not worth debating, for who can hold a conversation with such monstrous evil?

One of the cleverest moves is to define the debate in a way that excludes some ideas from consideration before the argument even begins. The technique involves designing a universe of "bounded discourse"—an arena in which some ideas can be debated and others cannot. The bounds always sound reasonable, whether they are or not. In the middle years of this century, any position that smacked even vaguely of communism was prohibited (sometimes legally prohibited) in public debate. More recently, in what should be an academic embarrassment, liberal theorists have spent much effort in crafting rules for public dialogue that leave well outside the universe of discourse points of view with which liberalism is uncomfortable—religious argument, for one.[2]

The purpose and effect of bounding discourse is to make some ideas not so much undebatable as inexpressible. In one sense, this is important to the proper functioning of democracy, because conversation, like every other human activity, can help define a people when it proceeds from common norms. Besides, one cannot build a nation in which everything is on the table for discussion: such a nation would stand for nothing, resting on no enduring principles, and could scarcely function because of the chaos created by an inability to predict what might change tomorrow. So, in America, we take off the table a commitment to equal opportunity, respect for private property, universal adult suffrage, and many aspects of individual liberty. We cherish them sufficiently that we put them in the Constitution. All these precepts, of course, are freely debatable, but if there were any serious prospect of their repeal, we would scarcely *be* America.[3]

The difficulty, however, is that the effort to bound discourse limits our horizons: the ideas we freeze out can never become dominant. Historically, every group that has found itself, for a time, in power has tried to take off the table ideas that were contrary to its own interests. So the antebellum Congress refused to discuss an end to slavery, the early industrial capitalists insisted that unions were un-American, and most American churches, until fairly recently, treated any question of enhancing the role of women in the worship service as a joke. This is the point, and it is also the risk: the rules of discourse are always made by those who hold power, and the ideas they rule out of bounds will almost certainly be the ones they dislike.[4] One of the many virtues of the First Amendment is that it creates a barrier (admittedly imperfect) against *official* drawing of the bounds of debate.

Political parties behave this way too. In the summer of 1996, I argued on the op-ed page of the *New York Times* that the Democrats, busily pointing their fingers at the Republicans for seeming to take the view that anybody who was pro-choice did not belong in the party, took essentially the same position with respect to people who were pro-life.[5] And although I received some mail insisting that I did not know what I was talking about, what I wrote was, and remains, essentially correct. Each party has been captured by one of the narrow abortion extremes. This is not evil in itself: I suppose the Democratic Party of the late sixties, for example, might have been described as captured by one of the narrow civil rights extremes. I have no objection to a party's adoption of a reasonable number of litmus tests for membership. After all, there is more than one party: if your views are unwelcome in one party, you can always try another. Besides, a serious political party should stand for something other than compromise: how else can one decide whether to join it? I only object when a party adopts litmus tests but pretends that it has not.

Religions, by their nature, have litmus tests too (or they should); and, also by nature, they tend to tell us what those tests are. In the major American religious traditions, there are clear litmus tests for membership, although the modern trend, at least among Protestants, has been to behave as though there are none. (A religion, of course, is free to have no rules if it wants none, but the problems of self-definition then become quite awkward.) Religions, like political parties, are entitled to have tests that exclude some from membership precisely because they are not all of America. Those who do not like the rules of faith or party need not join; or, if already members, they are free to leave. There are other denominations. There are other parties. There are other social clubs or colleges or bridge games. The ability of the dissatisfied to exit is precisely what creates the space for such private and quasi-private entities to enforce whatever rules they want on the members who remain.[6]

The political sphere is different. The only way to exit is by ceasing to be an active member of the polity, a fate the student of civility would not wish on any fellow passengers. As we have seen, democratic politics must, in a just society, have its limits; there will sometimes be a need to adopt what the political scientist Stephen Holmes calls a "gag rule"[7]—a limit on discourse for the sake of coherence. But if our republic is to remain fundamentally democratic, the boundaries of discourse should be broad, its exclusions few. Otherwise, the political sphere begins to resemble a private club, with membership requirements sufficiently restrictive that not many people are actually allowed in. Too many Americans already think that our politics fits that model; as we work to reconstruct civility, we must avoid the trap of supposing that politics can be structured the way we structure a political party, with a long list of positions that all right-thinking people must accept. Even thoughtful political philosophers have lately stumbled down this treacherous path, crafting elaborate theories that would exclude from democratic dialogue citizens whose views are not formulated in an approved manner. Perhaps needless to say, the student of civility must ever remain a skeptic of such ideas.

CIVIL LISTENING

. . . .

Yet exclusion, too often, is the American way: when we are not labeling our opponents as extremists so that we need not show them the respect of discussing our differences, we are explaining patiently that their views do not fit an ideal model of liberal democratic decision-making. In the end, the principle is the same: we conclude that those who hold wrong views are entitled to no respect.

This profoundly uncivil proposition is anticipated in Luther Willson's sermon on Christian love that opened chapter 6. Willson recognizes the human temptation to condemn those whose opinions are different from our own, but he warns that doing so violates the very principles of love that he has been pressing. We ourselves are as fallible as anybody else, Willson reminds us, and therefore "should never determine with respect to the character of any, merely from a knowledge of their particular opinions."[8] Indeed, one reason to value such virtues as integrity is precisely because they enable us to take the measure of a person's character without regard to whether or not we agree with his or her political opinions.[9] So take stock of the whole person, Willson cautions:

> How often do we find men, whose views we believe to be erroneous, yet whose characters are covered with integrity and virtue as with a shield. This fact, which I believe to be confirmed by general observation, should lead us to be candid and cautious in pronouncing sentence against any on account of supposed errors.[10]

Willson here proposes something that the student of civility should find attractive: Those who disagree with us, even on the issues that matter most, are not necessarily evil—they may just be misguided. They may be in error. If they are, the errors may be correctable. And to make corrections, we must explain the error of their ways. Already, then, Willson is implying the necessity of dialogue when we disagree.

But he is also making a deeper point. He reminds us of our own fallibility: we, like those with whom we disagree, are mortal and thus face the possibility of error. In other words, we ourselves could be wrong. Why does this matter? It matters in the dialogue that Willson proposes and civility demands. As the legal scholar Michael Perry has pointed out, conversation that admits the possibility of error is the only kind of conversation that love for others allows.[11] All too often, we enter dialogue with our opponents by listening with our mouths rather than our ears—that is, we listen only for the flaws, awaiting our chance to refute. We do not listen to this living, breathing specimen of God's creation with any sense of awe; we do not even listen with any sense of respect. We begin our listening with the certainty that our opponents have it all wrong. And I admit, with no small amount of embarrassment, that I as a law professor am well paid to help young people learn to approach dialogue this way.

But listening of this kind—let us call it *confrontational listening*—calls forth from us neither the awareness of personal fallibility that love for our neighbor entails nor the generosity of spirit that civility requires. It is, in short, not civil. Indeed, confrontational listening is not listening at all; it is not respectful and leads to no dialogue; it is just a more cautious and polite form of the screaming and incivility that has characterized too much of our history and continues to characterize our self-centered age.

In the Victorian era, ladies and gentlemen were taught what was called the "art" of conversation, and they were warned against refusing to engage in discussion with others (which was rude) and against discussing in a boisterous, combative way (which was even ruder). If the art of Victorian conversation sometimes involved a skill at evading discussion of difficult or embarrassing issues, it also carried a strong current of civility, as we have been using the word, for it demanded recognition "that those one talked to were also forms of life." In short, the very reason not to attack those with whom one disagreed was that they too were fully human, and fully deserving of respect. The well-mannered conversationalist would therefore listen as well as speak.[12]

Here we have another hint of how rules of etiquette, even in the perhaps over-mannered Victorian era, can carry useful moral messages. Confrontational listening signals others that they are, in your opinion, not worthy of respect. True listening—what we might usefully call *civil listening*—signals your belief in the equality of all people, because it treats them as equal, even if you dislike their views. "What my opponent has to say," the civil listener implies, "is as important as what I have to say. If you would listen to me, listen to my opponent with the same courtesy and the same care. I will do the same."

But civil listening is not easy, especially because it demands of the civil listener a considerable risk. Civil listening is part of civil dialogue, a loving and respectful conversation in which we try, for a moment at least, to experience the other side's world as our own. "Empathy" does not capture the idea, for empathy conveys no more than understanding the other's point of view; and, as any lawyer knows, understanding the other's point of view is simply a tool to use in crafting an effective reputation of the other's argument. (If you cannot make the best case for the other side, every debate teacher will tell you, you cannot make the best case for your own.)

The ideal of civil listening is best captured not in a simple word but in a simple explanation, and Willson's sermon suggests it. I am to make your interests, joys, and sorrows my own. Not simply to understand but to try to share. To listen civilly, to listen with love, is good not only for us but for others. Says Willson: "[I]t is the nature of love to make men happy; both those who feel its exciting influence within themselves, and those who are the objects of it."[13] Surely this is often true of dialogue: simply by our openness to what others have to say, we accord them a respect that they can hardly help noticing. And sometimes being heard is all they want: the act of civil listening can itself spark a civil response.

But what does it mean to be open to what others have to say? It means, quite simply, to acknowledge the possibility that they may be right. We must approach each other, even in disagreement, with openness, not cynicism. Cynicism is the enemy of reason, and thus of civility: it suggests a deep distrust of the motives of our fellow passengers, a distrust that ruins any project of treating others well because they deserve it. But if I expect you to listen respectfully to me and give me a genuine opportunity to convert you to my way of thinking, civility requires me to first listen respectfully to you and give you a genuine opportunity to convert me to your way of thinking. And there lies the risk. If I listen to you in a truly open way, not searching for the flaws in what you say but accepting as real the possibility that you are right, I place my ego, my very sense of myself, at hazard. In other words, instead of changing your mind, I might change mine.

And so we can now see a rule taking shape:

> *Civility requires that we listen to others with knowledge of the possibility that they are right and we are wrong.*

Like so much that civility demands, the choice to listen in a truly open way involves a sacrifice—and what we are sacrificing lies near the core of the self. For our sacrifice is of nothing less than the ego support that comes from the certainty of our own rightness. Our senses of ourselves are deeply bound up with our senses of *this-I-believe*, whether our *this* involves a party affiliation, a commitment to nonviolence, a position on abortion, or even (especially!) our belief or nonbelief in God. These central beliefs will be at risk if we enter into a truly civil dialogue, willing the other to try to convince us we are wrong, a dialogue we can join only by accepting, as Luther Willson admonishes in his 1816 sermon, the possibility that we may be in error. We may protect our *this-I-believe* by refusing to enter into a truly civil dialogue, one in which we listen with our ears rather than our mouths. But if our egos are so fragile (and they may be) that we refuse to give others the chance to show us our errors, if we think that dialogue is nothing more than our chance to convince our adversaries, not the other way around, we are, at minimum, committed to our incivility; more than that, we may after all be fairly subject to the very label of fanaticism that most of us like to pin on our opponents. For what is a fanatic but somebody who refuses to listen?

Certainly the willingness to listen with awareness of our own fallibility does not mean that we will not, in the end, decide that we were right all along. Nothing wrong with that, as long as it is a considered *decision*—that is, as long as we are confident that we have listened, truly listened with our ears, with respect and even love, that we have *civilly listened* to the other side. Even if we decide that we are right and the other side is wrong, our obligation of civility does not end. A part of our love for our neighbors is surely the capacity to forgive them for their transgressions . . . including their errors.

All of this works only if we are first prepared to listen—to listen civilly—to the other side, even when it is so much easier to demonize. The process of civil listening takes time, of course, and it may be that we of the too-busy generation do not think we can spare any from our dwindling hoard of hours. So civil listening is thrice a sacrifice: because we must hear views we may detest, because we must be open to the possibility of their rightness, and because we must steal the time to do it. But if we have no time to listen with love and respect to those who disagree with us, then we have no time for awe in God's creation, and thus no time for lives of civility.

CIVILITY AND THE INTOLERABLE

. . . .

Yet there are ideas that are genuinely dangerous, even in a thriving democracy . . . and it is not clear that our democracy is thriving. In our nation's history, the most damaging idea of all has been that some groups are inherently superior to others, an idea that sparked not only chattel slavery and Jim Crow but also systematic discrimination against non-Protestants throughout the nineteenth century and for a good part of the twentieth. So the student of civility must discover a way of dealing with those who hate others on the ground of their skin color, ethnicity, or religion. Are those who hate entitled to the neighbor-love on which civility rests? And, if their ideas are so genuine harmful, must we grant them the favor of listening civilly to them?

The theologian Donald W. Shriver, Jr., in *An Ethic for Enemies*, argues vigorously that the obligation to love others not only extends to but is in some sense intended for those who have done us terrible wrongs. He proposes "a collective turning from the past that neither ignores past evil nor excuses it" in order to make peace between those who have been enemies. And, in particular, he insists that those who have been wronged must forgo vengeance, lest they become the very evil they profess to hate.[14]

This is, of course, an old idea, and an exquisitely Biblical one. In chapter 6, I quoted from a sermon by the abolitionist preacher Charles G. Finney. In the course of the same sermon, he warned his audience against hating those who might oppose them:

> No one does anything for his friend which would be acceptable to God unless he would do as much for his enemies if he could. God can give him no credit for doing good to his friends unless he does it on a principle which would make him do as much for his enemies if he could. . . . I put this on the ground that God's law requires you to love all your neighbors—every neighbor; and if you have the spirit of obedience to God, you will.[15]

This is difficult counsel, and, as we shall see, few enough Christians follow it. But even if we take both Shriver and Finney seriously, how can we make their ideas work in practice? Shriver's examples are largely drawn from wars between nations: he is trying to explain how to make peace with people who have lately been trying to wipe your people from the face of the earth. Many societies on our unhappy planet are confronting precisely this problem, and they need our prayers as they do it. But how does the idea work in the United States? Does it mean that black Americans must be prepared to break bread with the David Dukes? Or Jews with the Louis Farrakhans? If we have reached stable, democratic consensus on anything, we have reached it on the proposition that racial and ethnic hatreds are wrong.

The judgment that an individual is racist (or hates on another impermissible ground) tells us something about his morality. But does it tell us how to evaluate other aspects of the person? Put otherwise, is it appropriate to separate the racism from the rest of what we know, to say, in effect, yes, he is a racist, and that is too bad, but what a brilliant surgeon! From time to time, we as a society have pretended to answer this question—but in fact, we have scarcely confronted it.

Take the case of Farrakhan. Should we say that Farrakhan's blatant anti-Semitism disqualifies him from participation in the needed national conversation about our common values? Or that it leaves him outside our responsibility to listen civilly to those with whom we disagree? Or that we should ignore the positive side of his message, his efforts to restore a sense of personal responsibility to the residents of the inner-city communities where it has been so shattered? If we do, we risk excluding a significant segment of the population. It does not much matter whether or not one is happy that he seems to have so many supporters. (I certainly am not happy about it.) It does not matter whether one thinks his views are hateful. (They certainly are.) It does not even matter that the Farrakhan phenomenon itself is in large part a media creation: sensation-seeking reporters have ignored the mainstream Islamic movement in America, which dwarfs his in size, preaches the universal brotherhood of man, and does not consider Farrakhan's pontificating genuinely Islamic. (All true.) What matters, rather, is that the principle that we could use to exclude Farrakhan is one we have neither the stomach nor the justification to apply across the board.

Consider what happens if we press the point too far. First, we have the case of Alexander Alekhine, the chess champion of the world in the 1930s and 1940s and one of the most brilliant players the game has ever known, who was also a virulent anti-Semite whose pathetic screeds against "Jewish chess" were published by Nazi newspapers with great fanfare. Alekhine is still Alekhine. We might not invite him to dinner, but we neither strip him of his historical title nor urge students not to study his games. We distinguish Alekhine the political man from Alekhine the chess genius. Similarly, the physicist William Shockley, a Nobel Laureate and co-inventor of the transistor, was an adamant racist whose belief in the inherent intellectual inferiority of black people was never shaken. But we do not pretend that he therefore deserves none of the credit for an invention that paved the way for the microprocessor and thereby changed the world. We do not delete his name from the roll of Nobel Prize recipients. We distinguish Shockley the political man from Shockley the scientific genius.

Literature, of course, is replete with examples. Despite the desperate apologies of his partisans, we know, now, that Charles Dickens was resolutely anti-Semitic, at least until his later years. (Fagin was no accident.) But schoolchildren across the nation still read his books and love them. T. S. Eliot's racism and anti-Semitism, according to his defenders, was a minor part of his persona and may have helped to fuel his art: a nicer man, evidently, would have been less brilliant. This is a remarkably silly explanation for his notorious monograph "After Strange Gods"—a sketch of an ideal society in which "any large number of free-thinking Jews" would be "undesirable"—for his support of openly anti-Semitic political movements, and for the slurs on Jews in some of his poetry.[16] It is no explanation at all for the Negrophobia in much of his work. But so what? We still conclude, as we should, that "The Love Song of J. Alfred Prufrock" ushered in a revolution in poetry and that "The Waste Land" is among the greatest poems ever written.

At a different level of literature, Robert Heinlein is routinely described as one of the great science fiction writers of all time and is ranked along with Isaac Asimov and Ray Bradbury as one of the three founders of the modern canon. But he must also bear responsibility for a frighteningly racist novel entitled *Sixth Column* (later reissued as *The Day After Tomorrow*), in which, following a war, the United

States is saved from its vicious "PanAsian" occupiers by the invention of a device that kills everybody within range who does not happen to be white. (I am not making this up; I only wish I were.)

There are examples from every arena of American public life: George F. Patton, the raving anti-Semite and charismatic military hero beloved of conservatives; Woodrow Wilson, the genteel racist beloved of liberals; Bear Bryant, the racist and celebrated college football coach; and on and on.* Indeed, many black intellectuals insist that Charles Murray, of *The Bell Curve* fame, is a racist, and although I think he is not (even though I think his thesis on the distribution of intelligence among ethnic groups is dead wrong), this perception by many African Americans does not, so far, lead the American right to disown him.

Unlike Alekhine or Shockley or Eliot, Louis Farrakhan is no genius, at least in the traditional sense. But it would be perverse to conclude therefore that we should be less willing to split him into his component parts and evaluate them differently. Otherwise we risk creating a sort of "genius license": if you are smart enough and accomplished enough, we can forgive or perhaps ignore your racism, but, in the absence of some exceptional ability, we cannot. Through such reasoning we wind up, as so often, with special privileges for the elite.

Actually, we do indulge a kind of genius license, or, more properly, an elite license: we are remarkably forgiving of the bigotry of intellectuals and the powerful. For example, the academic defenders of Paul de Man, the brilliant literary critic who was also a Nazi shill, have simply embarrassed themselves with their efforts to explain away his anti-Semitism. Similarly, we hear from time to time that the poet Ezra Pound was not really a committed fascist. So what if he never apologized? As Michiko Kakutani of the *New York Times* notes, "There are plenty of critics around to attribute imagined contrition."[17] Unfortunately, it often seems that if you are smart enough and accomplished enough, your fellow intellectuals will forgive you any transgression, as though brilliance in one field must translate automatically into moral uprightness. So if we

* James C. McReynolds, the openly racist and anti-Semitic Supreme Court justice appointed by Woodrow Wilson, is probably a poor example because he was utterly undistinguished as a jurist as well.

are very sure that a total exclusion is the appropriate punishment for Farrakhan, it would be better—and more civil—if we were able to be more consistent in our condemnations and stop pretending that the fact of genius is a license to hate.

I would not want the reader to misunderstand my point. I have no brief for Louis Farrakhan, whose words fully deserve the condemnation they receive. I do disagree, however, with the notion that people whose views are virulently hateful should be totally excluded from the possibility of the saving conversation, or that we can be sure that they say nothing worth listening to on any other subject. It is only through the process of *civil listening*—even to those whose views are hateful—that we can discover whether this is true. But even if we decide that the words of the hateful are as wrong as we thought, our duty to treat them with respect is in no way reduced.

Shriver calls on us to recognize "the humanity of enemies even in their commission of dehumanizing deeds," a sentiment the student of civility will readily endorse.[18] Lewis Smedes, who teaches at Fuller Theological Seminary, counsels us to find ways to forgive even the intolerable, wrongs that are so wretched that we have no intention of putting up with them. "Remember," he writes, "that forgiveness was invented precisely as a remedy for the wounds that intolerable wrongs leave us with."[19] We forgive, in other words, for our own good, because forgiveness helps us not to distort our best selves with hatred. And, thus undistorted, we are prepared to follow the hardest rule of civility, which is our obligation to love even those who mean us ill. We can fight hard to change their policies and to change *them,* as the civil rights movement fought with love and hope against segregationists, but the respect we owe them because of their equal share in God's creation does not turn on whether, on the issues we care about most, they are with us or against us.

CIVIL LISTENING AND OPINION-POLL POLITICS

Sometimes worse than the threat to civility from those who refuse to listen because they hate is the threat from those who pretend to listen but really do not. The Canadian journalist Harry Boyle is credited with the bon mot that candidates nowadays do not run for office—they pose for office. The student of civility, concerned about the etiquette of democracy, must worry over the truth of this proposition. None of our fine principles about dialogue or civil listening will mean very much if candidates are simply the products of marketing strategies, as substantial as sugar-sweetened cereals that arrive in attractive packages and contain no nutritional value. For our reconstructed civility to function, politics must be *about* something, and our politicians must stake out positions on the something that politics is about. But political consultants, and their constant polling, seem to be killing this possibility.

I quote a number of public opinion surveys in this book—perhaps too many. We Americans worry too much about what other people think and too little about what other people have to say. Polls tell us people's conclusions, not their arguments; we know what they believe, but not why. When we allow the polls to guide us, then, we are twice moral cowards: first, because we do not make up our own minds, and, second, because we do not demand that other people tell us the reasons for what they think. Moral cowardice of this kind is, in its turn, twice uncivil: first, because we do not do others the courtesy of arguing for what we believe, and, second, because we do not do others the courtesy of taking their views seriously enough to listen to their arguments. The great José Raúl Capablanca, chess champion of the world in the 1920s, once made a comment about chess books that should guide our politicians—and our journalists—as they look at opinion polls. They should be used, said Capablanca, like glasses, to assist the sight. Instead, he added, some people use them as if they conferred sight.

Surely we want our leaders, whether in politics, business, religion, or any other sphere of life, to be people who understand this distinction, people who will articulate for us visions of their own rather than mouth unthinkingly by rote what polls have told them are the values the rest of us hold. Luther Willson, in the sermon on Christian love we reviewed in chapter 6, put the point nicely:

A man without fixed sentiments of rectitude and goodness, however exquisite his sensibilities, exalted his genius, accomplished his education, or engaging his deportment, must, after all, be deficient in a wise consistency and uniformity of conduct. The splendour of his talents and speciousness of his virtues may captivate and allure, but, unless his character is supported by conscious integrity, solid worth, and practical wisdom, the partiality of prejudice will bias his judgment, the fluctuating influence of popular opinion will prevail against the decisions of conscience, and unsettle the rectitude of the heart.[20]

A candidate with Willson's "fixed sentiments of rectitude and goodness" might not, says the conventional wisdom, be electable. We need candidates, it is said, who are flexible enough to steer close to the political winds.

And yet I wonder whether this is so. The legal scholar Frederick Schauer points out how, very often, the great judges we celebrate are not those who follow the rules but those who break them—a process that often makes new ones: "We equate Solomon's wisdom with justice not because Solomon followed the rules in solving the dispute over the baby but because Solomon came up with exactly the right solution for that case."[21] Translated to politics, the point is this: we need leaders who, when necessary, reject both prevailing wisdom and the messages of the polls, leaders who stand for something when there is risk in doing so and who are willing to do the very hard but very civil work of trying to carry the unruly, self-absorbed American people along. Put more simply, civility requires that candidates for office respect the voters enough to listen to our actual concerns and then tell us what they really think. If we do not force them to do so, we deserve whatever scoundrels wind up in office.

One might answer, I suppose, that our nasty electoral contests are at best epiphenomenal: we must be cautious, one could argue, not to confuse effect with cause. Perhaps our angry politics simply reflects a more generalized anger of the era. It is not, then, the possibility of a civil language of politics that is collapsing around us, but the possibility of civil language at all. In fact, our common and familiar modes of expression have become remarkably mean, even violent. What has happened to our common language is the subject of the next chapter.

9

. . . .

Fighting Words

THE TIME has come to declare war on the violent metaphors that are besieging our language. We must smash them, crush them, track them to their lairs and eradicate every trace. We must not rest until we have wiped them out. They must be killed before they can multiply. Our strategy must be to slash and burn.

But they are wickedly clever, these metaphors. Demolishing their fortresses will not be easy because they build fortresses everywhere: not only on talk radio or in vicious lyrics, but in the ordinary conversation of everyday life. If there is a market for violent language, it is only because we have all come to accept it as normal. Violence done with words has become not merely acceptable, but mundane.

Item: In the fall of 1995, the coach of the Minnesota Timberwolves of the National Basketball Association said of his player Kevin Garnett, who jumped directly from high school to professional ball without benefit of college, "With weight and experience, this kid is going to kill people, big time."[1]

Item: In Suffolk County, Long Island, that same year, the manager of a state legislative campaign threatened to "rip the lungs out" of a man working for the other side.[2]

Item: Wall Streeters routinely describe people who make bad investments or foolish takeover bids as "having their heads handed to them."[3] (This phrase has evidently replaced the less colorful, and less violent, "losing their shirts.") And, of course, there are the "hostile takeovers," which, if successful, may lead to the "dismembering" of the target company, unless defeated by a "poison pill"

148

Fighting Words

defense. Later, the top executives of the dismembered company send their résumés to "headhunters."

Item: In 1995 a federal court appellate ruled that an employer did not create an illegal atmosphere of hostility toward women just because one of its managers said things like, "Sometimes don't you just want to smash a woman in the face." The gentleman in question, the judges explained in the case of *Gross v. Burggraf Construction Co.*, said equally nasty things about men, and so was not exhibiting any special bias toward women.[4]

And the list of violent metaphors goes on. We constantly threaten to make each other "eat our words." When our big ideas go bust, we have been "shot down in flames." Or perhaps "blown out of the water." Legislatures are always "killing" bills. (One of my favorite headlines from years past: SENATE KILLS ANTI-BUSING RIDER.) Bad plays or films—or books!—are "savaged" by the critics. And the casually graphic sexual language that so many of us use to show our anger—"F—— you!" and the like—does not refer to the romantic, the pleasurable, or even the consensual aspects of sex.

Psychologists who study emotion tell us that aggressive words are often used when aggressive acts are impossible.[5] So perhaps it is healthier to *talk* violently than to *act* violently. But that knowledge does not make nastiness any easier to bear—not when it is directed at you, or at someone you love, or at an institution you value. When an angry driver raises his middle finger at us, we do not sit and say, "Well, at least he isn't shooting." We are far more likely to grow angry, or at least shaken, and we may snap at the next person we see. In this way, as we saw on our automobile trip in chapter 1, incivility is a force multiplier, even if the forces that it multiplies are negative.

We Americans are a violent people. Our violent crime rate, although lately down a bit, remains the highest in the industrialized world—a fact that haunts the nation's effort to fight for human rights abroad.[6] That violence is contrary to the norms of civility should be sufficiently obvious to need no proof. But violent, aggressive language also violates the norms, because it does not treat other people as sharing equally in God's creation. Nastiness devalues the speaker as well because the unwillingness to restrain the urge marks the speaker as less civilized, more animal-like. Cleansing our language of violence is not simply a matter of politesse—it is a matter of morality. And, at a practical level, it is a matter of making conversation work. Nasty language, whether vulgar or violent or simply bigoted, does nothing to encourage a thoughtful and reasoned response. It sparks anger or shame but not dialogue. So it makes it harder for us to talk to each other, and thus hurts democracy.

I do not mean to suggest that displaying anger is always bad. True, we tend to think of anger as a negative—we refer to "loss" of temper, suggesting that it should have been kept—and the Bible admonishes us that a soft answer turns away wrath. But social historians have suggested that the belief that anger should be controlled is itself a market phenomenon, stemming from (among other things) the development of an industrial economy, in which, for an employee, a short temper was often a weakness.[7] Moreover, behavioral scientists believe that anger is functional. Because laboratory studies suggest that angry subjects have significantly greater self-confidence than others, and the potential for greater courage as well, some theorists argue that anger has been important in the establishment of civilization.[8] This makes sense. Anger surely made it easier for primitive humans to face down a deadly enemy or to prove themselves in a variety of ways to doubters.

Still, the fact that anger is functional—if it is a fact—offers scant defense for aping the language of anger in everyday speech, where we rarely spend our anger on such noble tasks as saving our families or building new cities. Instead, we allow the language of anger and violence to serve as part of ordinary conversation; we take the hateful as the norm. Indeed, whether or not the federal court in the *Gross* case (how aptly named!) had the law right, its vision of a workplace in which violent language is commonplace surely has the facts right, because we seem to accept such language as simply a part of our lives. *Gross* itself represents acceptance with a vengeance: the broader the swath of nastiness, the better the chance to gain legal protection. It may be wrong to hate only women or only African Americans or only Jews, but it is fine to hate everybody. Or to talk as if you do.

MARCHING AS TO WAR

. . . .

Of course, the use of the language of violence to make a point about something nonviolent is no recent invention. Many of the violent metaphors I have mentioned seem intended to capture the spirit of battle, perhaps as a way of inspiring the troops. Unsolicited tender offers are called "hostile takeover attempts" because the corporation that wants to remain independent might have the best chance to get what it wants if it imagines itself girding for war. In our metaphors, we gird for war all the time. President Johnson promised a "war on poverty" back in the 1960s, and we have been fighting it, albeit with waning national will and through a series of mostly losing engagements, ever since. (Vietnam was not LBJ's only well-intentioned quagmire.)

Violence itself, as Hannah Arendt persuasively argued, is instrumental: it is almost always used, especially by the state, in order to attain some end.[9] The same is true of violent language: it has a purpose, and language that compares our efforts to ameliorate our social ills to warfare should certainly be considered violent. Perhaps the rhetoric of war is meant to be inspiring, not least because it promises victory rather than stalemate. But the rhetoric has its costs—and not only because of the risk that we will inure ourselves to violence through talking about it too much. A significant problem is what we have done to our sense of what is valuable and good. The ideal of civility, the reader will recall, requires us to sacrifice for the sake of our fellow passengers. A real war requires real sacrifices, but our many metaphorical wars seem destined to be fought at lesser cost. Even when politicians promise us a war—on poverty, on drugs, on pornography, on crime—they always take care to explain that it will cost us taxpayers nothing and that we will somehow benefit in the long run. The wars we fight with words are evidently supposed to be fought for free.

Thus, in our zeal to reconstruct the language around metaphors of battle, we lose much of the moral force of our history and our culture. We lose much of what is special and sacrificial about war itself. Rather than calling us to sacrifice, our politicians promise us that we will prevail. Consider the deeply tragic (and frequently

misquoted) lines from Alfred Lord Tennyson's poem "The Charge
of the Light Brigade":

> Theirs not to make reply,
> Theirs not to reason why,
> Theirs but to do and die.

This is followed by:

> Into the jaws of death,
> Into the mouth of hell,
> Rode the six hundred.

These famous words remember the foolish, hopeless assault by
British cavalry on the Russian heavy guns during the battle for Bal-
aclava in 1854. Tennyson's public knew that the order to attack
should never have been given, which is one reason the poem so
effectively conveys an image of sacrifice, of duty-at-all-costs, of the
grim willingness to risk all for the sake of the common good. The
Light Brigade charges the enemy positions, even knowing that it is
almost certain to lose the battle. It is, at best, a suicide mission—
and one that might not even end in victory. But the Brigade
charges anyway, not for the sake of victory, but for the sake of duty.

Nowadays Tennyson's powerful words have evolved into the triumphant and melodramatic "Do or die," suggesting that if we do
our jobs right, we *avoid* death—that is, we win. Or turn it
around: the dead guys lose, which also implies that the losers are
the ones who are dead. This is a troubling ethic to teach our children, suggesting as it does that survival is more important than
duty . . . or morality. But we teach it constantly, because much of
our culture seems to rest on the supposition that the good guys
always survive.

Not long ago, I was one of several people asked by the *Los
Angeles Times* to select three films that would best illustrate the
American character to a foreigner unfamiliar with the nation. One
of my selections was *Star Wars*. I will admit that I enjoyed the film,
but I selected it principally for its cartoonized and oversimplified
model of violence and its relationship to morality. You can tell that
the Empire is evil because its minions run around (well, fly
around) killing people (and other intelligent life) quite indiscrimi-

nately.* And how do we beat them? Why, by killing even more efficiently than they do.

Indeed, the efficiency of killing by the good guys is a staple of modern American cinema. In the *Star Wars* movies, the good guys—the members of the rebellion—are outnumbered and out-gunned by the bad guys of the Empire, but, in the end, through pluck and careful screenwriting, the good guys manage to kill far more bad guys than the bad guys kill good guys. And none of the bad guys ever surrenders or is asked to: they are blasted out of the sky. Or out of space, their planet-smashing weapons blown to dust.

This is precisely the theme of the popular films starring such Hollywood stalwarts as Arnold Schwarzenegger, Steven Seagal, and Bruce Willis. Again, there are clearly marked good guys and bad guys. The good guys are generally outnumbered and outgunned—often by what the screenplay describes as terrorists, but usually the greedy, apolitical kind who want only money—and the good guys often are a mere good *guy*, for these modern heroes like to face entire armies of bad guys by themselves. But they always win. They shoot, maim, stab, and explode vastly larger numbers. Every bullet seems to find its mark. Every thrown knife finds a throat, every karate thrust a neck, every booby-trap a booby. They kill with sufficient efficiency to refute the military adage that warfare is labor-intensive.

And they are aided by the longtime Hollywood precept that the bad guys can't shoot straight. The bad guys are boobs indeed who, although they are able to acquire nuclear weapons (*True Lies*), take over battleships (*Under Siege*), and outwit the FBI (*Die Hard*), do not know how to guard prisoners properly (*True Lies*), post look-outs effectively (*Under Siege*), or even use hostages to best advantage (*Die Hard*). They are so stupid that the audience can be forgiven for thinking that perhaps they deserve to die for that alone. Violence? Violence is a triviality: the hero of the action-

---

* I did not mention in my comments to the *Times* the interesting similarity, now common in science fiction and adventure films, between the bad guys—the Empire—and the Nazi regime in Germany. Why has this device become so common? Probably because we all despise the Nazis more than any other group that has ever inhabited the earth, and the filmmakers want us to despise their bad guys by association. I remember reading somewhere a Catholic priest's comments on the Nazis who were slaughtered (some by Indiana Jones, some by a supernatural force) in *Raiders of the Lost Ark:* they did not die because they were Nazis, he wrote. The filmmakers made them Nazis so that we would not mind watching them die.

adventure film (as the genre is known) is expert at it. So expert that he often seems bored by the very violence he inflicts.

It would be surprising if we were not, aspirationally at least, the people we describe to ourselves in our rhetoric and display to ourselves in our art—the same way that it would be surprising if young people who love music about sex and drugs and violence were unaffected by it. So if we glorify killing in our films and our music, select aggressive metaphors in everyday speech, and declare that our every cause is a war, we are proclaiming ourselves to be people of violence. (Small wonder that we are able to glory in being the only nation in the industrialized world that possesses as many firearms as people.)

Naturally, and sensibly, we tend to be a little uncomfortable with this characterization. And so, in dribs and drabs, we try to do something about it. In June 1996, William Bennett of Empower America, Senator Joseph Lieberman of Connecticut, and C. Delores Tucker of the National Political Congress of Black Women announced a campaign (we had best not call it a war) against the record companies that distribute "vicious, violent, and vulgar music." They have a pretty good argument. The death metal group Cannibal Corpse, distributed by Sony, sings: "She was so beautiful I had to kill her," adding, "Couldn't scream, raped violently." (After that, the song gets worse.) Time Warner distributes the music of Ol' Dirty Bastard—a name some newspapers, understandably, refuse to print—who croons "Snatch a kid by the braids and cut his head off." The head of the Recording Industry Association of America huffed in response, "If they don't like it, don't buy it,"[10]—which is, I think, the whole point. If enough people don't buy it (or refuse to let their children buy it), perhaps the executives who do not mind distributing it will rethink their moral responsibility. That would be a rare triumph of morality over the values of the marketplace, which is why boycotts are such fine, and civil, ideas.

And, despite silly cries of censorship—the First Amendment contains no privilege against criticism—the unlikely coalition has had its successes. True, the boycotts might have increased sales briefly, for the forbidden always possesses an allure for the ill-raised young. But, in the end, Time Warner has sold its stake in Interscope Records. A few states, led by Texas, have recently passed "divestment" laws, which require their pension funds to sell stock in such companies. In their eagerness to look good, however, politicians have drafted the laws badly . . . or rather, broadly. The Texas statute bans state ownership of stock in firms that distribute music or videos that (among other things) depict scenes of gang activity or rape. As critics have pointed out, this language, taken literally, would ban *West Side Story* (gangs) and *Man of La Mancha* (rape).[11]

Conservatives are not alone in their effort to ban violent lyrics. Liberals sometimes do it too, and wind up looking equally silly. Is there too much violence in our cities? Perhaps our church services are to blame! Somebody must certainly think so, because there has been a strange move in recent years to sanitize Protestant worship—in particular, to remove what is seen as warlike imagery from the hymns. No, seriously. The Anglican Church of Canada, for example, has decided that its congregants are better off without the uplifting and triumphal strains of "Onward Christian Soldiers," evidently on the theory that "marching as to war" in the name of Jesus is not a good thing.[12] (Never mind that a survey of Anglicans at about the same time showed the hymn to be one of the ten most popular[13]—mere rank-and-file members apparently lack the moral smarts to make such decisions.) In 1988 the Methodist Church in the United States came within a whisker of doing the same. I assume this means that Anglican clergy in Canada, along with antiviolence Methodists in the United States, have also stopped preaching from the pulpit on the need for a "war" on poverty, or racism, or AIDS—wars that most Christians would surely feel called to fight.*

CIVILITY AND REAL WAR

. . . .

But it is an error to equate violence and incivility. To be sure, Erasmus himself, the father of the Western ideal of civility, was a committed pacifist. And small wonder. The concept of *civilité*, as we

---

* This is not the first time "Onward, Christian Soldiers" has faced a ban. At the celebration in Durban, South Africa, to mark the coronation of Edward VII, the hymn was banned by the British viceroy because of its lines "Crowns and thrones may perish/Kingdoms rise and wane."

have seen, developed in part as a reaction to the culture of casual violence that arose in Europe as the grip of Catholicism waned: humans had to learn anew how to treat each other. One purpose of *civilité* was to persuade people to discipline the urges to violence they might sometimes feel. And a strong Christian moral tradition holds pacifism to be the only stance that reflects genuine love of the neighbor.

And yet it is not obvious that this is the only answer. If I violently prevent someone from harming a child, it is difficult to see how I have been uncivil. Indeed, paradoxical although it may seem, civility may sometimes allow violence—or even encourage it. Consider the problem of war. Civility, the reader will recall, is sacrifice: submerging one's own immediate desires and interests in the love of neighbor that is the principal work of citizenship. Military service in time of war, in order to protect one's nation, is a very high form of civility, because the soldier puts at risk what many people value most—life itself. In doing so, the soldier may be called upon to kill soldiers fighting for the interest of another country, one which is, for that moment, the enemy. The morality of warfare is complex, and it is not my intention to summarize that debate here.[14] Suffice it to say that for the moral individual, taking the life of another human being, although it may be necessary, will always be difficult.* Soldiers who kill must live with the knowledge that their guns or bombs or missiles have destroyed the lives of other humans. Living with that knowledge is the other sacrifice that the men and women of the armed forces make for the sake of their country—and, ultimately, for the sake of civility.

When we honor our veterans, we recognize that they have risked their lives for the nation. But that materialistic view should not be the principal reason they deserve our thanks. Rather, we owe them a debt principally because they have taken upon themselves the moral burden of the willingness to kill for the nation. This is, for the moral individual, no easy thing. For many who kill, the memory never dies—even when they wish it would. Lieutenant Colonel Dave Grossman, a former Ranger and paratrooper, has expressed the dilemma eloquently in his book *On Killing*:

* I do not mean to deny the morality of pacifism. For the pure pacifist, there is no justification for taking a human life.

The soldier in combat is trapped within this tragic Catch–22. If he overcomes his resistance to killing and kills an enemy soldier in close combat, he will be forever burdened with blood guilt, and if he elects not to kill, then the blood guilt of his fallen comrades and the shame of his profession, nation, and cause lie upon him. He is damned if he does, and damned if he doesn't.[15]

Unfortunately, the rhetoric of war can obscure this point. Indeed, those who stay at home and support the war may not comprehend that the burden exists at all.[16] But the Christian tradition knows (although it has often forgotten this knowledge in our nation's violent history), because the requirement of loving the neighbor arguably prohibits all killing, even of the enemy. "Just war" doctrine, controversial though it is, developed to make this knowledge bearable.[17] And soldiers know, which is why, in order to get soldiers to kill, it is sometimes necessary to euphemize the act and demonize the enemy. Writes Grossman:

Most soldiers do not "kill," instead the enemy was knocked over, wasted, greased, taken out, and mopped up. The enemy is hosed, zapped, probed, and fired on. The enemy's humanity is denied, and he becomes a strange beast called a Kraut, Jap, Reb, Yank, dink, slant, or slope.[18]

I am old enough to remember vividly the KILL A GOOK FOR CHRIST buttons and bumper stickers of the Vietnam era. And I have learned, with some pain, of President Harry Truman's response to a letter from the National Council of Churches, questioning his decision to drop the atomic bomb on Hiroshima: "When you have to deal with a beast, you have to treat him as a beast. It is most regrettable but nevertheless true."[19]

These racist dismissals of the humanity of others doubtless made it easier to kill, but also made it impossible to defend the killing in the name of civility. Civility requires sacrifice, and the sacrifice may sometimes be of our sense of self, of *moral* self—as may happen when we kill. The more the enemy is caricatured and dehumanized, the less the sacrifice involved in killing him. The less the sacrifice involved in killing him, the greater the risk that the soldier may take pleasure in the task. When soldiers (or any of the rest us) come to enjoy killing, we have strayed very far from civility, and off in the direction of moral anarchy. Wars, like abortions and executions, involve killing, and therefore are justifiable (if we love our neighbors) only in the most fragile moral circumstances. A society in which any one of these practices is too common is a society that is morally obtuse about violence. Unfortunately, we seem to have accepted all three as common, even celebrated parts of life. That, too, is most regrettable but nevertheless true.

THE TELEVISED REVOLUTION

. . . .

And then there is the technology most commonly identified with the collapse of civility, the television—home of mean-spirited talk shows, casual sex, and even more casual violence. Although television raises many complex questions for the student of civility, it is the violence of television that concerns me here. Television has grown so violent over the past two decades that no serious researcher any longer doubts that overexposure to televised images of violence helps transform gentle children into brutal adults.

Since 1972, when the Surgeon General found a "preliminary and tentative" link between watching televised violence as a child and engaging in aggressive behavior as an adult,[20] the evidence of a strong connection has been pouring in. In 1992 the *Journal of the American Medical Association* published the first epidemiological study linking exposure to television violence to the commission of violent crimes.[21] The study, by Dr. Brandon Centerwall, argued that in the absence of television, the crime rate would be measurably lower. Although some of Centerwall's numbers seem a bit shaky, a number of very careful longitudinal studies have since confirmed his basic thesis: the children who watch lots of televised violence are not only more aggressive than others, but more likely to commit crimes.[22] Leaders of the American Academy of Pediatrics have pressed their members to counsel parents in television control along with talk about infant formula and vaccinations.

So, yes, television is violent, and violence is bad for kids. But here one wants to be cautious. To call exposure to violence the cause of incivility is like calling sugar the cause of a cavity. What causes the cavity is the refusal of the patient to discipline his consumption of sugar. Similarly, it is the indiscriminate and undisciplined use of the television—which is, after all, simply a tool—that may combine with other factors to turn an unformed child into an aggressive adult.

Moreover, violence is not the only behavioral problem related to overconsumption of television, and it may not be the most important one. Even parents who carefully screen the programs their children watch may be in for some unhappy surprises. For decades, controversy has raged over whether television does or does not shorten the attention span; in recent years, the nays appear to have it, but the pendulum could easily swing back the other way. The student of civility, however, is more concerned with a much better documented difficulty: too much television causes atrophy in the social skills we need to get along with each other.[23]

This tragic result is entirely predictable. Getting along with other people is like any other skill: the harder we practice, the better we do it. Children who spend many hours in front of the television are not practicing the skill. They are not practicing it with friends or siblings, and they are not practicing it with their most important teachers, their parents. If they do not learn the skill early, however, there is no reason to think they will learn it later—and so we raise generations of children who have not quite come to appreciate that they have fellow passengers on whose behalf they must often discipline their own urges. And so our incivility grows.

Unfortunately, lots of children have undisciplined exposure to television. The average child between ages two and eleven watches between twenty-three and twenty-eight hours of television a week, spending nearly one-third of his or her waking hours in front of the set.[24] Parents—evidently using the set as a baby-sitter—have demanded that the television industry cooperate by providing useful ratings, warning parents of objectionable content. The networks, whose natural concern is maximizing profits, not turning out good children, have demurred. Presumably worried that children (and adults) might not tune in shows with warnings indicating sex and violence—and thus would miss all the wonderful advertisements—they have offered instead an empty set of ratings purporting to tell parents which children can watch which shows. So the ratings, which each network does according to its own unpublicized standards, suggest the appropriate age at which children should be viewing the shows. A system of this kind represents the antithesis of a respectful civility, because it tries to make the decision for the parents rather than providing information to assist them.

A 1997 article in *TV Guide* argued rather desperately that television is not harmful to children as long as the parents are willing to supervise it.[25]* But we already knew this. The problem is that too many parents are unable or unwilling to supervise the television their children watch, and the television networks, knowing that millions of children are channel-surfing alone, nevertheless leave the equivalent of live ammunition lying around for the kids to play with. Indeed, the protests of the networks are beginning to sound a bit like the mantra of the National Rifle Association: television doesn't ruin children, parents ruin children.

Television programmers, shielded from significant regulation by the First Amendment, continue to insist that they are only providing the shows that the market demands. But the First Amendment demands more than so shallow an excuse. After all, the market produces the breakfast cereals and automobiles that the public demands without the need for constitutional protection for those industries. The authors of the First Amendment envisioned a more robust imagination—what in fairly recent times was known as news judgment—from those who would invoke its protections. The principal reason to protect freedom of the press is to encourage the press to take risks, especially the risks involved in challenging the government and other structures of power that could, without the First Amendment, shut critics down. If instead all the media do is feed their viewers what the viewers already want, an entire democratic tradition is being wasted.

Besides, to justify violent programming—or any programming—on the ground that people like it shows about as much moral vision as the pornographer. The pornographer, too, provides

---

* The article failed to disclose that *TV Guide* is owned by Rupert Murdoch, who also owns broadcast television stations, and therefore has an interest in how the controversy is resolved.

a service that many people want, and in his moral vision, that is doubtless reason enough; that he may also do harm is not a part of his calculation. All of us have a baser side to our natures, and the appeal to what is worst in us is the source of the pornographer's profits. Sometimes television programming, too, appeals to the bad part of our nature, which is not what civility demands. To advertise hard to stimulate demand is, in this context, like offering a bribe. The fact that a person might take the bribe is no evidence that the bribe itself is a good thing.

A WORD ON FREEDOM OF SPEECH

. . . .

None of the problems I have discussed in this chapter are amenable to regulation. The constitutional protection for freedom of speech makes it enormously difficult to restrict what people can say . . . or what networks can broadcast.

Yet the student of civility is necessarily concerned with the way we communicate. The social theorist Neil Postman has reminded us, with his typical polemic brio, that the study of language—including our own language—cannot be divorced from morality. The rules of grammar, he argues, are like any other rules: there is right and there is wrong. "[L]anguage," writes Postman, "distinguishes between the sacred and the profane, and thereby provides organization to our moral sense."[26] And although professional linguists are quick to argue that only description of language, not prescription of language, is theoretically sound, we must place limits on language in order to create community. The limits may not be legally enforceable—they may be nothing but very strong norms—but limits there must be to make conversation possible. After all, anything, even an act of aggression or violence, can be explained as somehow communicating an idea; but that does not mean that these violent word-acts are a form of communication that we need.[27]

I have in mind not the Orwellian task of constructing rules that make expression of some ideas impossible, but the more practical task of identifying some of the words and phrases we use (often unwittingly) to restrict or even prevent dialogue rather than enhance it. For example, in chapter 7, we discussed our tendency to describe our opponents as monsters, thus making conversation unnecessary. If demonization of our opponents were the principal (or the only) challenge our incivility presented to the spoken language, we might well survive it. But it isn't. In fact, so much that is uncivil has infiltrated the way we speak that it is difficult to hold a conversation in which incivility plays no part. I refer not only to the proliferation of vulgar and obscene words—especially in music and film—although that would be problem enough. I refer, rather, to our development of conversational habits in which we ourselves count for everything . . . and others matter not at all.

Civility certainly requires that we strive to eliminate from our vocabularies the nastiness and hatred, the violent language I have described in this chapter, and that we raise the consciousness of others about it, pointing out to them the import of the words they choose. We can mold this idea into a rule:

> *Civility requires that we express ourselves in ways that demonstrate our respect for others.*

What does this mean? Certainly that we should avoid "fighting words": we should not, for example, set out to make other people angry. This task in turn requires us to recognize that not everybody is angered by the same things. Decades of data support the proposition that men and women are not always angered at the same things. In particular, men tend to be angered by aggression, women by condescension.[28] More recent work evidently suggests regional differences too: a Southerner, for example, is more likely than other American men to become angry because somebody blocks his way in the hall.[29] But we cannot create many legal impediments. We certainly have the right to anger others. Indeed, hatred itself might be described as a constitutional right. The courts have not looked favorably on efforts to regulate "hate speech," even though some theorists argue that demeaning words targeting minority groups should be construed as acts, perhaps violent acts.[30] The courts have allowed the state to restrict the use of what have come to be called "fighting words," but only when the words are likely to provoke a violent response in the listener.[31]

So far, proponents of hate speech codes have not persuaded the judges that what they are trying to ban is anywhere near as bad.

One of the problems is that speech consisting of hateful ideas is still speech about ideas. The legal theorist Owen Fiss puts it this way: "Like pornography or for that matter much of art and literature, hate speech may appeal to our affective sentiments and be both the cause and the product of human action, but nonetheless is speech."[32] As Fiss points out, to conclude that hate speech is speech is not to say that it does no harm. This is where the classical liberal opposition to campus speech codes runs into trouble, trumpeting as it does the classical liberal claim that the cure for speech is more speech, and that truth will out in the end. This claim is often overstated and can even be dangerous. Its only focus is the thoughtful listener: more speech may indeed be the cure if all we care about is whose arguments will ultimately prevail in the battle for public opinion. Let them all come in! True, in these days of dialogue-by-television, we too often seem to mean, "Let all of them who have money or notoriety come in!" But the theory is nice even if the practice is bizarre.

On the other hand, not even the theory works if we place our focus not on the audience that might be persuaded but on the target of the speech, who might actually be harmed. Even if the harm is psychological, it is still harm. We might prefer to think of the targets of hateful speech as strong and stoic, ready to turn the other cheek—latter-day Jackie Robinsons all—but, even within this ideal, the pain of hateful speech would be no less real. Racial insults hurt. Sexual harassment hurts. Religious bigotry hurts. The pains are genuine and can be deep. Some speech has no speech cure. Words can wound, and wounds, left unattended, often fester. The idea that the wounds of racism, including the wounds of racist speech, will be healed if only we can find the proper incantation to pronounce over them—well, it is simply nonsense. Yet this revival-meeting spirit characterizes much of the criticism of the speech codes.

The notion that no form of speech offers harms greater than its benefits is ridiculous. Racial epithets, to take the example we have been discussing, are devoid of any utility other than to do harm.[33] So why do we not ban them, as anti-hate-speech crusaders have long advocated? We are well past the point in history where we believe that epithets contribute anything to democratic dialogue, so the reason cannot be that we are worried we might be banning an important moral truth. Nor can the reason be a simple mistrust of government power; we trust the state to regulate, for example, advertising. I suspect that the true reason—and, certainly, the reason with the greatest appeal to the student of civility—is that we are worried about the humanity of people we select to govern us. We see them in their human frailty, people no better than ourselves, and we wonder (or we should wonder) what, in their frailty, they would do with unlimited power.

There is an eternal human temptation to ban what we would rather not see or hear, and the temptation is surely strongest for those with their hands on the levers of power. The student of civility obviously wants to help those who govern resist that temptation. A judicial system that can review the laws for constitutional defects is not enough: judges, even Supreme Court justices, are just as human, and just as frail, just as open to temptations of power, as any other government officials. The best tool to help government officials resist the urge to ban speech they do not like is a norm of free speech so strongly inculcated that we will not ban even those categories of speech we *know* to be harmful—whether violent television programming or nasty, alienating epithets. If we refuse to ban what we know does harm, we are unlikely to ban what we simply dislike.

So free speech, although certainly a glory of democracy, is also one of its costs. The student of civility may love our democracy and the precious freedoms that are a part of it, but must never make the mistake of thinking that those freedoms come without cost—or that the costs fall equally on all.

CHANGING DIRECTION

. . . .

Civility, as we have seen, teaches us to discipline our desires for the sake of others. So much in our world teaches us not to: politics in particular proposes that what life is for is to allow us to get what we want. Politics and morality are always, perhaps inevitably, at war. They are at war now. Sad to say, politics is winning and morality is losing. If life is principally about gaining our objectives, there is no reason to treat others well, except, occasionally, as a tactic on the road to victory. (If I treat you well, you are more likely to vote for me.) Consider a simple example, common to our everyday experience: giving up a seat on a crowded bus or train. Suppose that Alan, a strong and healthy young man, is seated comfortably, when Beatrice, an elderly woman, heavily laden with packages, gets on the bus. Nobody else offers her a seat, so Alan gets up and lets her have his. Now, Alan gains no obvious advantage from this act, other than the satisfaction of having done what is right. The fact that there is no advantage to be gained surely explains why none of the other passengers offers Beatrice a seat. There is evidently no natural impulse that urges us to help—not when we must sacrifice our own comfort.[34] So when Alan decides to give Beatrice his seat, he is acting out of a learned impulse, not a natural one. The trouble is, fewer and fewer people are learning that impulse, because the institutions that should be teaching it are not doing their jobs.[35]

This concern is particularly pressing because the same moral weaponry helps us in another battle, now at its crucial point: the battle to keep all of social life from being swamped by the values of the marketplace. Markets work efficiently to provide us with the goods and services we want, but they cannot tell us what goods and services to want. In principle, a market draws no distinction between the desire to buy a new car and the desire to buy the services of a child prostitute. If the demand for a particular commodity is high, even making it illegal merely raises the price—as has happened, for example, with drugs. Thus, economic forces are considered not immoral but amoral.

Although I will have much more to say about markets in the next chapter, it is important here to note how similar are the values of the market and of politics. Both exist to allow us to achieve our desires. This is not bad in itself. But it is bad—in fact, disastrous—if we lack the morality to help us to control our desires. For example, some adults want to have sex with children. Law and morality work together to prevent this. Absent law, the market would fulfill these desires. Absent shared moral norms, there would be no law against it. There are groups (like the National Man-Boy Love Association) that wish to change the law. They will certainly fail, but only because of moral objections to their agenda. There is nothing in the nature of politics itself to guarantee their failure, just as there is nothing in the market to prevent the sale of that which is legal but immoral. Only a widely shared moral understanding can do that.

10

. . . .

Market Language and
the Linguistics of Incivility

IN 1990, the rap group 2Live Crew was prosecuted on obscenity charges (eventually dismissed) for some of the lyrics on its album *As Nasty As They Wanna Be.* A national brouhaha ensued. People who had never heard the music took firm positions. The controversy transformed a moderately successful and by most accounts mediocre album into a phenomenon. It also gave the English language a troubling new phrase. Here are some of its uses in the late 1990s: A blurb for Rosie O'Donnell's television talk show asks us: "Is civility back in style? Or are people (at the top) as nasty as they wanna be?"[1] An article about the campaign tactics of lawyers who want to be judges asks, "Can judicial candidates be as nasty as they wanna be?"[2] The football player Michael Irvin is described by a journalist as wearing "gangsta shades, gold chains and that nasty-as-I-wanna-be smirk."[3] A newspaper story on a Boston neighborhood where many college students live warns that "there are a few nasty-as-they-wanna-be book/video stores."[4] And let us not forget the Internet. The Associated Press has this to say of Internet Explorer 4.0: "Microsoft's Web browser lets computer users be as nasty as they wanna be."[5]

What difference does it make, the reader might ask, whether the lyrics of a song or the name of an album become a cliché? In the first place, the phrase itself reminds us of the source of our crisis, not because of its reference to nastiness, but because it implies that our personalities, no matter how offensive, should be wholly matters of our own choice. One is reminded of George Bernard Shaw's famous line, that the two things he hates most in the world are duty and his mother. Both *duty* and *mother*, of course, represent the possibility of not living entirely according to one's own will and desires: duty tells us what to do, and family (represented by mother) teaches us to do our duty. Countless messages in our uncivil era tell us that we have no duties unless we want to have them, even to our families.

A powerful source of the messages of self-interest and dutiless-ness is the marketplace—in particular, the language of commer-cials. One automobile manufacturer advertises its products with the slogan ON THE ROAD OF LIFE, THERE ARE PASSENGERS AND THERE ARE DRIVERS, adding the tantalizing invitation: "DRIVERS WANTED." These words appeal, of course, to our American tradi-tion of independence, especially in our cars. But what is the moral content of this slogan? Just this: it is better to be a driver than a passenger. The idea must be that drivers are in charge, whereas pas-sengers are not—and everybody who is anybody should want to be in charge. If everybody tries to be a driver, we turn out to be travel-ing through life alone. And if I am not a passenger, I can have no fellow passengers, and thus I need not worry about the others I may encounter. Isaac Peebles would spin in his grave.

We face some difficulty here, because the language of the mar-ketplace is reconstructing the language of civil society. The words we use in our everyday lives are being shaped by the forces of acquisitiveness and self-seeking that characterize what was once called *economic man*. We scarcely seem to be aware that the change is occurring, but we should think about it every time a child sees an advertisement on television and runs to his parents to pro-nounce a sentence beginning, "I want . . . "—and every time a political candidate encourages us to think of government as simply a bureaucratic Santa Claus that distributes the goodies we desire. The market pollutes our children, it pollutes our politics . . . and it pollutes our souls. Capitalism counsels that we should be acquisi-tive, and, lacking alternative sources of meaning, we go ahead and acquire. If not nasty, we are, at least, as selfish as we wanna be.

One might protest that this is a bit much to deduce from the title of a record album, that the phrase in question is but the title of an album, not a symbol of the market. But the title, properly understood, emphasizes the phrase *as they wanna be*—not the word *nasty*. It celebrates individual choice, including, obviously, the choice to do things that others find unpleasant (nasty). The difference between the selfish man's refusal to share his wealth with others (hurting the pocketbook) and his insistence on being offensive to others (hurting the spirit) exists only if we adopt, as the measure of morality, the market emphasis on dollars and cents.

Besides, we must bear in mind that a professionally recorded and distributed album is a commercial product. For all the pleasure it may bring to listeners, an album is, to the market, simply a commodity. It exists to be sold—that is, its very purpose is profit. Markets exist to allow commodities to be exchanged, and that is all to the good, an important component of human freedom. But nobody pretends that markets are friendly or even particularly civil places. Buyer and seller, cooperating on the surface, are in a sense adversaries: they do not trust each other and rarely have any concern for each other's welfare. And markets are not particularly moral places either. It is a truism of economics that markets are amoral: markets bring together willing buyer and willing seller but are not capable of evaluating the moral worth of a transaction.[6] If morality (or law) does not cause people to restrain their desires, the same free-market forces that respond to consumer demand by supplying breakfast cereal and razor blades will supply cocaine, hand grenades, and child prostitutes.

And markets can transform those who participate in them. Sometimes this is to the good, as when the limited market reforms of a Mikhail Gorbachev helped the people of the Communist bloc to understand the virtues of freedom. But when we come to think that because markets allow us to acquire, acquisitiveness is a virtue, disaster is on the way. The economist E. F. Schumacher put it this way: "If human vices such as greed and envy are systematically cultivated, the inevitable result is nothing less than the collapse of intelligence."[7] And as Don Eberly, president of the Commonwealth Foundation, has written: "Free markets by themselves do not assure a well-ordered and free society; they can even undermine the very virtues that produced prosperity in the first place."[8] That is why a morally thoughtful community limits the reach of the market, preserving a space that is relatively free of its influence, and creating and nurturing the institutions that fill that space and help us to construct our moral selves.

But we seem incapable of doing it. The theologian Cornel West describes what is happening in America today as allowing market values to crowd out nonmarket values. Such nonmarket institutions as family, churches, civic associations, private clubs, and neighborhoods—often collected under the name civil society—should ideally supply the meaning, the language of morality and value, that the market does not. Traditionally, supplying that meaning has been a special responsibility of the religious sphere. But there is some reason to doubt that the religions are doing their job.

Let us see what happens when they try.

THE DEFEAT OF THE MARKET?

. . . .

Early in 1997, the Vatican issued a sharp denunciation of the way that products are advertised in Western capitalist societies. A thirty-five-page report from the Pontifical Council for Social Communications, entitled *Ethics in Advertising*, called on those who commission advertisements, those who design them, and those who publish or broadcast them to accept their own moral responsibility for "what they seek to move people to do." The report argued that advertisements, like the media generally, invariably play one of two roles: "Either they help human persons to grow in their understanding and practice of what is true and good, or they are destructive forces in conflict with human well-being." Consequently, the council concluded, advertisements should be truthful; they should not violate "the dignity of the human person"; and they should reflect a sense of social responsibility.[9]

The document ignited a small firestorm among advertisers, many of whom questioned whether the Catholic Church should be speaking on this topic at all. "They're playing in the wrong ballfield," said one executive quoted in the *New York Times*. Added another: "We get into a very dangerous place when the Catholic Church or any other religious organization tries to dictate content.

Let the consumer decide. The free enterprise system provides its own policing."[10] And then there was this one, with echoes of the abortion fight: "They should stick to religion, and we'll stick to advertising."[11]

The critics are partly right. The document's emphasis on advertising's appeal to various irrational human faculties does not reflect current marketing theory, which treats advertising principally as a transmitter of information.[12] The report seems mired in the antiquated notion that successful marketing consists of "hidden persuaders" (to borrow the phrase Vance Packard made famous during the 1950s)—the idea that advertising is a sophisticated form of brainwashing, robbing the consumer of free will rather than facilitating consumer choice. Growing evidence suggests that consumers are far more autonomous and sophisticated than such simple models assume.

But the critics are mostly wrong, and, indeed, criticisms of the sort they offer miss the deeper truths that the report touches. Consider the most controversial aspect of the report, the reference to human dignity. The report explicitly condemned "appeals to lust, vanity, envy and greed."[13] The student of civility should be quick to see that the Vatican has a point: when we appeal to the baser side of human nature in order to sell a product, we are not living the loving respect for our fellow humans that civility demands. Instead, we are encouraging them to yield to their instincts, that is, to behave like animals. Unfortunately, there are all too few advertisements that could survive this test.

Yet the test matters. Civility, as we have seen, is sacrifice, and it requires us to remember that our actions must be morally justifiable. Advertising exists to sell products and services. As the Vatican statement conceded, that purpose is not bad in itself; on the contrary, supplying consumers with information that allows them to make rational choices is essential if market economies are to exist. But it is a very long way from conceding the moral value of advertising to conceding that all advertisements are of equal moral value. There is, first, the question (also raised by the Vatican) of whether there are some legal products that should not be advertised at all. That is the position, for example, that many anti-smoking advocates take with respect to cigarettes. But the greater challenge raised by *Ethics in Advertising* is to the content of the advertising itself. And here the student of civility must admit that the Vatican has an excellent point.

To take the most obvious example, it strikes me as bizarre that anybody would patronize Calvin Klein, given the sexualization of its models, even the very young, that has long been a mainstay of its advertising. Not long ago, the firm removed billboards in New York City that critics considered little better than child pornography. (The prominent advertising executive Jerry Della Femina responded to the Vatican statement this way: "It would have been just as easy to send a telegram to Calvin Klein and spare the rest of us."[14]) But, of course, that is just why people buy: so much advertising is aimed at convincing us that we are not attractive enough and can turn our lives around if only we wear the right clothes or cologne.

Sexualization is powerfully antithetical to civility. Civility calls us to see God in all people, to feel a sense of awe as we come into the presence of somebody new, but the sexualization of a model, or of anybody else, is in a sense dehumanizing, for it creates a kind of nonhuman, a creature we are intended to desire sexually but not to relate to in any other aspect of (his/her/its) being. This problem, I suspect, is what Pope John Paul II had in mind when he warned that a man who looks at his own wife with lust is committing a sin.[15] He did not mean that married couples should not want to make love and enjoy doing it; he meant, surely, that it is sinful for a husband to see his wife (or a wife her husband) only in the dimension of sexuality, denying the spouse other aspects of humanity (and of loving marital intimacy) in the rush to celebrate him or her as an object of sexual desire.

And the sexualization of advertising does not damage the dignity only of the models and actors; it also damages the dignity of those at whom its message is aimed. Audiences, in fact, should understand it as a rather grave insult. Appealing to potential customers at the level of some base instinct is not only repugnant but disrespectful of their humanity, for it supposes us to be guided not by the rational faculties that set us apart from other animals, but by the instincts that make us resemble them.

For all of those reasons, *Ethics in Advertising* is quite correct that some advertising is an affront to human dignity. But the Vatican statement is also correct that not all advertising is. The principal point is that those who prepare advertisements, like those who pay for them and those who publish or broadcast them, must recognize the moral dimension of their work. In the Western religious traditions, human communication is a gift from our Creator; using it in a way that demeans is immoral. The Qur'an, for example, is particularly detailed in explaining to the faithful the limits that God places on how one does business in the market.*

Translating this religious understanding into secular terms, the rule would be that a decision on how to shape an advertising campaign, no less than a decision on any other human action, must be disciplined by an understanding of our obligations to our fellow passengers—including the obligations of generosity and respect that civility demands of us. Thus, we can see the germ of a rule, by combining what we have learned in this chapter and the previous one:

> *Civility requires resistance to the dominance of social life by the values of the marketplace. Thus, the basic principles of civility—generosity and trust—should apply as fully in the market and in politics as in every other human activity.*

What does this mean in practice? The civil advertiser certainly does not mislead, but more than that, the civil advertiser does not seek customers in a way that demeans either the customers themselves or the models and actors on whom the advertiser may rely. This argument implies that the moral advertiser sometimes accepts inferior results in the market, but civility often entails sacrifice of the desires of the self for the sake of our fellow passengers. "This is the most effective way to sell my product" is not a moral argument.

This does not mean that advertising offensive to dignity should be banned. Not only would drawing a line be difficult, but, as we saw in chapter 7, there is no reason to suppose that the state can be trusted with such power. In other words, the market will contribute to civility rather than incivility only if advertising execu-

* The famous prohibition on usury is crystal clear in the Qur'an (see Surah 2.275–84). To comply with the rule and yet attract depositors, banking institutions in Islamic countries frequently offer depositors shares of stock, on which dividends are paid, rather than interest.

tives can be persuaded to make it so. This, too, *Ethics in Advertising* got right: "The indispensable guarantors of ethically correct behavior by the advertising industry are the well-formed and responsible consciences of advertising professionals themselves."[16] But, as the harsh responses to the Vatican's report make plain, the consciences of the executives will not well-form themselves. What we saw with respect to negative advertising is true here too: only public pressure will bring about an atmosphere in which ads enhance rather than demean human dignity. Only a mighty effort to free ourselves from the shackles of market language will enable us to create the pressure. And only a religious understanding of the world offers us the tools we need to make the effort.

The reader might object, of course, that our secular moral understandings are entirely sufficient to solve the same problems. One wishes this proposition were true, but recent history has not borne it out. Neither liberalism nor conservatism has proved adequate, in theory or practice, to attack the violations of human dignity that occur from advertising that sexualizes or in other ways appeals to our baser instincts. At least, liberalism and conservatism cannot do it without the aid of a belief in a transcendent good—the aid that religion supplies.

Liberalism cannot do it because it cannot articulate a theory of why the sexualizing of other human beings is wrong—a proposition that antipornography feminists have discovered when trying to enlist liberal allies to fight degrading images of women. At bottom a theory about individual choice, liberalism has difficulty explaining why that choice should extend to, say, whether to end a pregnancy but not to whether to buy pornography . . . or, for that matter, whether to grab for a third car. I once saw a libertarian bumper sticker that captures the point precisely: I'LL KEEP MY LAWS OFF YOUR BODY IF YOU'LL KEEP YOUR LAWS OFF MY MONEY. And liberalism has never successfully escaped this paradox. If sexual freedom is to be unlimited, it is difficult to see why economic freedom should not be. The claim that the second does harm and the first does none is tenable only if one surrenders to the market method of valuation and decides that only money, not the dignity of the human spirit, counts.

Besides, liberalism is trapped by its own fantasy, that it is possible to have a state that is neutral among competing conceptions of the good life, allowing people to live as they choose. As long as all conceptions are equally good, liberalism will never be able to supply us with the moral armament that we need to assist us in deciding what we should want; liberalism merely protects our ability to fulfill those wants. This is an important task—freedom matters!— but it is not an adequate public philosophy for a society that wishes to be civilized.

Liberal theorists recognize the paradox but have no way out. Many have come to focus on the schools, hoping to educate (read "indoctrinate") children out of making illiberal or irrational choices—that is, choices with which the theorists disagree.[17] Some, evidently a bit impatient with democracy, have tried to use our all-purpose contemporary tool, the Constitution, as a device to prohibit the expression through politics of positions that liberalism abhors.[18] Others, desperate to find answers but trapped by the liberal wariness of religion, have argued that we should adopt the techniques of contemporary marketing in an effort to alter behavior.[19] But the truth may be that only a resurgence of genuine religiosity can do the fundamental work of change that needs to be done.

Conservatism fares little better, split as it is between two very different movements, the social conservatives and the economic conservatives. Social conservatives, who tend to be heavily evangelical, would certainly insist that religion play a strong role in creating social meaning and would have no trouble dispensing with advertisements that sexualize. But economic conservatism's emphasis on free markets in which consumers are assumed to be both sovereign and autonomous strips it of the weapons needed to criticize any advertising, except, perhaps, that which is actually false. This was the argument of the executive who responded to *Ethics in Advertising* with the cry that the market should decide, but what the argument misses is that the media culture that generates the objectionable advertising also influences who we are and what we want—and thus affects our decisions about what to consume. It hardly makes sense to call on the market alone to decide, when the market itself is influencing those who make decisions.

So if the values of the market are to be prevented from reshaping us, religion must take the lead. *Ethics in Advertising* is a first effort, and a good one. Resisting the incursions of the market into other areas of social life is a challenge that should unite all of America's religionists, for the blurring of boundaries strikes at the heart of what makes religion religion: the unique ability to call us to contemplate the ultimate questions of human existence. Economic conservatives, insisting that the market is the solution, are unable to see that the very same ideology of uninhibited choice that makes the market so dangerous also fuels our societal refusal to re-create a distinctive morality of sex . . . or of family life.

The unwillingness of movement conservatives to take on the problem of corporate power has been disquieting to many Christian evangelicals who are with them on other issues. Evangelicals, by tradition, tend to be suspicious of all concentrations of power and certainly have no love for large corporations or the very rich. In fact, some data suggest that evangelicals as a group are more economically liberal than most Americans.[20] But Republican candidates, who court evangelical votes with bold talk about social issues, tend to ignore their views on economic matters.

From time to time, I find myself wondering whether the next truly great President, the one who will unite broad and diverse segments of our broad and diverse nation, will be economically liberal and socially conservative, wrapping both in a genuine and deep religiosity. Oddly, the candidate in recent years who has come closest to fitting this description has been the speechwriter-turned-journalist Pat Buchanan, whose nativist and often nasty appeals to the worst in the American character have masked his deft merger of family-values conservatism and populist economic activism. Perhaps the day will come when a mainstream candidate, without Buchanan's xenophobic instincts, will present the same package.[21]

MARKET POLLUTION

. . . .

This brings us back to 2Live Crew and the other rap groups that nowadays face such scathing criticism for violent or sexually explicit lyrics. Their defenders insist that the artists who make such music are expressing a genuine anger, even anguish, or that their songs are a mirror held up to the world—the world that we have bequeathed them. But these defenses, accurate or not, are beside the point for the student of civility. What is true and sad about contemporary music is its limitless emphasis on fulfillment of the self: whether it is about sex or violence, drugs or money, the music sends the message that what matters is that *I get mine* (even if I sometimes have to kill you to do it). There is an animalistic, uncivilized quality to that demand, but it is not something that rap artists invented. It is, rather, the fundamental value of the marketplace, the fulfillment of the wants of the individual, set to music.

Outside of the genre of Christian music, there seem to be all too few popular songs that call anybody to sacrifice for anybody else. Some songs are about pain, some are about anger, some are about hatred, and many are about love or sex or both; but it is difficult to find the music that teaches us to give up a part of what we value for the sake of making a common life with our fellow passengers. Popular music may be about gain, or it may be about loss, but it is, almost entirely, about us and our desires.

But why should music be different from anything else? We have already seen how electoral politics has been reduced to a parade of candidates making dubious promises to give us, painlessly, the things we want. Universities are also becoming market-driven. The content of the curriculum, once a sovereign and jealously guarded responsibility and privilege of the faculty, is more and more given over to student preference; the departments and courses that are popular survive and thrive, and those that are not get the ax.* The market of student choice, not the professional judgment of the teachers, drives the decisions.

American religion, too, is taking on that coloration. Nobody wants to be preached to. Nobody thinks anybody else should be preached to either. When my wife and I moved to New Haven and tried to find an Episcopal church to attend, people asked us whether we were liberal or conservative in our politics—assuming, wrongly, that what we wanted was a church where we would be assured each Sunday from the pulpit that all our political convic-

---

* This is quite independent of the related problem of political pressure, from left and right alike, to offer some courses instead of others—pressures to which universities seem more and more inclined to yield.

tions coincided with God's will. But so much of religion is like that now: rather than challenging the faithful to do what is difficult, preachers share with them only the part of God's word they want to hear.[22] And so the worship of God, too, becomes an embodiment of the values of the market, language carefully selected to fill the pews—and the faithful carefully shopping for congregations that will offer them comfort rather than challenge. So the churches, too, have decided that survival is more important than autonomy.

Yet religion retains the power to help us focus, as Tillich wrote, on the ultimate questions. By helping us to see that we are God's, religious faith can help us to understand what truly matters. At its best, religion accomplishes this not through the creation of fear (although seven of ten Americans believe in hell[23]), but through inspiration. In particular, by calling us to live according to the great principle of loving the neighbor, our religious traditions can help to shape our moral selves in order that we might defeat the incursions of the market. But religion can do this only if it is willing to challenge us to sacrifice our own desires, instead of telling us that whatever we want to do is fine.

WHO SHAPES WHOM?

If our moral selves are created by the forces of civil life rather than the forces of the market, our moral selves can shape the choices we make in the market—about what things we want to buy—and thus can influence the choices the market offers. When school-children in the early 1990s went home and begged their parents not to buy tuna from companies that fished in ways that harmed dolphins, the resulting purchase decisions changed what was on the shelves: suddenly, every firm was selling dolphin-safe tuna.

Corporations nowadays are tripping over each other to demonstrate how environmentally friendly they are. Recently, I bought my son some pencils for school. The package was emblazoned with the legend DOES NOT CONTAIN RAIN FOREST WOOD—presumably because some consumers were asking. This responsiveness to what motivates buyers is what free-market conservatives have in mind when they answer a complaint about corporate behavior with the cry, "Let the market decide!" What this really means is, "Let consumers decide!"—that is, let those who are sufficiently disturbed by the objectionable corporate practice respond by changing their own market behavior. If you don't like the gas mileage of car A, buy car B instead, and if enough drivers make the same choice, the firm that builds car A will redesign it for better mileage. If you don't like firm F's investments in nations ruled by oppressive regimes, buy firm G's stock instead. And if you don't like tuna X because the nets that catch the fish also kill dolphins, choose tuna Y instead. In this way, our language of morality controls the market—by adjusting our preferences. But the language of the market is not supposed to return the favor.

I will admit to a certain eerie dissonance, being so in love with a country that is sure it wants to save the tuna and the rain forest but is not sure it wants to save its central cities. These priorities strike me as scrambled.* But at least they are priorities. Unfortunately, the tuna revolt was an all-too-rare exception to a depressing trend. We hardly worry at all about the environmental records of the corporations that cut the wood for our furniture or the working conditions of the laborers who pick our produce or sew our clothes. The literature has long been full of the many reasons that consumers are often unable or unwilling to put their stated preferences into their market choices.[24] But my concern is civility. When we are unable to use morality to discipline our desires in the marketplace, it is a sure sign that civility is collapsing.

The same discipline must attach to those who work in the marketplace. The law professor Azizah al-Hibri has written movingly of the conflicting demands of his Muslim faith and the needs of clients during his time as a corporate lawyer. The Islamic prohibition on taking unfair advantage of others in business dealings, for example, is rarely the lawyer's credo. Al-Hibri traces the conflict to America's cultural insistence that the way things already are is neutral and objective: "It is only when the dominant ideology is questioned that its systematic shaping of our lives and laws becomes visible."[25] That shaping is precisely what religion should give us the power to see—

* Infuriated readers may e-mail me at carter@mail.law.yale.edu.

and to resist. So when critics argue that the Vatican should not have issued *Ethics in Advertising*, they are really saying that they do not want anybody to interfere with their effort to teach consumers to value what marketers want—no, need—them to value. The student of civility, however, will prefer to battle against the encroachment of market values into the rest of social life.

Do not mistake the point. I am no anticapitalist. Markets are vital to progress: we have not yet found a more effective means for producing wealth or distributing goods. The amorality of markets poses scant threat to a nation that possesses a highly organized set of institutions that do speak in a moral voice, but it is deadly for a nation that has none. In America, civil society yet survives, but there is less of it than in the past, and less of it than we need. We have few sources of moral investigation. Thus, the language of the marketplace, the language of wanting, of winning, of simply taking—the language of *self*—is supplanting the language of community, of sharing, of fairness, of riding politely alongside our fellow citizens in Isaac Peebles's passenger compartment. When the values of the market teach us the words to use, whether in our common life, our civil society, or our political contests, our speech is bound to reflect the market's amorality. Unfettered by moral bounds, we are likely to speak on impulse, and our favorite subject will be our desires: we will resemble animals with the facility of speech.

So although a loss of respect for our fellow humans is at the heart of our incivility crisis, a concern for civility is not solely a concern about how we treat others. It is also a concern about preserving the aspects of our social life that provide us with moral armament. Without the aid of those institutions—once again, religion very much to the fore—we will be unable to resist the growing domination of our social life by the amoral values of politics and the market. The institutions that should sustain social life as an independent sphere and thus help civilize the young are collapsing around us, weakening, in turn, our children's moral armor. We must do battle against this trend, because young people will gain the strength to resist the incursions of the political and market values that teach us to fulfill all of our desires only if they are *taught*— by word and by example—how to do it. And the lessons we teach through our examples must be lessons of sacrifice for others.

THE CIVIL ORGANIZATION

. . . .

The market, of course, has much to do with how our business firms are organized, but so does culture. A more civil culture will have more civil firms. A few years ago, I participated in a seminar with a German executive who had recently moved to the United States to help run his corporation's interests here. He professed himself astonished at the American boss's way of telling subordinates what to do. Why, he asked, do Americans give orders by asking questions? He was talking about the way that so many supervisors would say things like, "Would you mind having that report on my desk by Monday?" or "Would it be a problem for you to work late tonight?" He pointed out that the requests are not requests: "Yes, I would mind," or, "Yes, it would be a problem," are not acceptable answers. So why bother, he asked, to pretend to care what the employees think about what they are asked to do? Isn't the whole thing a farce?

The question is a nice one, and I have certainly heard other executives, from Asia as well as Europe, ask it. The answer, I suspect, lies in the effort to preserve a culture of respect for others, even when the others stand below us in a hierarchical relationship. I do not pretend that this never looks ridiculous or even malicious—one thinks, for example, of the genteel slave owners who were absolutely convinced that they were loved by those they owned. And I do not pretend that this approach does not cloak the actual power relations in a firm. But, as we saw in chapter 2, the role of civility is often to help make tolerable aspects of life that might otherwise prove intolerable. The cost to the boss of being polite to a subordinate is relatively low; the payoff in employee dedication may be quite high. In other words, the boss's exercise of good manners may be efficient.

But the student of civility prefers a deeper, more satisfying reason to put what seem to be commands in the form of questions. And civility offers one: The fact that an employee is an employee does not lessen the duty of respect that he or she is owed. To be polite only to one's superiors or equals in the corporate hierarchy is to violate several of the rules of civility that we have reviewed.

One's employees are entitled to precisely the same degree of respect because, as we have seen, they hold a precisely equal share of God's creation. Naturally, one may be polite without turning a command into a request. Nevertheless, as long as we all understand the language of the civil organization, the use of the question format can be a way of exercising authority with delicacy and careful thought—both characteristics that civility favors.

I remember from my days as a law clerk to Justice Thurgood Marshall the way that one of Marshall's Supreme Court colleagues, Justice Lewis Powell, would always begin his interrogations of the lawyers presenting arguments: "Counsel," he would murmur in his soft Virginia accent, "would you mind if I asked you a question?" Now, Powell was an old-fashioned Southern gentleman, and he was simply being polite. But it is important to understand that he was not really asking permission. No lawyer would dare say, "Yes, I would mind"—not to a justice of the Supreme Court. Yet that is the very point of the story. The fact that a justice of the Supreme Court, who did not need to ask permission, did so anyway, showed a profound and almost warm respect for the lawyers who came before the bench.

Nowadays, management consultants always warn employers to be sure to be respectful toward their employees and to show the respect in more ways than mere good manners. Work teams are replacing hierarchical command structures, and most industries are better for it. Campus-style architecture, with employees in the same division working on the same floor, is replacing the office tower, with senior executives at the very top and decreasing layers of prestige as one goes further down. (Some architectural critics refer to this as the *feminine* replacing the *masculine* in office design—an overstatement, but an intriguing one.)

But it is not enough for the workplace to *look* more civil. The workplace also should *be* more civil. In particular, employees should have the sense that if they take questions or concerns to supervisors, they will be treated with respect—and thus be taken seriously—rather than brushed aside or criticized. This suggests in turn a need for corporations to be welcoming to would-be whistle-blowers.

Consider a standard case in the business ethics courses today.

Beech-nut landed in serious difficulty in the 1980s after allegations that it was selling bottles of baby apple juice that actually contained nothing but flavored water. The firm wound up in trouble with regulators as well as with the public, which lost a degree of confidence in the venerable firm. (My wife and I at the time had a very young child, and, rationally or not, we stopped buying *all* Beech-nut products for a while.) Beech-nut wound up paying a fine of $2.2 million and settling a class action suit for another $7.5 million. In addition, several executives were convicted of criminal offenses.

How did matters go so wrong? Evidently, the company switched to a new and untested supplier of concentrate in order to save a few hundred thousand dollars a year. When a Beech-nut researcher went to his boss—let us call the boss Timid Manager—to report that the supplier appeared to be providing an impure product, the boss chose to cover the problem up. The company continued to sell the adulterated "juice" to the public until regulators got wind of the problem, at which point Beech-nut shipped large quantities of the product overseas. And why did Timid Manager behave as he did? He would say later that he acted as he did for the good of the company, but it appears that he may have been concerned about what *his* bosses would think if the news got out.[26]

The civility dimensions of the case are two. At the most obvious, the firm failed to create an atmosphere in which Timid Manager felt comfortable as the bearer of bad news. This inhibited conversation and thus inhibited civility . . . and the damage was immense. The second dimension involves not the firm but the executive. When we conceive civility as a duty to love our neighbors, the duty is not limited to those cases in which loving the neighbor is easy to do. The firm's customers are neighbors too, and the duty to love them surely includes the duty not to do them harm when it can be avoided—for example, by selling flavored water and calling it apple juice. The fact—if it is a fact—that Timid Manager himself might have been punished for bringing the news forward does not spare him the duty to protect the public.

Finally, we should not forget that a recognition of the firm's duty of civility can protect not just the public but workers as well—and not just whistle-blowers. For example, one might look at the problem of sexual harassment as a reflection precisely of the willful refusal to follow civility's rules. Some critics are uncomfortable with the theoretical basis for sexual harassment law, but that may be because we tend to describe it as resting on principles of nondiscrimination rather than principles of civility.[27] When a supervisor repeatedly asks an employee for a date, or when workers express attitudes that result in the "hostile environment" that can sometimes constitute harassment, what they are really being is uncivilized. We have already seen that the reduction of human beings to stereotypical categories exemplifies the very opposite of civility's requirement that we come into the presence of other human beings with awe. And we saw earlier in this chapter that viewing an individual in a purely sexual dimension refuses to recognize that person's humanity at all. Were children taught the principles of civility from a young age, sexual harassment might not disappear, but there would surely be less of it, and we would have a cleaner, simpler reason for calling it wrong.

CHANGING DIRECTION

. . . .

Our relatively free and robust markets have made America rich and powerful, the envy of the world. And yet, what made it surprisingly easy to overthrow the civility of the fifties was also our remarkable economic position: our wealth, our technology, our military might, our very success as a world power. The unwise tendency among theorists has been to consider civility as among our higher-order needs, something that wealth can purchase once our more basic requirements are satisfied. This may be correct if all we mean by civility is the maddeningly complex web of rules that we collect in the term "etiquette."

But consider some of the other purposes that civility serves. Civility, as we have seen, enables us to cushion the impact of the many slights and indignities of everyday life. Following the local rules of civility signals our willingness to discipline our desires for the sake of membership in the group. Acting in a civil manner demonstrates our respect for our fellow human beings. Viewed in this way, many basic rules of civility are plainly functional—that is, we can readily see how rules of civility are generated, and why most people would decide over time that following the rules was in their self-interest.

Wealth, however, changes this calculation. With resources enough, we can purchase other cushions for the indignities of life. We can, for example, abandon the posse, and other traditional means of group protection against harm, in favor of burglar alarms for our cars and homes.* We can abandon the relative civility of the front stoop and the backyard fence, choosing instead to obtain information through television or computer, but without interacting with other human beings. And the less need we have of other people, the greater the risk that we will begin to devalue them.

It may be, then, that it is incivility, not civility, that is among our higher-order needs; that only a wealthy people, protected by its science and technology, can afford the mutual disrespect that the loss of civility breeds. The way we use the fruits of our science, in short, may be leading us to care less for one another. In Erasmus's terms, our technology may be turning us back into barbarians.

---

* My Yale Law School colleague Ian Ayres points out that installing a burglar alarm, or at least affixing an alarm company's sticker to a window (what legal theorists call "specific deterrence"), may be viewed as an act of incivility. Why? Because, he says, there is little functional difference between putting a sign on my house that says "Burglar Alarm Equipped" and putting a sign on my house that says "Break into Somebody Else's House, I Don't Care Whose, as Long as It Isn't Mine." On this point, I suppose my family's commitment to civility must seem weak: our house is equipped with both a burglar alarm and a decal proclaiming its presence.

II

. . . .

Some Technologies of Incivility

Yet science is no enemy of civility. In the era of the singular American truth, a faith in science was virtually a part of the national creed. Americans believed in both the inevitability and the morality of progress.[1] The future would be better than the present, and scientific advance would lead the way. The market for science fiction exploded. Everybody understood that science would change the world, and everybody was excited about it. Visitors to the New York World's Fair—and to Disneyland too—wanted to see what tomorrow would look like. When Vannevar Bush, an adviser to President Eisenhower, published a popular book called *Science: The Endless Frontier* in 1958, he was following, not creating, a trend.

Even today, with our national faith in technology shaken by such phenomena as the Dalkon shield scandal, the Three Mile Island near-disaster, and the stubborn persistence of AIDS, most Americans continue to welcome technological change. Some find the Internet scary, others worry about which food additive will next be linked to cancer, but, for the most part, we seem to believe that when things break, American know-how can fix them. We count on science to cure diseases, design safer cars, warn us of hurricanes, and invent faster computers. We still count on science, in fact, to improve our lives in ways of all sorts. What we do not count on science to do is to change who, fundamentally, we are. And yet that change is occurring, and the student of civility should be worried.

CIVILITY'S VIRTUOUS INEFFICIENCY

· · · · · · · · · · · · ·

Since Aristotle, it has been a commonality of the Western tradition that people do not automatically do good. There may be many reasons for this. Doing good may be difficult and doing evil easy, and we may choose the easy path. Or we may be deficient in the skills that are needed to tell which is which. Or we may be unpersuaded that the categories good and evil exist. Or we may just be greedy and self-seeking. Whatever the set of reasons, we are tempted constantly by wrong, and theologians and philosophers (and political leaders too) have obsessed for centuries about how to assist us in resisting the temptation. Thomas More, in *Utopia*, imagined an ideal world in which everybody does the right thing, even when it is costly, and does it by instinct and without complaint. Our world is more complex because we ourselves are. In particular, we are often slaves to our instincts, and thus often in need of encouragement, incentive, and perhaps training to choose self-discipline over instinct and right over wrong. In other words, we need to be civilized.

This matters to the student of civility because civilizing us is what civility is for. Rules of civility (as we have seen) are also rules of morality, dictated by the imperative to love our neighbors. But unlike the denizens of Utopia, we do not always obey the rules just because morality commands it. Many rules of civility have survived for centuries (and many more for decades), but we must not pretend that every good rule survives just because it is good. Some good rules survive because they are functional—that is, because we, and our society, get something out of them—and many rules of civility are among them.

To be sure, a *defense* of civility on the ground of functionality is insufficient; merely functional rules of civility lack moral importance. If we follow a rule because doing so seems to be in our self-interest, we may be doing what is wise, we may be doing what is human, but we earn very little moral credit. We are merely doing what leaves us better off. Rules of civility, as we have said from the outset, often require sacrifice. Not that rules of civility cannot be efficient. Many rules of civility that are good rules because of their moral content—their embodiment of the basic requirement of loving respect for all—may *persist* because they also happen to be functional. For example, a moral rule that prohibits the use of words in a way that directly harms others may also be functional; if you refrain from insulting me verbally, I am less likely to harm you physically.*

More complex rules of civility may also be functional—but may also be sensitive to technological change. Consider a simple rule of civility, one that follows easily from the basic requirement of loving the neighbor: I must get to know the neighbor, that is, I must make connections with other people, be involved in a wider circle than myself. Can we describe this rule as functional as well as moral?

I think the answer is yes. Suppose that one goal in life is to obtain information. By "goal" I mean something that we do by instinct, something we are wired for. So suppose we want, as a matter of wiring, to know about the world around us. Information helps us to protect ourselves, to enrich ourselves, and generally to survive. Now imagine a time when communication technology is relatively primitive—another way of saying that the act of communicating (especially over long distances or with large groups of people) is quite expensive. One efficient (that is, low-cost) means of gaining information in such a society would be to get to know other people, who might then pass on information from their own various networks and sources. The more different people an individual knew, the more information he or she would obtain. And if, as I propose, a supply of information is vital to survival, then evolution would over time select for people with greater skills in getting to know others.

But it would be the necessity of obtaining information—not the mere existence of the skill—that led to its continued exercise. If we are required to get to know other people in order to obtain information, then the goal of obtaining information causes us to behave in a civil fashion—because getting to know other people,

---

* Aficionados of evolutionary psychology might further argue that ancestors with a genetic makeup that influenced them toward insulting others would be less likely to survive: over the millenia, they would be disproportionately killed off by those they insulted (assuming the availability of language). This would suggest that human beings are today *biologically* less likely to insult others than we were thirty or forty thousand years ago. If this is so, I shudder to think what that earlier world must have been like.

forming those human connections, is a part of being civil. We are following a moral rule for instrumental reasons.

This in turn suggests that any process that allows us to obtain information without getting to know other people militates against civility. Thus—potentially—anything from reading a daily newspaper to surfing the Internet can leave us less civil, simply by separating the process of getting information from the process of getting to know other people. This does not make any new communications technology immoral, but it does serve as a reminder that our ability to obtain information without connecting to other people should not keep us from connecting to other people. Ironically, then, ease of communications might actually cause our skills at keeping connected to atrophy. A principle that was once functional now seems unimportant. Thus, it requires an act of will to maintain our morally desirable habit—our civil and civilized habit—of keeping in touch with others.

The example is simple, but the point is vital: if we follow rules of civility because they are useful and efficient rather than because they are morally required of us, the rules will fall away as technological and other changes make them less useful. So retaining our civility in an era of rapid scientific change requires us to be deliberate, not casual, about doing what morality demands and teaching it to our children. The problem can be fixed, of course—but only if we first recognize what it is and why it exists.

THE SALES CALL . . . AND OTHER HORRORS

. . . .

Let us begin with a common and irritating occurrence. As you sit down to dinner with your family, the telephone rings. When you answer, you find that you are being offered a subscription to the local paper or invited to donate to the volunteer fire department. And although you may enjoy reading your local paper and admire the volunteers who keep the city from burning to the ground, if you are like me, a wave of frustration passes through you, and you face the serious temptation to say something rude. Although the direct marketing industry insists that they exist, I have yet to meet any people who are actually pleased when somebody calls at mealtime, hoping to sell something.

Like many people, my family has adopted a firm rule to deal with these intrusions: No matter how desirable the product or service being sold, no matter how noble the cause, we politely inform callers that we never respond to telephone solicitations. We invite them to send us any literature in the mail. (They never do.) If they persist, we warn them once, then hang up.

Now, query: Who is being uncivil? My wife and I for refusing to listen to the sales pitch? Or the salesperson for calling at the dinner hour? To answer that question, we must consider not simply the dynamics of the conversation—the general problem of how the student of civility, trying to see God in all people, confronts a sales pitch—but the technology around which the tale revolves. That technology is the telephone.

The telephone, which came into widespread use fairly early in the twentieth century, is a marvelous invention—so marvelous that when Alexander Graham Bell applied for his patent, a worshipful Supreme Court allowed him to skip the legally required step of building a working model of the device before it could be patented.[2] Nowadays few devices are more ubiquitous in America. Our nation boasts nearly two hundred million telephone *numbers*. The instruments themselves are evidently uncountable, but, certainly, America has more telephones than people.* We tend to think of our phones as labor-saving devices, increasing the efficiency of both our business and our personal lives. What we tend to leave out, if we even notice, is that our love affair with the telephone almost certainly has made us less civil.

How can this be? Consider something as basic as keeping in touch with our friends. The telephone makes it easier and cheaper to do so—but also changes dramatically the nature of the interaction. Before the widespread use of the telephone, we had two means of keeping in touch with friends: stopping in for a visit or writing a letter. Each involved a significant investment of time and perhaps resources; in other words, maintaining friendships automatically called us to sacrifice. And, by making those sacrifices, we

* We also have, as of 1998, approximately one portable telephone for every ten people—a much greater ratio than the ratio of ordinary phones to people in much of the world.

showed our friends repeatedly how greatly we valued their friendship. Correspondence, in particular, not only preserved and nurtured a relationship but provided a record of it, a testament to its enduring character.

We invest far less in our friendships when we decide to call rather than write or meet in person. There is no permanence, nothing enduring, and no significant investment. At the same time, we demand much more of the friends we call. The telephone carries an air of immediacy: callers seem to think it our duty to drop whatever may be going on at the moment, whether it involves family, prayer, work, or a favorite hobby—or to offer an adequate excuse for not dropping everything—all because they have chosen that instant rather than some other to indulge the urge to punch a handful of digits on the control pad of a lightweight construction of silicon, copper, and plastic. The telephone caller intrudes unasked into the privacy of the home, and yet it is the one who is called who, if refusing to talk just then, is considered rude.

Consider the connection of telephones to the business world. Suddenly, everybody is essential to every decision. It grows increasingly hard to find peace and quiet on a train or a street corner or even in a restaurant because of the number of indispensable people who must carry on loud conversations on cellular phones lest the office discover it can get along without them. (One wishes that Isaac Peebles was around to write the rules.) The cherished wall between the space of commerce and the space of social life is further battered when the telephone allows work to intrude into the most private moments of our lives.

This is not to say that the telephone is not, on the whole, a boon to business. The ability to keep in touch with coworkers can be a great convenience. The ability to call a store or an airline can be enormously helpful (depending on how long we must endure "music on hold"). The ability to close deals without leaving one's desk can increase profit. But in the wrong circumstances, the telephone can lead to trouble.

A number of years ago, I came across a study by two industrial psychologists who insisted that the widespread use of the telephone in business was making us less, not more, efficient. According to their research (as I now recall it), the telephone creates two separate pressures that can actually slow business activity. First, employees are more willing than in the past to pass a decision on to the boss, simply because it is now always possible to reach the boss. Second, the boss wants to be involved in every decision, simply because it is now always possible to reach the employee. As a result, less authority is delegated, discretion vanishes, and businesses spend more and more time in conversation (aided by the telephone) and less and less time on making and implementing decisions. The telephone, in short, has created the possibility (which some professions, like law, seem to exemplify) of reducing all work to a single, endless meeting. According to the two psychologists, the added cost of this eternal conversation is sometimes more than the savings generated by the efficiency of communication.

Inefficiency is not, of course, evidence of incivility; on the contrary, as we have seen, inefficiency is often one of the virtues of civility, for the sacrifices we make for others are what define the depth of our commitment to the principle. And yet the same features of the telephone that may make it, in some circumstances, an inefficient technology, also make it an uncivil technology.

Let us return to the sales call. In the era before telephone solicitation, if I wanted you to buy my product and could not get you into my shop, I probably would have to come to your house. And at once, an entire panoply of considerations of civility would be activated. In the first place, I would have to invest time and resources: going door to door is quite a bit more expensive than going phone number to phone number. Already, by deciding that you are worth that investment, I am practicing a form of civility, for I am according you greater respect if I prepare to meet you in person than if I simply meet you by phone.

Second, if I meet you in person, I must be better groomed and on better behavior than if we meet by phone. I must work harder to make the good impression on which my sale depends. I must watch not only my words but my nonverbal cues: how I stand or sit, what I do with my hands. I must make eye contact. I dare not let my attention wander. This extra work is the extra measure of devotion to the other that civility requires.

Third, by meeting you in person, I prevent either of us from being anonymous to the other. As psychologists like Richard Sennett and sociologists like Lyn H. Lofland have pointed out (and as practical experience confirms), it is far easier to be polite to people we know than to people we do not.[3] When I take the trouble to sit or stand face-to-face with you, I am taking the risk that I will see God in you—a happy circumstance that will force me to be civil.

Of course, telephone solicitation is much less expensive than door-to-door sales, and the products or services we may buy are that much cheaper. But the convenience comes at great cost to the project of reconstructing civility. That is not the fault of the telephone; nor is it really the fault of the companies that train salespeople to call at the dinner hour. It is the fault, rather, of all of us, for letting the technology transform us. The telephone has made it possible to dispense with many precepts of civility; rather than considering whether to keep them, we have simply let them die.

Many other technologies deserve their share of the blame for our incivility crisis. I have already mentioned the automobile. Other critics have cited everything from the microwave oven (family cooking, a great civilizing activity, bites the dust) to the birth control pill (so does sexual abstinence, or, more precisely, the link between sex and marriage). Television probably gets more blame than any other technology for our incivility crisis, and most of the criticism it receives is deserved. (See my discussion of violence in chapter 9). But there may be worse on the horizon.

CYBERSPACE

. . . .

Civility, as we have seen since the start of the book, requires a sense of commonality, of shared experience. The rise of cyberspace is the apotheosis of the ideal (if it is an ideal) of individualized experience. Although the personal computer market is now more or less mature—meaning that there are fewer first-time buyers—the market for online services is exploding. The online world is what creates cyberspace, a virtual "place" where we seek new information, encounter new people, buy new products, and have new fun.

The appeal of the cyberspace culture is to autonomy: we can choose our own experiences. Thus, the online world represents the ultimate fissure (so far, at least) in the rock on which civility has traditionally rested: the notion of the existence of shared truth. The sociologist Sherry Turkle argues that we are truly postmodern now: the information age has destroyed the old concept of "unitary truth" so that now "[t]here is only local knowledge, contingent and provisional." The Internet encourages a new hierarchy of understanding, Turkle tells us: the precedence of "simulation over the real."[4] What matters is not what is, because there is no *is*—what matters is what we can manufacture.

Why should this pose a challenge to civility? The journalist Kurt Andersen describes the problem thus: "Not only is every citizen entitled to his or her opinion but he or she is entitled to deliver it instantaneously, studded with chunks of fake information, to the whole world."[5] And entitled to persuade those who instinctively doubt the claims of authority. So in the fall of 1996, Pierre Salinger, no less, announced his possession of a secret document that proved TWA flight 800 had been shot down by an American missile—unaware that he had been snowed. The document was bogus but had been posted on the Internet months before.

Salinger is hardly alone. Consider the black helicopters. Millions of Americans evidently believe that their government secretly uses black helicopters to ferry troops from place to place as it prepares for a United Nations occupation of the United States under the Zionist Occupation Government. (Or something like that.) What? You don't know about the black helicopters? Or maybe you haven't heard of ZOG? Maybe you don't believe in either? Well, they are all staples of Internet bulletin boards and chat rooms. Are they real? Imaginary? It scarcely matters, and Turkle is correct that the term *real* is losing its meaning: in the new information age, every one of us is entitled to an individualized reality.

When cyberspacers rave about black helicopters and secret missiles, most of us laugh. But they are only doing in a somewhat more open manner what the tailoring of information allows the rest of us to do more subtly. For a fee, the *Wall Street Journal* will deliver to you each weekday an online summary of the news—but only the parts of the news that interest you. (In the jargon, this is known as *pull*, meaning you choose what to get, as opposed to *push*, meaning you allow someone else to choose for you.) No need to wade through articles on subjects that do not catch your fancy; no need to be informed on topics that you do not select for yourself, or do not even know to ask for; and no need for the newspaper itself to exercise any judgment whatsoever. And the *Journal* is not alone: every media service is working on ways to provide you with only what you want to read.

This sounds like more autonomy, but can it actually be a good idea? In the old days, you would leaf through the paper, happening upon the news that the editors thought important: again, in the jargon, *push*, now pejorative, rather than *pull*.[6] The unexpected article on an interesting subject, the latest tragedy in a part of the world you had never before considered, exposed you to a wider community; the news judgment of the editors helped create our common experience. But now you can skip all that held us together and create a world in which the only facts that matter are the ones you yourself choose to know. So not only do we no longer share experience, we do not even share information: I have mine and you have yours, and each of us is equally entitled to our facts.

The metaphor of a marketplace of ideas collapses against this postmodern onslaught. John Milton's romantic paean to freedom to publish, the *Areopagitica*, presents a vision of truth as somehow rising from the cacophony of public speech by virtue of its own shining nobility. Civil libertarians have long proclaimed that the cure for bad speech is good speech. As the Supreme Court wrote in 1974, "However pernicious an opinion may seem, we depend for its correction not on the conscience of judges and juries but on the competition of other ideas."[7] What speech breaks, in other words, speech can fix. This theory is at the heart of freedom of speech. But the theory presupposes the existence of a conversation somewhere, with willing speaker meeting willing listener, because truth will out only if we hear it alongside falsehood. Civility presupposes that conversation as well, but the tailor-made pseudo-facts of the online world deny it. The most shiningly noble and generous astrophysicist, willing and able to explain how she knows that extraterrestrials are not hiding behind the tail of Comet Hale-Bopp, would scarcely know where (that is, with which audience, which Website) to begin.

In the online world, users may tailor not only facts but entire communities to fit their preferences. Thousands of users now spend many hours each week "living" in virtual communities, each with its own residents and laws and even politics. In these virtual communities, users interact with others whom they know only in their online personas, which may be quite different from who they are in their offline hours; thus the "residents" of virtual communities become, in a sense, self-created. Many users describe their virtual communities as more welcoming—and even more real—than the world in which they spend the rest of their time.

A related aspect of cyberspace that arrests the attention is the ability of the user to morph—not so much to *pretend* to be something else as actually to *be* something else, at least as far as other users know. Users commonly claim a whole range of accomplishments that they lack. Indeed, it is not unusual for cyberspace users to pretend to be members of the opposite sex. (They are known as MorFs, a pun that also abbreviates "male or female.")[8] Bulletin boards on all subjects are full of notices that begin, "A woman wants to know . . . ," presumably to arrest the attention of the users, mostly males, who surf the Web—but who knows if the notices are actually posted by women? Because nobody knows anybody else, there is no way, in the confines of an online chat room, to refute or even to mount an effective challenge to another user's claim. Users are taken as they are found: if I say I am an astronaut or a drug addict or a Pulitzer Prize–winning poet or a friendless high school sophomore, then, as far as cyberspace is concerned, I am one. Of course, in reality, I could be anybody: a drug addict *pretending* to be an astronaut, or vice versa. And because this is true, and everybody knows it is true, nobody can quite be sure of the bona fides of any claim that any other user makes. So the information that users glean from each other is not only contingent but very possibly worthless.*

---

* Because everybody knows that everybody else may well be, in effect, living a fantasy, interesting arguments sometimes arise over whether participation in online sex (sometimes known as "text sex") with strangers represents cheating on one's significant other. Fortunately, we need not resolve that issue here, although I must say that it seems to me indistinguishable from at least "talking dirty," as it used to be called, with another.

The next epoch of online sexual experience is expected to involve sex with what is, in effect, a humanoid robot, controlled by one's online partner—whom one will view virtually, if at all—or controlled by the computer itself, in accordance with the user's previously stated desires. (The technology is available but not yet in widespread use.) At the risk of seeming to rush to moral judgment about a crisis not yet upon us, I would think this somewhat over the infidelity line, as well as deeply uncivil in its weird sexual narcissism. But I gather that some within the rising generation have very different ideas.

Marketers also disguise themselves on the Internet, and the technology makes it easy. Some Websites conceal specialized programs, known as "cookies," that plant themselves on the hard drives of users who visit the site, allowing marketers to find out where they come from and where else they go, and thus to target sales efforts more precisely. Others use a practice known as "word-stuffing," luring users to a commercial Website through the use of a rather simple (but, among Web sophisticates, unethical) technique to fool the computer programs that drive Internet search software.[9]

These MorFs and other deceptions are reminiscent of the rise during the nineteenth century of what the historian John Kasson calls "social counterfeits," people who took advantage of an earlier American revolution, the sudden confusion over social roles in the cities that led to the idea that a person's appearance and deportment formed an index to his or her character. Social counterfeits were people who learned "to exploit for their own selfish ends the possibilities of unstable and illegible identity as well as the ambiguous relationship between the social exchanges of respectable society and the economic exchanges of the marketplace." And so there were prostitutes who pretended to be ladies, beggars who feigned ailments to prey upon the newfound sense of noblesse oblige, forgers who seemed to be gentlemen, and that great American invention, the "confidence man"—the swindler who was, to all appearances, as genteel, and therefore as trustworthy, as anybody could ask.[10]

In American society, we have never quite shaken the nineteenth-century illusion that we can judge people by how they present themselves, and we often take it to troubling and uncivil extremes—as, for example, when we judge people by their skin color. In the online world, it may be that younger users are untroubled by MorFs because they are of a generation that has come to question the nation's obsession with appearances. We face, in other words, a fresh wave of confusion about roles—which presents, of course, a fresh entrance for the confidence tricksters. Some of them already have. So we continue to hear grim stories of grown men luring young boys and girls into, first, online sex and, later, actual sexual encounters.

We do not know, yet, exactly how to protect young people from the dangers of the online world while allowing them access to its benefits. It is no easy thing for parents to supervise children who are hooked up to the Internet, who almost certainly know more about the technology than their parents do, and who may spend long hours online, much of it in the privacy of their bedrooms. Parents worry about what their children are encountering in this new cyberworld: pornography? suicide manuals? bomb-making instructions? The litany runs through the head of many a parent— and the headlines of many a newscast, even though it is the very rareness of such encounters that makes them newsworthy.

Nevertheless, the supervision problem is present, and the student of civility surely wonders what to do about it. In 1996 the Congress passed a hastily drafted statute called the Communications Decency Act, and in 1997 the Supreme Court duly consigned it to that historical dustbin into which unconstitutional infringements on free speech are tossed.[11] A wave of software packages that allow parents to block objectionable Websites has hit the market, but all suffer from the same weakness: most parents need to ask their children how to use the programs, and if the children can be trusted to explain properly, they can probably be trusted to surf the Web on their own.[12]

There are more prosaic solutions too. For example, some families, concerned about what their children encounter in cyberspace but reluctant to stand over their shoulders, locate their computer in a central location, like the kitchen or family room, so that using the computer is an activity that one rarely performs in absolute privacy; it becomes more like reading a book in the easy chair in the corner while brothers and sisters play a board game and parents watch the news. This solution actually improves civility, because it integrates the use of the computer into family life and reduces the likelihood that the child, off alone in his or her bedroom, will lose social skills as more time is spent online. But none of these answers are substitutes for raising good children—children we adults can trust to make wise judgments not only in cyberspace but in the larger world into which we finally launch them.

Finding answers is imperative, because more access—and thus more confusion—is coming. Michael Dertouzos of the Massachusetts Institute of Technology, in his book *What Will Be*, describes research on the Bodynet, which will essentially allow us to walk down the street embedded in a cocoon of digital information. We will do research, chat online, stay in touch with the office, and play video games everywhere we are, all without the bother of any hand-held device.[13] The wonders of the ordinary world—the colors, the sounds, the smells, the sheer life, excitement, unpredictability of it—will eventually fall away, replaced by a self-created existence, a virtual world tailored to our liking. We will eliminate our fellow passengers the way the fellow got rid of the world in the classic *Twilight Zone* episode: flick a (virtual) switch, and we can pretend that the real world is the myth and the mythical world the real one. Or maybe I should not say *pretend*, for once we are shrouded in our Bodynets, it may turn out, as Turkle implies, that it is the so-called real world that is contingent and our individually constructed cyberworld that is real.

The more we are able to tailor the world to our liking, the less civil we are likely to be. Civility requires us to act with love toward our neighbors, to sacrifice on their behalf, but the cyberworld proposes that we have no neighbors—or that we can know no unimpeachable facts about them, or even that we can actively reinvent them. It is easy to be rude online precisely because the people with whom we argue are faceless, somehow no more real than the machine that transmits their words to our screens. And so, safe behind our anonymity, and taking advantage of theirs, we say things that we would not dream of uttering face to face.

Surfing the Web one afternoon, I came across a bulletin board started by a young mother who wanted advice about raising her children—in particular, about whether and how she should be assessing the character of their friends. Now, this is a puzzle with which all morally thoughtful parents are forced to wrestle, so I took a peek inside to see what I might learn. What I learned, according to some who had left postings there, was that Young Mother, as I shall call her, was a "silly bitch" for establishing the bulletin board incorrectly. Other users posted comments that were not quite as gently welcoming. But this is scarcely surprising: veteran users of the Web are famously nasty to those who are new to the medium ("newbies"). Efforts by the major Internet service providers to craft codes of civility have, thus far, done little to remedy the problem.

But direct rudeness is only the tip of the proverbial iceberg. A larger chunk is Turkle's point: the notion that there is a basic, solid truth somewhere out there shatters as the sources of information become more diffuse. Some of the users of Young Mother's bulletin board posted serious suggestions; others posted answers. The ultimate challenge of the online world is that we can search until we find the answers we like. If we find our arguments refuted on one bulletin board, we can go in search of new virtual neighbors, folks who will agree with us, on the next. We will share little in common with others if we are able to build for ourselves worlds that reflect only what we have decided in advance is true. And the time we spend in these artificial worlds is time we might otherwise have spent using—or, in the case of young people, simply developing— the skills at social interaction on which civility ultimately rests.

President Clinton, in his 1997 State of the Union address, proclaimed that the Internet is becoming "our new town square,"[14] but I am not sure that this is a town where the student of civility wants to live. Still, we should not make too much of the purported revolutionary character of our new online world, warns Marilyn Gell Mason, head of the Cleveland Public Library, in a perceptive essay in *Daedalus*. "Digital information," she writes, responding directly to Turkle,

> is not a revolution but a development, albeit a fast one, and information is only part of what it takes to achieve knowledge. In the end it is not the speed of the information or even the information itself that will give our lives meaning. It is still what we do with it that matters most.[15]

But even if what we do with information matters, what counts as information matters too. What Turkle has pointed to is not simply a more rapid flow of information, but a change in the nature of information itself. And the change may be more fundamental than even Turkle contends. It is not just that knowledge is local and contingent; it is that the basic line that modern Western thought has drawn for two centuries, the line between fact and belief, is disappearing even from the public mind, which is where it has been sustained in an era of academic doubt. Knowledge nowadays is a matter of reaffirming what we already believe. There is no real conversation. Evolutionists visit pro-evolution Websites, and creationists visit pro-creation Websites, and each side can look at the evidence that its worldview considers reliable and assure itself that the other side is nuts.

This helps explain why conspiracy theorists love the Web: it is so easy to find other people who agree with one's conspiracy theory. But it should be no surprise that people whose views are not widely shared seem not to be concerned with facts. (To the devout conspiracy theorist, the very absence of confirming evidence may itself be evidence of the conspiracy.) Conspiracy theorists, and others who desperately want evidence to support their beliefs, no matter how often their mythologies are debunked, continue to press them with almost religious zeal.

We sometimes forget that Leon Festinger's famous theory of cognitive dissonance was originally elaborated in the context of religion. Festinger's argument (which the passage of time seems to bear out) was that when events in the world seem to "disconfirm" the central beliefs of a religion, its adherents, rather than abandoning the faith, often embark on forceful and even exuberant missionary work. Why should this be? Because, says Festinger, of the need to reduce the discomfort, the dissonance, between what is believed and what is observed: "[I]f more and more people can be persuaded that the system of belief is correct, then clearly it must, after all, be correct."[16]

The online world seems to be the place to eliminate dissonance more thoroughly than any religion ever did. You can spend your days and nights metaphorically surrounded by anonymous people who will gleefully assure you that your most unlikely fantasies are the reality—gleeful, because you are simultaneously assuring them. In this mutual affirmation, you can deny the truth of anything from outside your circle that may contradict what you already believe. In fact, you may ignore the outside altogether. If this behavior took place anywhere but online, we would doubtless mutter about a cult. The student of civility must surely view it with despair.

None of this is likely to be solved by regulation. Even if one is a great fan of solving problems by regulating them (which I am not), there are the obvious difficulties of deciding what to limit and deciding how to enforce limits in this evolving and not-quite-controllable medium. And there is the obvious difficulty (and blessing) that our Constitution protects free speech. Whether all that occurs online should be considered speech, or, if not, which parts are really something else, are topics we are a good long way from being ready to tackle. As the legal scholar Lawrence Lessig has sensibly predicted, if we were forced to decide now just how the First Amendment should apply in cyberspace, "we would get it fundamentally wrong."[17]

INTERMEZZO:
THE IMPERFECTION OF INFORMATION

Of course, as we have already seen, the notion of singular truth has been an illusion from the start. This does not mean that notion is postmodern puffery—but we have always had the most profound disagreements over what they are. Of moral truth this has been obviously true, although survey data refute the old saw that there is no American consensus on values. What the rise of cyberspace and its tailored factual world makes plain, and what academics have long insisted, is that the same dissensus characterizes our search for truths about the material world. The postmoderns have always been right on one point: information is inherently imperfect. It is not that the real world, the *is* out there, is contingent and in a sense the creation of our minds, but that our *perceptions* of that real world are contingent and in a sense the creation of our minds. But here is where the postmoderns go wrong: the contingent nature of our perceptions does not mean that all perceptions are equally valid. It only means we make mistakes.

But so what? The human heuristic is such that we learn from our errors. As the biologist and essayist Lewis Thomas has suggested, our mistakes mark us as human and lead to progress. We move ahead, says Thomas, through "exploration," which "is based on human fallibility." If there were no wrong paths, there would be nothing to explore. "The lower animals," writes Thomas, "do not have this splendid freedom. They are limited, most of them, to absolute infallibility." The lower animals, according to Thomas, seem programmed by nature not to err in important ways: "Fish are flawless in everything they do." We seem programmed to err, and thus to learn.[18]

But this optimistic assessment is correct only if we are able to recognize that we are making mistakes. We cannot learn from our errors if we do not recognize them as errors. A community that shares a core belief that there is such a thing as bedrock material truth is able to recognize mistakes and learn from them. A community that fundamentally disbelieves in the idea of truth will, by definition, make no mistakes, and so it can send undesirables to the gas chambers and teach that the world is flat and make no apologies. And a community whose cognitive dissonance leads it to search only for additional evidence that what it has believed all along is true—never for evidence that it just might be mistaken—can never make true progress. More and more, we Americans are falling into that last category.

A decade or so ago, the newspapers published accounts of a controversial study of teenagers who had undergone abortions. The study, undertaken at a public high school, purported to show that young women who had ended their pregnancies were health-ier mentally and emotionally and performed better in school than young women who had carried their children to term.[19] I say "pur-ported to show" for two reasons: First, I have never examined the study itself, only read the news accounts, and so I cannot speak for its validity. Second, anyone who follows data in the abortion area knows that young women who are well-to-do are much more likely to have abortions than young women who are poor, and that pregnant women who are white are more likely to have abor-tions than young women who are black. Thus, the results of the study could reflect not the effects of abortion but the effects of being a member of a favored versus a disfavored demographic group.

On the other hand, the study could be precisely right. What is intriguing is how many pro-choice people leaped to the conclusion that it was right and how many pro-life people leaped to the conclusion that it was wrong. I have encountered many people on both sides of the issue who have strong opinions about the study (at the time it was published it was quite well known), but I have yet to find someone who both possesses a strong opinion and has actually read the study itself. So it turns out that we do not even need the cyberworld to get us to tailor facts to fit our previously held opinions. Too often, all we need are opinions.

THE TRAP OF SCIENTISM

. . . .

Perhaps it was inevitable that we would twist matters around. Our faith in science, although it has been dying for two decades, remains strong enough that we often succumb to the lure of *scientism*. Scientism is the effort to disguise as science things that have little to do with science, in the hope of making them look more attractive—in much the same way that a fisherman baits a hook hoping the fish will think it is food, or the way that a politician often quotes Scripture hoping the audience will think the politician's preferences are the will of God.

The story of the abortion study illustrates the trap of scientism: if I have already made up my mind, the good science must support what I have decided, and the science on the other side is bad science. This tendency helps explain why scientists often fare so badly in the courtroom. Forensic science—science that is used to assist in deciding a legal question—should be an important part of our judicial practice. Unfortunately, instead of science in the courts, we see what critics have called "junk" science but is really scientism: the manipulation of the scientific evidence and the scientific method to reach the desired results. As one commentator has pointed out, "Despite lip service to the contrary, lawyers frequently perceive forensic scientists as strictly utilitarian tools of the lawyers' trade."[20]

A well-known example occurred in the Supreme Court's 1954 decision in *Brown v. Board of Education*, when the justices rested on the tentative conclusions of social science that school segregation was harmful to black children.[21] Probably the Court read the studies correctly, but the choice to use them helps illustrate the trap of scientism. When data are presented in support of a moral proposition, the implicit message is that the moral claim is only as strong as the data. If racial segregation is wrong because social scientists believe that it is harmful, the message is that, if you think the social scientists are wrong—or if later research proves them wrong—then racial segregation is just fine.

What has this to do with civility? Everything—because what makes scientism attractive is the hope that one can win a moral argument without discussing morality. The irony of scientism is that it simultaneously acknowledges and denies the traditional vision of singular truths. On the one hand, scientism is deeply postmodern, treating scientific knowledge as infinitely malleable, able to reach any result, support any argument. But that is only in the construction of scientistic argument. In its public presentation, scientism treats science as settled and clear, a collection of irrefutable if unexplainable facts—not the asker of difficult questions but the provider of easy answers. The debater who goes to scientism wants the audience to understand that only a flat-earther would disagree.

Scientism's exaltation of scientific results (but not scientific method) is a transparent device for avoiding debate. If I make a scientistic claim, my message is that I have not mere opinion but actual science—hence, *truth*—on my side, suggesting that anybody who disagrees with me should simply shut up and go away. This attitude treats those on the other side of whatever may be the underlying moral issue as though they cannot possibly have anything important to say, and certainly nothing persuasive. Scientism thus denies my opponents the fundamental respect that is derived from the requirement that we love our neighbors. There is no trust. There is no generosity. There is no hope of civil listening because there is no listening at all—there is not even any conversation.

Despite its tendency to deaden dialogue—or perhaps because of it—the lure of scientism is tremendous. In the early 1980s, it ensnared the pro-life movement, which wasted precious political capital on the ill-conceived Human Life Bill, a declaration, backed by scientific evidence, that human life begins at the moment of conception.[22] Never mind that life itself—to say nothing of its beginning—does not even have an agreed scientific definition. Or that the morally difficult question about abortion is not whether the fetus is human (most people tell pollsters they think it is), but whether the pregnant woman owes that human an obligation of support. At the same time, one may make the pro-life case with some force whether the fetus is thought to be human or not: the deliberate destruction of a struggling new life, whether or not it is called human, is a terrible tragedy.[23]

The left, too, has been a victim. Thus, we see the gay rights movement enthralled by the idea that scientific evidence shows a genetic tendency toward homosexuality.[24] Never mind that nobody has been able to replicate the one study of DNA on which the claims are based, or that (according to news reports) the researcher himself has been investigated for possible fraud.[25] Or that the pressing moral question on all matters of sexuality, for heterosexuals and homosexuals alike, is not what set of biochemical reactions causes people to feel particular urges, but which of our many urges we should allow to influence our lives. One can make a perfectly sensible gay rights argument on the basis of the right to privacy— it is neither the state's business nor the boss's what consenting adults do behind closed doors, and viewed through the lens of civility, the Supreme Court looked very bad in holding otherwise.[26] As in *Brown*, to rest the case on a controversial scientific claim may weaken the more important moral claim.[27]

In each case, questionable science is being used to buttress a claim that proponents have actually reached on some other ground. The proponents, however, are uneasy stating the chain of reasoning that has led them to their moral conclusions. So they try science instead, which perhaps seems more "objective." But that is the other side of scientism's trap: it persuades us that our strongest moral convictions are useless in public debate unless we can repackage them as the conclusions of natural science. Scientism thus betrays a lack of faith in our ability to conduct dialogues on moral questions.

These, then, are the two ways in which we abandon civility when we go to scientism: we manifest a mistrust of public moral conversation, and we demonstrate a disbelief that our opponents might have anything useful to say. When democratic dialogue becomes infected with such mistrust and disbelief, the conversation simply stops.

12

· · · · · · · · · · · · ·

Law, Tolerance, and
Civility's Illusions

To BE CIVIL is not to suspend moral judgment; but to be civil
may sometimes mean tolerating conduct of which you disapprove.
You may, for example, believe that smoking cigarettes is wrong and
yet be unwilling to interfere with the freedom of your fellow citizens to choose to do it. In this, a sensible civility tracks the tension
between two important aspects of the role of morality in a free
society. On the one hand, freedom unrestrained by clear moral
norms begets anarchy. On the other, moral norms that have the
force of law often stifle freedom. This tension is inevitable in a
nation that wishes to be both moral and free. But nobody can (or
should want to) sustain the tension indefinitely; sooner or later, on
every question on which we might disagree, the side of freedom or
the side of restraint will have its way.

Consider the most divisive moral issue in American history, the
only one over which we fought a shooting war among ourselves:
slavery. In the first half of the nineteenth century, abolitionist sentiment spread rapidly through the young nation. Already by the
1830s, proslavery and antislavery partisans had met in violent con-
frontations. Everybody knew that the argument might end in warfare. Yet, as the historian William Lee Miller has shown, the
antebellum Congress turned parliamentary handsprings to avoid
serious debate on the issue.[1] After all (as many Northern members
evidently reasoned), the fact that slavery was immoral did not
mean that the government should ban it. To many of the self-

described abolitionists, it seems, slavery was one of those moral issues on which citizens might agree to disagree; in a free country, it was not the task of those who disliked the institution to force their morality on those who thought it was fine.

This course of moral cowardice in the guise of civility and toler-ance ended in civil war, and more Americans died in payment for that error than in any other war the nation has fought. Although the example is a hard one, the message should be clear: civility does not require that our lives, private or public, be morally empty. I may disagree with you in the most civil and respectful way while nevertheless working for laws that ensure that you will no longer be able to do what it is you are doing.

Nowadays we often hear the argument that it is wrong for you to impose your morality on me. It is offered as a defense against laws on everything from drug use to sexuality to taxes to abortion to smoking to guns. But the argument is, as it has always been, simply blather. If I happen to believe that private property is immoral, and also happen to covet an automobile that you are dri-ving, it is only an imposition of your morality on me that calls the car your property and allows the state to punish me should I act out of my morality instead of yours. And if you answer that most people agree with you that I cannot take the car you say is yours, all you are saying is that the majority should be able to impose its moral sentiment on the minority.

The mythology of modern liberalism has been that it merely establishes a set of background rules that are themselves somehow devoid of moral content—and morality is the decisions that we make about how to live our own lives against those rules. But philosophers on both the left and the right have successfully exploded the myth. The proposition is an ancient one, but bears repeating nevertheless: practically all laws, whether they forbid me to take your car, outlaw racial discrimination, or coerce the pay-ment of taxes, impose somebody's morality on somebody else. Every law either prevents me from doing something or forces me to do something. The understandable American tendency is to pre-tend otherwise, as though laws against car theft are without moral content, whereas laws on abortion are dripping in moral judgment. This tendency assists us in evading moral argument but is, of course, deeply uncivil. As we have already seen, moral conversation is vital to the survival and progress of a democratic people.

And even when we choose (as we usually do) not to give our moral judgments the force of law, we still can, and sometimes must, offer moral criticism of the words and actions of our fellow citizens. There is nothing uncivil in this. We can respect the autonomy of our fellow citizens—their ability to make up their own minds on tough questions, especially questions about how to live their lives—and still let them know when we disagree with their choices. Civility is not a vow of silence.

In this chapter, we will consider the role of tolerance and appropriate forms of moral criticism within a polity characterized by civility.

THE RIGHT TO BE IMMORAL
. . . .

In the penultimate scene of the 1995 film *The American President*, the embattled President of the United States, played by Michael Douglas, defends his paramour, played by Annette Benning, against charges that she once participated in a demonstration in which an American flag was burned. He never denies that she did it. Instead, in the best political tradition, he cleverly goes on the attack: Our precious constitutional freedoms, he tells the White House press corps, include the freedom to burn the flag. Although this fuzzy non sequitur leaves unclear precisely what point the screenwriter was trying to convey, the implication is that there is something un-American about criticizing a fellow citizen for burning the flag. Why? Because flag-burning is a constitutional right.

Now, it is true that what once was called flag desecration— including burning the flag in protest—is a constitutional right, protected by the First Amendment. Although it may seem a bit of a stretch, the person who burns a flag to make a point is trying to send a message and is thus exercising the right to free speech. The Supreme Court so decreed (by a vote of 5–4) when it decided *Texas v. Johnson* in 1989.[2] The case involved one Gregory Lee Johnson, who burned the flag at a demonstration during the Republican

National Convention in Dallas in 1984 while he and his fellow protesters intoned, "America, the red, white, and blue, we spit on you." Although rather tame by the standards of, say, the Days of Rage protests in Chicago in 1969, this is nevertheless rather offensive stuff. But should it be illegal?

The state of Texas thought so. Johnson's stunt led to his arrest. I Iad Texas possessed the wisdom born of hindsight, it would have charged him with some property destruction violation. That would probably have been an easy case, because the flag he burned was stolen by another protester from a public building.* Instead, perhaps trying to score political points, the state charged Johnson only with desecrating the flag.

The prosecution blew up in the state's face.

The Texas courts threw out the prosecution on First Amendment grounds, and the Supreme Court agreed, ruling that Johnson was being punished for "his expression of dissatisfaction with the policies of this country." The core meaning of free speech, the justices explained, is that the state cannot punish only the views it dislikes. That is why, for example, courts have routinely held unconstitutional so-called hate speech codes when adopted by public universities.[3] Not only do the codes propose that the state should sort the ideas that may be expressed, terming some objectionable and others not, but many supporters propose that the state should sort the groups that merit protection, shielding from offense some and not others.[4] One could easily defend an anti-flag-desecration law as a ban on hateful speech that does harm: antics like Johnson's no doubt cause enormous pain, for example, to the families of those who gave their lives in defense of the flag and what it represents. One could easily use similar arguments about harm to defend any ban on speech the government detests. After all, as the legal scholar Michael McConnell has pointed out, America's first "hate speech" statute was the seditious libel law adopted in the late eighteenth century to protect the public officials of the fledgling nation from "unfair" criticism.[5]

Hate speech is bad. Burning flags is bad. People who agree that

---

* The cleaner First Amendment case involves a flag burner who destroys a flag that he owns, not one he has swiped from a public building or, for that matter, grabbed from a spectator at a parade.

they are bad should not be reluctant to say so. But to allow the state to ban such speech, whether in the name of equality, or security, or nationalism, or any other high-sounding ideal, trusts the government with more authority than a democracy can afford. So even though desecrating the flag is somewhere between puerile and contemptible, I think the decision correct. "It is poignant but fundamental," Justice Anthony Kennedy wrote in a concurring opinion, "that the flag protects those who hold it in contempt." Including Gregory Lee Johnson—and Annette Benning's character in *The American President.*

Fair enough: the flag burner in the film could not be fined or jailed for her action. Yes, she had the constitutional right to do what she did, and that freedom is indeed precious—but none of the rest of the fictitious President's diatribe makes any sense. I can fight for the right of my fellow citizens to express their opinions by burning the nation's flag and still criticize them—be furious with them!—should they choose to do it. My fellow citizens have the right to be racist too, but I have the right to say that to be racist is to be wicked, and I do not tread upon their rights by saying so. There is a constitutional right to desecrate the flag, but I have the right to say that it is immoral to exercise it, and that right to criticize is at least as precious. The fictitious critics of Benning's character could defend her right to burn the flag even while insisting that doing so revealed an important deficiency in her character. So Douglas's fictional President was actually saying nothing at all when he suggested that the criticism of the flag-burning was inappropriate because it is a constitutional right.

But the nothing he uttered has become a weirdly common one in our standardless age. More and more often, we speak as though the exercise of a constitutional right is immune from moral critique, as though "I have a right to do X" carries the same content as "I am beyond censure when I do X." One thinks of the Berkeley student who attended classes naked and responded to critics by claiming constitutional right.[6] He was wrong on the law, but even had he been right, he was wrong to think that a right is a shield from moral criticism. Criticism is the beginning of dialogue, and, in a vibrant democracy, dialogue is what citizens do.

During his 1996 campaign for the Republican presidential nomination, Texas Senator Phil Gramm told audiences that he owned "more guns than I need but not as many as I want."[7] Taking the senator at his word, what is the subtext, the message he was sending his audience? Just this: that Gramm, if elected, would protect the right to own as many guns as we want. Maybe that is a constitutional right—I am not quite sure—but even if it is, that fact does not mean that it is morally correct to do so. Like Annette Benning's flag-burning character, like the naked Berkeley student, the citizens who exercise their right to bear arms in a morally thoughtless manner are the fair subjects of criticism. If you believe that it is possible to own too many guns—that there is a level of love for weapons, as for wealth or anything else, that is immoral—you violate nobody's rights by saying so.

The distinction I have been defending suggests what I suppose is obvious—that free citizens must enjoy a degree of freedom to engage in immoral activities. This conclusion also follows from the definition of autonomy, which is a respect for the ability of our fellow citizens to figure out for themselves a vision of the good life. The ideal of autonomy is the centerpiece of liberal democratic theory: the state sets out certain background rules to make sure that nobody infringes on anybody else's theory—so we have the protection of property and so on—and then we all go off in search of our visions of the life well lived. Another term for autonomy of this kind is the famous line from the Declaration of Independence, "the pursuit of happiness." Within broad limits, we have freedom to pursue our own versions of happiness, and the state cannot interfere. But as we rush off in pursuit of what we want, or even what we need, the principle of autonomy provides no shield against the criticism of our fellow citizens, who may think that what we are doing, even if legal, is simply wrong.

Justice William Brennan, writing for the majority in *Texas v. Johnson*, made this point in language the student of civility will surely recognize and even cheer: "The way to preserve the flag's special role is not to punish those who feel differently about these matters. It is to persuade them that they are wrong." But we can persuade the flag burners that they are wrong only if we are willing to tell them so. And conversation of that kind will be possible only if neither the flag burners nor their critics are deceived by the illusion that the exercise of a constitutional right provides a wall against criticism.

THE MYSTIQUE OF PURE TOLERANCE
. . . .

As we have seen, civility is a tool with which our society civilizes us: rules of civility matter precisely because they contain moral content. At the same time, they help us to create a world in which democratic dialogue—respectful conversation among citizens—is possible. And, very often, that democratic dialogue is precisely about which moral vision to impose. That is why civility does not require a suspension of moral judgment and must not make us reluctant to impose moral judgments on each other. On the contrary: civility creates the spaces in which a democracy discusses what it most values. Nowadays lots of Americans seem reluctant to join public moral conversation, seeming to fear what others might say in return. This is a tragedy. A society that refuses to speak the language of morality is more fearful than free.

This fearfulness is evident in our frantic attachment to the ideal of tolerance. In our Western inheritance, the concept of tolerance comes down from John Locke, who thought it the only way to avoid religious warfare. But Locke never imagined tolerance as a way of avoiding moral discussion; on the contrary, what gave the concept its power was his vision of a society in which most people believed most of the same things. The differences (principally in mode of Christian worship) that he wanted his fellow Englishmen to tolerate were smaller than the similarities (in fundamental moral and religious belief) that knit these diverse believers into a single nation.[8]

Unfortunately, we have come to speak of tolerance as an end in itself, as though nothing in our nationhood depends on the morality we share in common. But tolerance has no moral content of its own.[9] Why not tolerate theft? Why not tolerate arson? Why not tolerate wife-battering? We might say the answer lies in the harm that the practices do, but then it is not tolerance that determines what to allow and not to allow, but a theory about harm. In the evocative jargon of philosophy, tolerance is doing none of the work.

Moreover, the idea that we should value tolerance ultimately turns back on itself. I once served on a panel with an academic who explained, with perfect and unembarrassed sincerity, how our commitment to tolerance must make us "intolerant of intolerance." By "intolerance" he evidently meant any moral position different from his own; by refusing to tolerate those who disagreed with him, he undermined his own effort to elevate tolerance to the status of an important democratic value. But his failure is no surprise. Tolerance is more a strategy for living together than a moral position to be defended for its own sake. Tolerance, as we nowadays use the term, is not only unimportant in a democracy, but it also confuses more than it enlightens.*

Suppose that the legislature is considering a law that would make it illegal for Maria to own a particular type of gun that some consider an assault weapon and she considers a sporting rifle. If she opposes the law, it is not enough for her to march boldly behind the banner of tolerance. She is engaging in conduct her opponents think sufficiently wrong that they consider it, literally, intolerable. Maria acts far more civilly if she confronts the arguments actually made by the other side than if she simply behaves as though the fact that she very much wants to do what others want to ban is, by itself, a reason not to ban it.

When our ability to do a thing is threatened—whether we speak of owning a gun, ending a pregnancy, sacrificing animals, or sleeping with whomever we please—a demand for tolerance is merely a substitute for a clear argument on behalf of the freedom

* Liberalism's contemporary love affair with tolerance is fascinating, given the rejection of the concept by much of the left following the publication of *A Critique of Pure Tolerance* in 1965. The *Critique* included now-famous essays by Herbert Marcuse ("Repressive Tolerance") and Robert B. Wolff ("Beyond Tolerance"), essentially arguing that capitalism had so much power in America that voices seeming to offer radical alternatives were drowned out. There was then the appearance of tolerance, but in practice, a narrow set of views dominated public discussion. The implication was that the voice of capitalism had to be stifled (that is, not tolerated) so that the voices of radical change could be heard.

Marcuse's essay had a particular impact on the radicals of the day. He argued that a commitment to the marketplace of ideas presupposes that most people are reasonable enough to reject the most destructive ideas. If most people cannot be trusted to reject these dangerous ideas, Marcuse proposed, then the only solution is to limit the ability of other people to offer the ideas in the first place. The spirit of this proposition—censorship because people cannot be trusted—lives on in proposals to regulate everything from hate speech to Internet "indecency"; its popularity is easy to understand because it allows us to win without actually bothering to argue against those who disagree with us.

Although Marcuse and Wolff were wrong about the need to stifle the voices that seem to be too strong, they were clearly right about the tendency of capitalism—in the form of consumerism—to offer messages so strong that other messages often have trouble breaking through. Thus, in an earlier, more radical voice, they were complaining about the tendency of the values of the market to crowd out other values. They simply failed to hit upon religious revival as the solution.

that is threatened; it is an effort to win, we might say, without fir-
ing a shot. The temptation to cry tolerance is sublime, because it
casts one's opponents as narrow-minded fanatics bent on interfer-
ing with basic freedoms. But, like most temptations, this one
should be resisted. It deadens democratic dialogue and betrays an
uncivil lack of respect for those on the other side of the question. It
also evidences a lack of moral confidence, suggesting that there is
risk in meeting the opposition in debate. As we have seen (chapter
5), there is always risk in genuine conversation, but that very riski-
ness is precisely what makes it genuine.

Abortion again provides a useful example. Pro-choice editorialists
are forever counseling tolerance from pro-life activists; this is the
import of the thinly reasoned bumper sticker reading IF YOU ARE
AGAINST ABORTION, DON'T HAVE ONE, which, to the ardent pro-
lifer, surely makes about as much sense as IF YOU ARE AGAINST
THEFT, DON'T COMMIT ONE. If you consider abortion to be a
moral wrong because of the harm that it does to the fetus, it is difficult
to see why, in the name of tolerance, you should distinguish between
a fetus that inhabits your own body and a fetus that inhabits somebody else's. To be sure, one might offer sophisticated moral reasons in
favor of the distinction, but a call for tolerance does not supply any of
them. So, once more, tolerance is doing none of the work.

Unfortunately, abortion rights supporters spend so much time
avoiding debate that the outside observer might be pardoned for
wondering whether they are afraid of conversation. They ask
courts to draw imaginary lines around abortion clinics, creating
zones, on public thoroughfares, into which anybody may enter
except pro-life protesters. Often, the courts comply.* The fear and
frustration that lead the clinics to seek protection of this kind is
understandable, and it is undeniable that pro-life protesters are
often uncivil and occasionally violent, but the practical effect of
this tactic is to enlist the aid of the state in making one side's
protests ineffective. (I wonder whether the many self-styled civil
libertarians who sat these battles out, or who sided with the clinics,

---

* Of course, it is possible to take a bad idea too far. In February 1997, the Supreme
Court struck down the innovative but blatantly unconstitutional notion that every
patient entering a clinic might carry her own floating zone with her, a protective "bub-
ble," as advocates call it, shielding her against confrontation by pro-life demonstrators.

would have felt the same ambivalence about a similar zone outside a nuclear power plant.)

Nobody likes to be criticized, least of all in the course of exercising a constitutional right, but the state is not supposed to choose sides. When pro-choice activists ask it to, they imply that they think the other side should not be allowed to make its case—that on this issue, to borrow Stanley Fish's phrase from chapter 2, the marketplace of ideas should be shut down. Like the conservative critics of the antiwar movement during the Vietnam era, they seem to think that those who disagree with them vehemently enough to be irritating should not be heard. Pro-lifers, it seems, should tolerate pro-choicers, but not the other way around. It does not serve the cause of civility, however, to try to make one's opponents disappear.

In chapter 5, I mentioned the comment by the (acting) head of Planned Parenthood that there are no bad reasons to have abortions, as though an unwanted pregnancy places a human being beyond the usual moral requirement that we do only what is right. I quite recognize that many abortion rights supporters see matters this way. But how can this be so? Consider the right to vote: inalienable, nearly sacred, purchased in blood, certainly fundamental to democracy. Surely we would not say there are no bad reasons for casting a vote. Were I to vote for a candidate because his campaign manager slipped me fifty dollars just outside the polling place, we surely would all agree that I had committed a moral wrong, that I had cast my vote for a bad reason. Similarly, I would think that to vote against a candidate of whose race, religion, or sex I disapproved would be casting a vote for a bad reason. And it would be bad to vote for a candidate because I hoped he would use elected office to oppress people of a particular race or religion—or even because I liked the cut of his suit or the shape of her nose.*

There are bad reasons to do all the things that we possess funda-

* One cannot distinguish the example of accepting fifty dollars for my vote by saying that I am harming someone (the body politic?) by casting my vote on this ground—not without a theory that explains why I do less harm when I vote for the candidate whose nose I happen to like. Indeed, some sociologists have pointed out the enormous advantages we grant to those, men and women alike, who fit the society's conventional notions of beauty. Besides, it is far from obvious that the harm I do when I cast a vote for a bad reason is greater than the harm I do when I commit other acts—choosing a job, say—for a bad reason. One bad vote among thousands or millions will change nothing, but a bad choice of a job might have devastating effects on my employer or my family.

mental rights to do: bad reasons to marry, bad reasons to bear children, bad reasons to take a job, bad reasons to quit one, bad reasons to choose a college, bad reasons to go to church, bad reasons not to. And, Planned Parenthood notwithstanding, there are bad reasons to have abortions. It is not uncivil to point them out.

In fact, sometimes it is uncivil *not* to criticize others. One of the sacrifices that love of neighbor requires of us is the willingness to accept the anger and dislike that often result when we offer even constructive criticism of others. In the Jewish tradition, many scholars argue that correcting the errors of others is an obligation.[10] In the Christian tradition, Jesus preached love for others but still criticized people—often quite harshly—for their transgressions against God's law. And so we have another rule:

> *Civility allows criticism of others, and sometimes even requires it, but the criticism should always be civil.*

This proposition helps explain why grade inflation is not only dangerous but actively uncivil: When college professors give easy grades, we show that we do not respect our students enough to face their fury or disappointment. We make no sacrifices on their behalf but instead require sacrifices of others, both the exceptional students, who are unable to distinguish themselves because the merely fair students earn grades every bit as good, and the marginal students, who believe they know more than they do because we gift them with grades their work does not earn.

Criticism, when offered, should certainly be civil; because it is respect for others that should lead to our willingness to be critical, the criticism itself should also reflect that respect. In chapter 1, I mentioned the nineteenth-century tradition of hissing bad performances at the theater that culminated in the carnage of the Astor Place Riot. Although the mores of the time apparently accepted hissing and interrupting as forms of criticism, those practices are today seen quite properly as uncivil. The practice of hissing (like the riot itself) indicates a mindless, moblike quality to the critical activity; but such thoughtless and instinctive action, even when understandable, is unlikely to be civil. This suggests that we should be wary of criticism offered in the heat of anger and that we will probably be more civil—to say nothing of more accurate—if we wait to criticize others until we are cool. But we should not avoid needed criticism simply to serve our own convenience, which includes the desire to be liked. Whenever we are moved by self-love—and the desire to have others like us is nothing more—there is a good chance we will wind up uncivil.

This leads us back to the question of abortion. Except for the most dedicated pro-lifers, few Americans want to criticize women who seek abortions, because the decision is a highly personal one, made in intensely difficult circumstances. Yet even most supporters of abortion concede that not all women who seek abortions have equal moral claims. Surveys make clear, for example, that only a tiny constituency supports abortion as a means of birth control.[11] Yet, although abortion rights supporters prefer to talk about pregnancies resulting from rape or pregnancies that threaten the health of the mother, birth control turns out to be the most common reason abortions are sought.[12]

Similarly, not all forms of abortion are moral equivalents. The American public, those who are pro-life, those who are pro-choice, and those who are somewhere in between, is overwhelmingly opposed to what have come to be known as partial-birth abortions: an operation during which the entire fetus is delivered, with the exception of the top of the head, and the physician then vacuums out the brain.[13] (Four out of five Americans would outlaw *all* abortions in the last three months of pregnancy.[14]) The fact that we agree to be civil does not mean that we must cease to point out grim truths. Sometimes we can make a moral criticism simply by stating facts.

The feminist author Naomi Wolf, avowedly pro-choice, made this point with some power in a 1995 essay in *The New Republic*. In the essay, which followed the birth of a child, Wolf warned her fellow feminists to be more measured in their objections to the tactics of pro-life activists. For example, by protesting the display of graphic photographs of aborted fetuses, noted Wolf, abortion rights supporters may be trying to evade an unpleasant truth that intellectually honest arguments would accept: abortion does kill *something*.[15] (Whether or not one wants to call the fetus a human being, the argument that something with its own genetic code is simply a body part is not accepted by scientists with respect to the development of any other living creature.)

Wolf's acknowledgment promotes civility because it elevates the pro-life conception from a position of presumptive fanaticism or misogyny to one that is worthy of respect: it turns out that the other side is within rather than without the universe of rational discourse. This implies that it is not ridiculous for pro-life forces to refuse to abandon the field of battle whenever somebody cries "tolerance": they are, as their chosen name suggests, fighting for the protection of what they consider a *life*. The fact that others might disagree hardly makes their position ridiculous, to say nothing of oppressive. And, once the pro-life position is treated as rational, it becomes plain that no call for tolerance can possibly carry the day. This might well mean that agreement is impossible, but the task of civility is not to mask our disagreements; the task of civility is to remind us, even as we disagree, to treat each other with the respect that our shared humanity deserves.*

To be charitable, I suspect that what Jane Johnson of Planned Parenthood was trying to say was that abortion is so precious a right that we should not legislate against it based on the pregnant woman's motivation for seeking one. In other words, the state should not decide which reasons are good and which bad; that is the pregnant woman's own business. Many scholars evidently share this view.[16] But, if this argument is correct, then surely we shouldn't keep me from voting for the candidate who slips me fifty dollars. After all, why I cast my vote is my own business—isn't it?

TOLERANCE AND SHAME

Of course, were we to encourage conversation about good and bad reasons to have abortions, we might discourage some women who would otherwise end their pregnancies. That, I think, is one reason

* It is by no means my intention to exempt from severe criticism the frequent incivility of the pro-life side—not just the handful who commit acts of terrorism and murder, but the many who seem, in their rhetoric, to call for death for doctors who perform abortions. I do not belabor the point in my text because I take the incivility of such activities, and such words, to be common ground.

that pro-choice forces so heartily resist the conversation. It is as though they believe in the protesters' rights only as long as the protesters are unseen and unheard: a Nixonian vision of the First Amendment. But it is the purpose of democratic dialogue to change people's minds; if, through moral conversation—frank discussion of right and wrong—a citizen is persuaded to choose a different course of conduct, that is democracy, not coercion.

This can be true even when the dialogue has its effect because it makes somebody feel bad. Consider the case of welfare policies aimed at encouraging unmarried teenage mothers to live with their parents. Henry Cisneros, while serving as secretary of housing and urban development in the Clinton administration, warned that programs of this kind might force young women into situations in which they would feel ashamed—because of family disapproval, for example. This would be a particular risk, said Cisneros, in the nation's socially conservative (and heavily Roman Catholic) Hispanic communities.

But a complete answer to this concern is contained in the two words, "So what?" If young people who have children prior to marriage feel ashamed, the reason may be that they have something to be ashamed of.* It would be wrong to punish them harshly—by ostracizing them from their communities or by cutting off all public benefits for their children—but there is nothing wrong with forcing the parents to face the societal disapproval of what they have done. We as a nation are so enamored of the idea that all of us should feel good about ourselves that we tend to forget that we sometimes need to feel the moral anger of others. If, as most Americans believe, and as Hillary Rodham Clinton wrote in her book *It Takes a Village*, it is wrong to bear children prior to marriage, we should trumpet that message at every turn; social pressure is an important means for communicating it. The great tragedy is that unmarried fathers often behave so irresponsibly that it is impossible to track them down so that they can get the message too.

* The fathers have as much reason to be ashamed. In fact, they often have more. It is wrong for a man to help bring a child into the world and then to refuse to marry his child's mother. It is more wrong still for him to do it more than once, as too many men do. And more wrong than either of these is for a man to abandon his children, a far too common occurrence—and not only in the case of teenage welfare mothers.

The message is desperately needed. All our politicians talk about supporting or rebuilding the family, and they generally mention that the family is the building block on which the society rests—but still they do not go far enough. The embarrassing and scary truth is that our national trend toward sundering marriage and child-bearing is a big part of what is making us uncivilized. The family, parents working together to raise their children, is perhaps the greatest civilizing invention of the Western world. It does no violence to the ideal of civility to point out that we are worse off when we forget this fact. And it is no answer to say that pointing it out will make some people feel bad. A society that believes in civility necessarily believes in morality, and it is in the nature of talking about morality that some people will feel the heat of criticism.

TOLERANCE, CIVILITY, AND THE VIOLENCE OF LAW

. . . .

In a self-governing society, our moral disagreements should ideally generate moral conversation—conversations marked, one hopes, by the *civil listening* we discussed in chapter 8. But conversation in a democracy is only a means to self-governance, not an end in itself. And no matter how hard we try to be civil, no matter how hard we try to listen in an open way to those with whom we disagree, the chances are excellent that when the conversation ends, we will continue to disagree. At that point, the one who has managed to sway a majority must make what can be the harder decision: deciding not what the right answer is, but what to do about it. We must decide whether to ban what we have decided is wrong.

Even if laws make moral statements, we should be cautious in considering whether to enact our moral visions as laws. What at last decides us should not be how certain we are of our rightness, but how willing we are to be violent. On the first day of law school, I always remind my new students of a fact that all of us know but most of us forget: the police officers who enforce our laws go armed. Why do they do so? Because it is possible that their efforts will be resisted. They might need their guns in order to make others obey the law—or accept the punishment for their disobedience. Consequently, every time we enact a new law, we create the possibility that violent means will be required to transform the new law's command into reality. What I tell my students is a lesson I learned from the late, great legal scholar Robert Cover: law is violence.[17]

Consider a rather simple law: when the traffic light turns red, we are supposed to stop our cars. Suppose that one evening I disobey the law, cruising through a red light. A police officer sees me, pulls me over, and gives me a ticket. I do not pay the ticket. I do not go to court to dispute it. Perhaps I think stoplights are immoral. Or tickets are. Perhaps I am just being selfish. Eventually, I am tracked down. A letter arrives from the state: because I have been delinquent, my fine is doubled. Maybe tripled. I ignore it. I no longer believe in the justice of the state. To coerce payment of money from me for the way I choose to drive my automobile is unconscionable, I decide. An officer comes to my house to haul me down to court. I refuse to go. He says he will have to insist. I tell him that he is infringing my freedoms. That he is imposing somebody else's morality on me. He says he is just doing his job. I notice that he is wearing a sidearm. I tell him to get off my property before I—

And what would we right-thinking people have the officer do? If he is to uphold the law, he must ultimately use force, perhaps aided by other officers. It is possible that I will die, there in the doorway of my home, defending what I take to be my rights. If you say that the officer is correct to use force, then you are saying that the rule about stopping at red lights is one that you are willing to kill to enforce. If you say he should not use force, then you do not really believe in the law.*

I emphasize this point not because I am against traffic laws; like everybody else, I am for them. I simply want us to admit, before beginning any discussion of law, that laws themselves, whatever

---

* It is no answer to say that I am being punished for my resistance to the law, and that it is my own resistance that has provoked the officer's violence. That simply pushes the entire argument back a step, but the result is the same: if violence is appropriate in overcoming resistance to the law, then the law is violent. Nevertheless, I have no doubt that the police officers in Birmingham in 1963 consoled themselves with the proposition that it was only the resistance of the civil rights marchers, not the violence inherent in the law itself, that provoked them.

their content, are in a sense ultimately uncivil, because they are, at their core, ultimately violent. Acknowledging the inherent violence in all law does not imply that law is inherently bad. The soldiers who defend our country, like the police who enforce its laws, are willing to be violent, but they are not in consequence bad people. The inherent violence in law should make us cautious, however, as we sift through our moral convictions and try to decide which ones should be laws. For if we are honest with ourselves, we must ask each time: "Is this one worth killing for?" If the answer is *no*, then for all that we may think our conviction correct, we should resist its imposition on others through law.

In the abortion example we have been discussing, the question is starkly posed to each side. If the Supreme Court ever reverses *Roe v. Wade,*[10] pro-life activists will suddenly be faced with the hard decision on what, if anything, to permit, and what, if anything, to outlaw. And any effort at a ban should be accompanied by the same inquiry: Is this worth killing for? Because, in the end, resisters may refuse to stop performing abortions. Meanwhile, with law in its current state, pro-choice forces should undertake the same inquiry every time they seek an additional limit on the speech of their opponents: Is this worth killing for? Because, in the end, protesters may refuse to stop protesting.

This is a hard test, but it is at least an intellectually honest one, because it forces us to face the violence that inheres in any enforcement of law. Coercive means to achieve our ends are, by definition, never peaceful. So we should use law carefully—one might even say prayerfully. At the same time, we should not be morally squeamish. Even if law implies a willingness to kill, we should not assume that we will kill to enforce every law. Despite decades of research, we know relatively little about why people obey the law. We do know, however, that Americans often seem eager to obey laws, even laws they consider wrong.[19] So whatever law is imposed in our seemingly unruly society, most of us will follow it just because it is the law. But some, always, will not, and the question we must always ask ourselves is how violent we are willing to be to bring the dissenters into line.

CIVILITY, DIALOGUE, AND
BISHOP SEABURY

. . . .

The ideal of civility allows and even encourages criticism of others (as long as it is civil); but the same ideal discourages the automatic resort to the violence of law whenever we believe that others have done wrong. And so, another rule:

> *Civility discourages the use of legislation rather than con-*
> *versation to settle disputes, except as a last, carefully consid-*
> *ered resort.*

The better route to restraining our urge to unlimited self-indulgence is not to make self-seeking illegal but to remind one another that it is immoral. Samuel Seabury, bishop and guiding spirit of the early Episcopal Church, made this point in a sermon he preached in 1777. Seabury argued that cultivation of the "benign and friendly" aspects of human nature was the only way to avoid the division and violence that would come from following our "malevolent dispositions." Without the gentle parts of our character, we were monsters:

> Strike all the tender feelings, all gentleness and kindness, and meekness and benevolence, from the nature of man; give a full scope to the malevolent passions, the vindictive dispositions of his nature, and see what would be the consequence. . . . The malevolence of wolves and tigers would fall far short of the malevolence of man. Every violence that you can conceive—rapine, and bloodshed, and murder, would ravage and desolate the earth.[20]

But surely we could prevent all this by making these terrible crimes illegal? Contemporary social science teaches that the answer is no:

> Democratic societies require normative commitment to function effectively. Authorities cannot induce through deterrence alone a level of compliance sufficient for effective social functioning. Society's resources are inadequate to the task and some basis of normative commitment to follow the law is needed.[21]

In other words, if we have to rely on law alone to get us to behave ourselves, we are in serious trouble. Seabury agreed and put the point with greater eloquence and evocation:

> No laws would be sufficient to restrain the impetuosity of the passions; no punishments of force enough to prevent the perpetration of evil: For that murder is now so seldom committed in the world, is probably more owing to the tender feelings of the human heart, than to any laws, human or divine, or to any dread of punishment.[22]

Once more, Seabury returns to the "tender feelings" that we must somehow inculcate in human beings if we are to have a society at all. And where do those feelings come from? Seabury offers a simple answer, and an unsurprising one, given that he earned his bread as a bishop: "To bring about this happy state by restraining the malevolent tempers of our nature, and by cherishing those of a kind and benevolent tendency, is the proper business of reason, the grand aim of religion."[23] But not religion alone:

> The laws of civil society, the laws of God, the tender, sociable and humane feelings of the heart, all concur to restrain the inordinancy of passion, to bridle the lust of revenge; and all these united, and assisted by education, are sufficient to answer the purpose.[24]

Education and religion, then, are the sources for establishing the "tender feelings" that Seabury and the student of civility would agree are the basis of civil society; they are the sources as well for the "normative commitment" to that society that social science and common sense tell us is also required. And how do we introduce children, these unformed animals, to education and to religion so as to teach them the principles of civility and thus to civilize them? We begin, of course, with the family. The interaction between family and religion, and the relationship of both to civility, will occupy the final section of this book.

III

Civilizing the

Twenty-first

Century

13
· · · · · · · · · · · ·

Where Civility Begins

IF AMERICA is to be civilized in the twenty-first century, it must begin by civilizing its children, teaching them about the necessary balance between instinct and desire, on the one hand, and doing what is morally required, on the other. How do we do this? When I think about how the elements of good character are transmitted from one generation to the next, I like to borrow an old metaphor—the model of the three-legged stool. The three legs are the home, the school, and the place of worship. If all three institutions work together, mutually reinforcing the moral understandings that the others are teaching, then the children are likely to learn what they should. If any one of them fails—if even one of the legs should break—then the task is much harder, and perhaps impossible. The metaphorical stool topples.

Nowadays the model may seem outdated. Many adults (including, sadly, many parents) do not feel comfortable teaching children that some choices are right and others wrong; many more adults simply do not think they have the time. The nation's houses of worship, as we have seen, preach less and less about right and wrong. As for the schools, despite the introduction of a handful of curricula aimed at "character education," too few teachers seem to want to take on the task, and too many parents seem to want to dump the entire project of teaching good character on the schools. But if the work of teaching children what is right goes forward, it must begin—as so many good things do—with the family.

Family is the most important institution in America. Just about everything of lasting value starts there. In particular, the family is the place where the training of the next generation begins. Personality forms. Habits that last a lifetime take root. Skills of moral reasoning are learned.[1] So if we are to solve our incivility crisis—if we are to build a more civil national culture, and thus a more sacrificial and trusting one—the family must be the foundation. That is how civility begins:

> *Teaching civility, by word and example, is an obligation of the family. The state must not interfere with the family's effort to create a coherent moral universe for its children.*

If families are to do this work, they must have room to breathe. We must cherish the freedom of the family not only to raise children everybody else likes but to raise children who look at the world differently, and value the things of the world differently, than our market-dominated culture tends to teach. Only in this way can we raise a generation ready to resist rather than be overwhelmed by the many forces we have been describing that conspire to make sacrifice for others seem to be a waste.

SACRIFICE AND THE TRAINING UP OF CHILDREN

. . . .

The student of civility should properly understand family not simply as an entity but as an act—an act of loving and intimate sacrifice. Family, at its heart, is not something that people *are* but something that people *do*. Christianity teaches that a family is a place where we die to the self. What this means is that by taking on the responsibility of marriage and children, one accepts the impermanence of mortal existence—and the ultimate irrelevance of human desire. For a family, as a place of love, is also a place of duty, a place where our obligations to others supersede our pursuit of the yearnings of the self. The way in which we who are adults carry out these duties (or fail to carry them out) helps our children to understand the first and greatest sacrifice that parents make.

Morality is learned, not innate. Unless that learning is to be entirely haphazard, every parent should undertake the difficult exercise of deciding what moral lessons a child must learn and trying to create, as far as possible, a world that reinforces them. As the psychiatrist Robert Coles points out in his best-selling book *The Moral Intelligence of Children* (1997), children both need and expect moral coherence. Despite all the widespread vision of our era as hopelessly relativistic, mothers and fathers instinctively understand this. Surveys make clear that most parents want their children to learn clear moral rules—not just the coping skills featured in the "values clarification" curricula that enjoyed brief and unfortunate popularity in the eighties.[2] One of the reasons religious parents fight so tenaciously to limit what their children learn in school is precisely that they believe in the need to shield their children from some aspects of the world in order to help them to form the consciences that will guide them as adults.

But how? In his posthumous memoir, *The Gift of Peace*, Joseph Cardinal Bernardin tells the story of how he fell off a porch rail at age four or five, and his father, shoulder still bandaged from recent cancer surgery, leaped over the rail and scooped up his child. Writes Bernardin: "As he held me in his arms, I could see blood soaking through his shirt. He paid no attention to himself; all he wanted was to be sure I was all right." And Bernardin, writing at the verge of his own death, then adds: "My father's ability to transcend his own illness and share in the joy of his family and friends now inspires me as I try to do the same."[3]

In this account, we see both cause and effect of civility in the family. First, the father, acting out of love, sacrifices his own comfort, possibly his own health, to console his child. Then, decades later, the son still remembers the story and tries to act out of the same sense of sacrificial love. Like all good things, civility builds on itself: children who see their parents willing to set aside their own concerns for the larger good are far more likely, upon reaching adulthood, to do the same.

Now compare a very different story. As I was finishing this manuscript in the spring of 1997, the newspapers carried the account of a New Mexico man who pled guilty to conspiracy to commit aggravated assault with a dangerous weapon after sharpening the chin strap of his son's football helmet to a razor's edge. When his son, a high schooler, played his next game, the referee and four players were slashed by the strap, one of them so seriously that he required hospitalization. The young man who did the damage explained to the judge, quite unpersuasively, that his father sharpened the strap in order to protect him.

And what is the lesson taught by the father's conduct in this second episode? That victory, the advancement of the self, is sufficiently important that we should be willing to risk serious harm to others if that is what it takes. That message, of course, is profoundly anti-civil—indeed, it is barbaric in Erasmus's sense—but it is the message that many families today teach their children. A seemingly small thing, like parents who bicker constantly, letting the chips fall as they may, teaches the same lesson of thinking only of self: the cost, the sacrifice for the sake of civility, comes in postponing the argument until the children have settled down for the night (and then resolving the dispute civilly). An obviously large thing, like the number of couples who divorce despite the children—or decide not to marry at all—also teaches lessons about what it is that adults truly value. And then there are the everyday things, like driving above the speed limit because our own convenience matters most. All that we do with children is teaching, which means that nothing we do to or within the family can be done casually.

When parents are asked how to strengthen values in America, the number-one answer is that parents must spend more time with their children.[4] What kind of time? The answer, I think, is not the infamous "quality time," but rather a kind of "moral time," time in which we are quite deliberate in demonstrating to our children right rather than wrong behavior.[5] Whether we are instructing our own children or mentoring others, adults must not simply while away the hours but help teach, by word and example, the basic moral norms and traditions we share in common. It is through learning these norms that children begin to become civilized.

This task requires hard work. It means, for example, that parents must strive to be civil in their dealings with others: rude shopkeepers, wayward drivers, and the irritating anonymous army of sellers-by-telephone. It means that adults must model for children the old-time virtue of not saying behind people's backs what we would not repeat to their faces. It means that spouses who tend to fight must learn to forgo the dubious pleasures of arguing nastily in front of the kids. The point is not that the family must follow the advice of those nineteenth-century etiquette gurus who proposed that verbal disagreements should be avoided altogether.[6] Indeed, we should not try to eliminate all bickering simply because it is often unpleasant. It can also be functional. In the particular context of the family, social scientists have long understood that nagging (at least of a husband by a wife) is functional, for it provides one of the very few potential sources of control for the partner in the marriage whom law and custom often make the weaker of the two.[7] (Which suggests that the more equal the marriage, the less the partners should nag each other.)

But married couples also should not follow the advice of game theorists, who recommend the strategy known as tit-for-tat in any contest requiring cooperation, which the family certainly requires. When one party defects—the jargon for ceasing to cooperate—the other party can best avoid defeat by also defecting. In many forms of competition, tit-for-tat is an effective strategy. In a family, it is a strategy for disaster. Yet many parents follow it: If one spouse gets mad, the other gets madder. If one shouts loud, the other shouts louder. If one does wrong, the other does wronger. Life in such a family is a little like wars in the Middle East: who did what to whom first becomes less important than who is going to do what to whom next.

The adults in the family have a very different moral responsibility, imposed by the norm of civility: the responsibility to discipline the desire to be mean to each other, even in response to meanness, and replace it with an attitude of mutual respect—not because children should be unaware that adults ever disagree, but because children need to see evidence that adults can disagree and yet respect and even love each other, and can demonstrate that respect and love even as they disagree. These are hard guidelines, for they mean, in short, that the need to discipline our instincts never ceases.

Teaching civility to the next generation also requires the establishment of clear rules of respect and simple good manners in the household. I am not referring to the problem of teaching children where the fork goes in a table setting, although learning those rules, too, involves self-discipline of an important kind. I have in mind the rules that govern the way members of the family behave. One naturally begins with the magic words (see chapter 5), but, beyond that, the family should try to implement the other positive duties of civility. For example, we saw back in chapter 4 that civility involves an affirmative duty to do good. Consequently, the rules of the household should include rules about kindness to strangers. My wife and I serve one meal a week in a soup kitchen, and we take our children along whenever we can, to help them understand their duties to others. The many families who make similar—and much greater—volunteer efforts are teaching the same lesson.

None of this is easy, because it requires a discipline that little in our self-indulgent age urges upon us. Any number of well-meaning reformers have proposed legislation to make it easier for adults to model sacrificial behavior: time off from the job for charitable work, mandatory pro bono activities by lawyers, tax credits for volunteering, and the like. Although I understand the impulse behind such ideas, I fear they do not touch the root of the problem, which lies in human will. It may be that what we need are the tools to help us sacrifice for the sake of sacrifice.

Besides, even if we manage to establish civil time in the home, we will but have scratched the surface of the influences on our children. The parent who is concerned about civilizing the next generation must pay attention to what goes on outside the four walls of the home as well.

THE DUTY TO MONITOR

. . . .

Children learn what they see. Their first role models are their parents. So the way that parents behave matters. But children are also embedded in a larger moral world, in which other adults—and other influences—play crucial roles. The parent who wants to raise a virtuous child is therefore careful about the corners of the adult experience to which the child is exposed. Although a part of the job of every parent is to prepare children for the world, another part is to protect children from that world, by creating a coherent moral universe in which fundamental truths about right and wrong are reinforced. The ancient human tradition has been to create this moral coherence in large part by raising children in religious communities.[8] The duty of parents to love children, which includes the duty to die to the self, to do what is best for the children rather than for the parents, may often mean doing for the children what others criticize or mock. One thinks, for example, of Jehovah's Witnesses determinedly refusing to allow their children to celebrate Easter or Christmas, or of evangelical parents doggedly requiring their children to sit out classroom education on sex. But one need not choose examples from religion. Consider the case of a mother who decides to put her career on hold because of a conviction that her children need and deserve her full attention. The point is in every case the same: The construction of a coherent moral universe for one's children often requires sacrifice. In particular, if the moral universe is very different from what the rest of the society believes, the family risks isolation and alienation—and yet must still, in the end, do the sacrificial work.

Many parents around the country have organized groups to try to share this work. For example, the Safe Homes Network is a program under which member parents pledge that there will be no parties for children or teens in their homes without a parent present, and that no alcohol or other drugs will be available. The program allows other parents the security of knowing that they are sending their children out into the world only to places where some approximation of the values they are trying to teach will be present.

Of course, such networks function well only if parents are able to trust each other to do what they have pledged to do. For many parents, that hope may not be enough. Trusting when there is risk is, as we have seen, an element of civility, but it is very hard to do so when one's children rather than oneself are taking the risk. Moreover, for all that groups like Safe Homes Network are admirable, they are also a sad signal of how far from the ideal of neighborhood we have tumbled: we are forced to demand promises and rules to ensure moral consistency in our children's world because we no longer know the people who live around us well enough to make our own judgments of them.

When religion depended strongly on geographic community, the faith itself helped supply the moral discipline that could reassure parents that their neighbors held the same values they did. So, in a sense, parents who join Safe Homes and similar organizations are trying to duplicate what religious communities once did and, for many, still do: creating a moral world with walls around it within which children can grow and thrive while learning the wisdom of the tradition.

This is an activity that must be undertaken with some caution. In particular, the construction of a community within which children can grow in a moral tradition is the proper work of families, not experts. If we lose that focus, if we try to professionalize the creation of moral meaning, we very likely will cripple rather than aid the ability of families to do that vital work. The longtime community organizer John McKnight, in his book *The Careless Society*, collects evidence of the way this professionalization has hampered community efforts to build problem-solving expertise in fields from medical care to alleviating the effects of poverty.[9]

But how are parents to do this work? It is not enough for parents to decide which moral lessons they wish to teach, although that is hard enough. Like so many tasks, the work of creating moral meaning for children rests crucially upon the collection of information. In particular, parents must understand what influences their children face in everyday life: what they learn in school, what music they listen to, what television shows they watch, where they go on the Internet, what they do with their friends. In short, parents who are trying to model civility in the home need to know what the competition is.

Monitoring the activities of children need not be unduly intrusive. For example, as I mentioned in chapter 11, some families monitor their children's Internet exposure by locating the computer in the kitchen or family room, instead of a child's bedroom. The job of parents would, of course, be easier if the market cooperated—if, for example, purveyors of indecency and incivility online or on television or over the airwaves would exercise a degree of restraint. Alas, those who make money by circumventing the wishes of parents are hardly willing to be sacrificial in helping to raise good children. Why would a television network offer viewers detailed rating information about its programs when information might cause parents to steer their children away? There is too much money to be made by going around parents and encouraging children to yield to temptation.

Here is one trick that some record companies use. A song is recorded in the studio and distributed on compact discs with offensive and vulgar language, but the demo versions that are given to record stores to allow children (and parents) to listen before buying have many of the offensive words removed or bleeped out. So a concerned parent who wants to know what his children are listening to and asks the store clerk for a demonstration, will hear one version of the song and approve the purchase—and the CD to which the child listens at home will have another. This is not an act of civility; it may, however, be an act of moral fraud.

On the other hand, it is not unusual. The corporate world, no less than the political world, is full of firms that try to wiggle through the defenses parents erect around their children. Whether they sell unhealthy music or unhealthy food, they are a principal source of the outside influences that pose the greatest challenges to parents who wish to build a world of bounded moral meaning for their children, and for the same reason that we have already seen: the message of the market is that what matters most is the satisfaction of immediate desire.

Deciding what children should be shielded from is an excursion into ideology and faith, not science. Different eras make different choices. For example, the treatise on civility that Erasmus wrote back in the sixteenth century included instruction on how young boys might resist the blandishments of prostitutes.[10] In today's terms, his choice of what subject matter to include might seem shocking. But in the Europe of Erasmus's time, prostitution was widely and publicly practiced, and encounters with prostitutes were part of a boy's everyday experience.

In this light, it is useful to consider today's controversies over AIDS education for schoolchildren, especially information on the use of condoms. Many people sincerely believe that encounters with sexual danger are a part of the everyday experience of young people, and these genuine fears, as much as any ideological program, surely account for the pressure to include such material in the school curriculum. If local communities agree, teaching about risk, and risk avoidance, might be a good idea. But the state, even acting in the guise of its public schools, must never substitute its judgment for that of rational, loving parents: thus, every family must have the option of excluding its children from morally objectionable instruction.

Sometimes—as with condom distribution programs—advocates protest that if parents are allowed to interfere, the programs will not work, because they rely on a promise to students that their use of the program will be anonymous. If counselors have to check names to be sure parents have granted permission, the argument runs, the guarantee of anonymity is lost, the students cease to trust, and the program fails. The result, supposedly, is that fewer young people use condoms, and that is said to be bad. When the New York City Board of Education considered an anonymous condom distribution program, parental protests were met by exactly this argument.[11]

But my answer as a parent is: So what? If an educational program can be made to work only if parents have no part in it, then it is not an educational program that belongs in the schools. Even when, as in the case of an AIDS curriculum, the program is founded on the school's empirical claim that most children will in fact be exposed to sexual danger and must thus learn to avoid it, parents must be free to say, first, that they are building for their children an empirically different world (and thus the chances of exposure are smaller), and, second, that they are building for their children a morally different world (and thus will teach them distinctive tools for coping). If a school rejects these possibilities, it is pressing an ideological program in the guise of an empirical proposition.

MONITORING THE PARENTS?

The courts, unfortunately, are generally unable to grasp these simple matters, even though the Supreme Court all the way back in 1925 ruled that parents and guardians have a fundamental right "to direct the upbringing and education of children under their control."[12] In exercising that right—which is also a solemn responsibility—a child's parents should try to create the morally coherent world that Robert

Coles describes. Because all families are different, each child's moral world would then be distinct; naturally there would be overlap, but there would be diversity too. A truly civil society would nurture the ability of parents to create those individual moral worlds for their children. Unfortunately, much about modern society proposes instead to build a single moral world in which all parents are required to raise their children. As parents of two magnificent children, my wife and I occasionally feel as though the state views the family as a little citizen-making factory, which must be run according to government specifications lest we lose our license. Lost in the march toward regulation of the family is the traditional notion that the family is prior to the state, which means that the state did not create the family and has only a very thin power to regulate it.

The theologian Michael Eric Dyson, in his book *Between God and Gangsta Rap*, writes movingly of being stopped by the police in Hartford, Connecticut, after some bystander saw him spanking his son in public and called the authorities.[13] Now, this has lately been a tricky point. Most parents spank their children, and most say that it is acceptable to do so, especially for dangerous behavior.[14] And, despite controversy, most doctors and nurses also continue to consider spanking to be an important and appropriate means of discipline.[15] Children have been raised that way for as long as there have been children. I was spanked as a child and somehow survived. My wife and I certainly took the time to slap our two children's bottoms or hands when they were young, usually for truly dangerous infractions, like running into the street. And our children, like most others whose parents occasionally spank, seem none the worse for the experience.

But a handful of experts (challenged, it must be said, by a majority of other experts) have decided that it is a bad thing to do, that a spanking is inherently abusive, a form of violence. This weird new argument that it is always wrong to strike a child seems to be catching on. The newspapers occasionally carry stories of arrests for the offense. Family-values conservatives have made the right to spank a cause célèbre in some parts of the country, citing it in support of the Parental Rights Amendment and other legislative goals. It is certainly true that there are abusive parents who cannot tell the difference between firm, sensible discipline and physical harm. But should the state readily assume that any parent known to spank a child is among them?

Consider once more Michael Dyson's tale. After Dyson, who is black, spanked his son, he was surrounded by six white police officers, who shoved him against his car, refused to believe that he was a professor (at the time he taught at Hartford Seminary), and, at first, refused to say why they had stopped him. They finally allowed him to go free after he offered a powerful and yet poignant rejoinder: "I can assure you that I love my son, and that I wasn't hurting him," Dyson said, adding: "I spanked my child now so that he wouldn't one day end up being arrested by you."[16]

The racial overtones of the incident are both infuriating and inexcusable—and they are also more typical than most white Americans might prefer to think. The relationship of black Americans to the police has long been, and continues to be, a somewhat ambiguous one. But racism we have already condemned as fundamentally against the principles of civility, and so that is not the aspect of Dyson's story that interests me at this point. My concern is what the incident says about civility in the relationship between the state and the family.

To take the more obvious point, it will become increasingly difficult for parents to discipline children if they fear that the police are constantly looking over their shoulders. Many parents tell stories of being informed by a child—jokingly?—that harsh punishment will result in calls to the child abuse hotline, the telephone number helpfully supplied by the child's school. Given the public presumption of guilt that attaches in such cases, the matter is no joke. But such results are predictable in a world that shows its concern for abuse by putting into the heads of children the germ of the idea that their relationships to their parents are adversarial.

Sadly, a growing number of parents evidently see their own relationship to the state as adversarial too. Some conservative activists, occasionally straining both civility and credulity, insist that a plot is afoot: I attended a panel discussion at which a prominent evangelist warned that the public schools were trying to turn heterosexual children into homosexual adults. And yet liberal theorists do their best to provide substance for such silliness. The public schools in particular are a place where, many theorists believe, children should be weaned away from the religious traditions of their parents. More concretely, according to a vast literature, children should be taught a set of supposedly democratic values that are at odds, sometimes intentionally, with the values of the coherent moral world that their parents have designed.[17]

Remarkably, contemporary liberal theorists are unable to come to grips with the totalizing implications of this analysis: it turns out that the state does after all have the power to stifle the construction of centers of dissent from its preferred meanings, as long as it gets to the potential dissenters while they are children. And some liberal theorists not only applaud the effort but wish the state would do more. For example, Amy Gutmann argues that the state should require public and private schools alike to teach a set of basic values on which liberal citizenship rests.[18] Bruce Ackerman suggests that parents should be required to send their children to the "liberal schools" he wants the state to fund in order to inculcate the ability to think critically.[19] Many other liberal theorists have made similar arguments. And all of them share a common starting point: the assumption that the state is likely to make wise decisions and parents are likely to make bad ones.[20]

Often the argument is explicit. The legal scholar Ira Lupu, for example, argues that "compulsory education laws reduce the risk of totalitarian control or abuse of children"—the parents, we should understand, being the potential totalitarians.[21] And the legal scholar Suzanna Sherry, in an otherwise quite sensitive effort to balance competing positions, lets slip this unfortunate claim: "[L]eaving most educational choices to parents or the democratic process . . . assumes, probably erroneously, that parents, whether individually or as a voting majority, will not make serious, virtue-threatening, education-stifling mistakes."[22] The implication is that if we follow instead her reasoning about the values that education should inculcate, we will avoid these serious mistakes.* One sees similar claims—if anything, more forcefully put—in the work of Ackerman, Gutmann, and others.[23]

Now, in the first place, history suggests that the state has often made bad decisions, not good ones, about how and why to run its

---

* To Sherry's credit, she does conclude that vouchers of some kind might be necessary as a protection for exit rights—a proposition that most theorists of liberal education heatedly reject.

compulsory schools. The deeper problem is that the family becomes, in this liberal vision, not a fundamental institution on which the society itself rests, but a little citizen-making factory, existing by sufferance of the state and principally to do the work the state requires. If the state decides to standardize its citizens through the device of standardizing its children, it is evidently the responsibility of the parents not to resist that effort, but to assist it—or to get out of the way. Nothing else can explain, for example, the terrible decision by the New York Court of Appeals allowing parents to withdraw their children from an objectionable sex education curriculum only if the parents agree to make sure that the children receive all the information that the curriculum contains.[24]

This notion—that the state should shape its young people to get the right kind of adults—was decisively criticized by the Lutheran theologian Dietrich Bonhoeffer (in his posthumously published *Ethics*) on the ground that it misapprehends the relationship of education to the idea of family, and of family to the idea of children. Wrote Bonhoeffer: "The human will to reproduce can never be interpreted as a purely social, economic, religious or biological obligation." Why? Because reproduction (in the Western religious tradition) flows from marriage, and "marriage existed before the development of any of the other bonds of human society." Thus, for Bonhoeffer, the free choice of a husband or wife must be absolute. And so must the free choice on how to raise children. He objects to efforts by the state (and possibly the institutional church) "to direct and shape the coming generation." Why? Because the supposition that children of only one kind should be raised "constitutes a disastrous interference in the natural order of the world." Those who try "deliberately deprive themselves of unsuspected human forces."[25]

The idea that the unsuspected is valuable implies that we should be glad not to know in advance how the next generations will think about the moral issues that so divide us. And so we see another basic rule of civility:

> *Civility values diversity, disagreement, and the possibility of resistance, and therefore the state must not use education to try to standardize our children.*

If we really want a world full of people who will surprise us, we have yet another important reason to cherish religious diversity, for the religions, in their subversive way, have the capacity to produce people who will surprise us constantly. But the religions will not be able to do this if the state acts as arbiter of the moral vision that children should be taught. When the state decides what moral truths children should believe, it necessarily interferes with the ability of parents to raise their children to believe a different set of moral truths. Indeed, the liberal schooling model, stripped of its pluralist pretensions, seems to hope that all children in the end will come out the same.

If nobody took these theories seriously, there would be no problem. But many people do. Some very powerful polemics have been written in support of the proposition that family is no longer trusted by bureaucrats—Dana Mack's 1997 book *The Assault on Parenthood* is a particularly well-known recent entrant—and the widespread popularity of the Parental Rights Amendment is one result.

Although Dyson is no conservative, the implication of the story he tells is actually very similar. The message of his protest is surely that the judgment on how to discipline a child belongs to the parent, not the state. This does not mean that the state should countenance actual abuse of a child, but we create enormous difficulties when we presume that any use of physical force against the child is problem enough for the state to become concerned. We often hear it said that if we are to make an error, we should make the error on the side of protecting the child. This is a wonderful theory without any practical implications, other than the disruption of family life. Unless we as a society are prepared to assume that most parents are abusive (which would lead to very interesting problems of definition), I think we should err in the other direction: we should err on the side of assuming that families are loving places with the best interests of children at their hearts. Consequently, the state should intervene when the case is clear, not when the case is marginal. This approach may seem contrarian—some will no doubt think it harmful—but it is important and proper unless we think that on the whole the state is more likely than the median family to make the right child-rearing choices, including the right choice on when and how to punish. In a nation that truly believes in both civility and the family, the discretion of parents over the raising of children is a precious freedom that we must not surrender.*

DOES MARRIAGE NEED DEFENDING?

. . . .

Children matter—but children are not the only reason marriage matters. We frequently hear that children are a sacred trust, a gift from God—which indeed they are. Most parents would surely agree, which is a very good thing. One only wishes that more people would remember that our spouses—and our very marriages— are also sacred trusts, also gifts from God. We often seem to forget that children are best raised in families, so that when an adult is blessed with a child, it is not simply that child who is a trust, but the family unit—of whatever kind—within which the child is born.

From the beginning, God made no perfect families. Mine is not perfect. Yours is not perfect. Throughout the Bible, families are as messily dysfunctional as any group one might find today on a soap opera or the evening news. This is so even of the very first family, as the theologian Paula M. Cooey points out:

> As the story of the first human family, [the story of Adam and Eve] narrates human differentiation within relationship in terms of faithfulness and ultimately betrayal, in terms of both responsibility and freedom. The story . . . focuses on faithfulness to and betrayal of other creatures and God, as well as human faithfulness to and betrayal of one another.[26]

And yet, with all its flaws and failures, family always outlasts its critics: in every culture we know, in every nation that exists, family, in some form, survives and even thrives. One could scarcely want more evidence of either its functionality or its fundamentalness.

---

* People often tell me that this argument echoes the pro-choice position on abortion. That is true. That is why I often tell lecture audiences that the pro-choicers on abortion and the family values conservatives have much more in common than they may think: they simply prefer to draw the line on state intervention at different points, one to build a wall around the individual, the other to build a wall around the family. Civil dialogue and civil listening could, I think, tease out these commonalities and their implications.

To be sure, families have changed. In the United States, the past four decades have been a time of particularly remarkable and sweeping changes . . . and not all of them are what one might predict. A 1997 Gallup/*USA Today* survey tells us that in some ways the family of the late nineties resembles the mythical family of the fifties more than the family of the fifties did. For example, some 63 percent of families say grace or give thanks before they eat family meals, compared with 43 percent in 1947. (So much for the decline of religion.) In 1952 many more Americans believed that wives dominated their husbands than the other way around; today those figures are reversed. And wives are less likely today than in 1952 to be the ones who proposed marriage.[27]

But it is important not to make too much of these figures. Since the number of couples living together without marriage has skyrocketed (a fourfold increase since the 1970s) and the number of children born to unmarried women has also taken a sharp jump (to 26 percent of all births in 1995), it may be that what has shifted is the identity of people who are married. For example—and this is just speculation!—if socially conservative Christians are more likely than others to marry today, they would say grace before meals and might well believe that the husband is in charge. People who would have married and not said grace fifty years ago are perhaps today less likely to marry at all.

I mention this possibility because something is happening to discourage people from marrying. Indeed, it is ironic that the Congress overwhelmingly passed the Defense of Marriage Act, limiting the effect of same-sex marriages, which have state sanction nowhere, at a time when marriage desperately needs defense from serious threats: the threat of divorce, the threat of battering, the threat of illegitimacy, the threat of couples not bothering to marry at all. There is no government program that can solve these problems, but a renewed religious commitment in our private lives can—and may therefore be the only way to save this glorious institution on which most Americans believe the nation rests.

Many of these problems are frankly the fault of men, men who do not take seriously the responsibilities of either marriage or fatherhood. When feminists argue that we live in a world that teaches men to behave as though women exist largely for their pleasure, they have a point. The challenge is to find ways of training men to behave better. And although some religious teachings have been complicit in the oppression of women, religion nowadays has a vital role to play in helping men to understand their obligations.

Consider the organization known as Promise Keepers, which was founded by the former Colorado football coach Bill McCartney. Promise Keepers, concerned about the number of men who abandon their wives and children, holds huge rallies at which married men recommit themselves to their vows and single men vow to keep the promises they will one day make. The group offers such messages as "Any man who thinks promises were made to be broken should see what it does to his family," a line that may sound simplistic but at least places the focus where civility says it should be: on others rather than the self.

Some feminists are suspicious, bashing Promise Keepers as a group that wants to restore men to positions of control over women. But this criticism, weak on the facts to begin with, seems in any case inapt, given the magnitude of the crisis. Either the abandonment of a family by the husband and father is a problem or it is not. If it is not, then masses of unequivocal data are somehow mistaken. If it is, then Promise Keepers is doing useful work. Nothing could be simpler. If the liberal suspicion of the group rests on the fact that it preaches God's word, that is merely evidence of how far out of step with the nation some liberals have become. Most Americans believe in God and believe that God's will should be obeyed. So if a group of God-fearing men want to gather in a football stadium and vow to do what God wants—to stay with their families—everyone who thinks either God or family is important should stand and cheer.

Some critics of Promise Keepers, however, see something much more sinister at work. Pointing out that the group encourages men to resume their "natural" or "God-given" role in the family, the critics suggest that Promise Keepers is somehow keeping women in thrall. That "natural" role is seen as patriarchal, the vision of the family with the husband and father at the head.

The first problem with this criticism is that, even if true, it demeans the choices made by the 30 to 40 percent of women who each year decide to enter "traditional" marriages, in which the husband is head of the household.[28] Unless we are to become mired in the false-consciousness swamp, where nobody's choices but the self-centered critic's are genuine, we must suppose that many of these women are doing precisely what the liberal state encourages, pursuing their own visions of the good. That a critic might prefer that these women choose a different vision (and thus a different kind of marriage) is hardly reason for their husbands to abandon them.* Indeed, the creation of centers of different, resisting social meanings is a large part of what civility is about.

The second problem is that even if the critics are right, and the traditional patriarchal family is bad, it hardly follows that a family that consists of a woman raising children on her own is better. It may be worse, at least for the children—which is certainly what the data suggest. The point is not that no woman can raise children alone, for many children raised by single or divorced mothers will thrive, but that, in aggregate, children raised by a lone parent are worse off than those raised by two on almost every social yardstick we possess.[29] Which means that there *is* a crisis, and everybody who cares about children should be grateful for help.

Does this mean that the student of civility must conclude that husbands and wives should not be too quick to divorce? Of course. One of the many reasons that adultery violates the norm of civility is precisely that one spouse allows himself or herself to be led astray by desire rather than duty—as though the marriage vow, which usually includes a rather explicit promise of fidelity, is a triviality. The husband and wife have a duty to love each other because of

---

* Some feminist critics of the traditional family have proposed using the tax code to give women incentives *not* to become homemakers—that is, to punish them for choosing to spend full time raising their children—evidently on the theory that the government should give them a push out of the home. Certainly it would be immoral to create official barriers to the choice of women to enter the paid workforce. But it is just as immoral to create official barriers to the choice of women not to.

Others have argued for some sort of vouchers, paying women and men alike to stay at home with their children. Although I quite understand the theory behind this idea, I fear that it would further weaken the already sagging barriers between the sphere of family and sphere of commerce, because it seems to accept the scary market vision that caring for children is not a worthwhile activity unless it is remunerated. Moreover, it suggests that spending time in the raising of children is a sacrifice, and perhaps one not really worth undertaking if there is no money involved. When everything in the world carries a price tag, nothing in the world is priceless.

their circumstance—the fact of their marriage—and the vow that underlies it. The duty is not lessened because one of them falls in love with somebody else.[30]

When civility is conceived as involving moral duties rather than mere rules of etiquette, we can understand the family as requiring the deepest and most profound duties of respect: not only does the mother owe the child, but the father does too, and the spouses owe each other. This last point bears particular emphasis. In the mysterious and depressing American view of the family, married couples owe each other love only as long as they actually feel the emotion itself. The very old answer that Christian theology offers is that love is an activity, not a feeling, and the obligation to do love is wholly independent of the happenstance of whether one feels love. And so we see another example of how the teachings of traditional religion can help guide our decisions away from the path of mere desire and toward the path of civility.

14

. . . .

Uncivil Religion

RELIGION, religion! We may exalt it or vilify it, we may be comforted by it or irritated by it, we may seek it out or flee from it, but the one thing we seem unable to do, in a society we often describe as secular, is escape from it. The United States offers as fabulous a religious diversity as any nation on earth. Ours is not a Christian nation in the strong sense in which some conservative activists seem to think it should be, and, in all likelihood, we never were.[1] But we also do not have the religion-free public life for which some liberal activists yearn. As the historian Richard Lovelace has pointed out, "[a]ny political landscape with this much God-talk going on may be divided, but it is religiously alive."[2] Although religiosity is notoriously difficult to measure, the one thing that seems pretty clear is that Americans possess an awful lot of it.[3] Religion is at the heart of America, and no amount of academic or journalistic wishing will make it go away.

Unfortunately, there is a growing perception (at least in elite journalistic and academic circles) that religion is the enemy of civility, that religious activism is a danger to our politics, and that the language of religion is either irrelevant or harmful to the rest of social life. For example, the literary theorist Stanley Fish, in the article I mentioned in chapter 2, argues that the reason we cannot all "just get along" in America is precisely our religious diversity. According to Fish, the trouble with religious citizens is that, far from wanting to participate with fellow citizens in the marketplace of ideas, they necessarily want to shut it down. In this, Fish and others who claim that religion is an obstacle to civility echo the famous line from Rousseau on the dangers of religion in the civic space: "[O]ne cannot live in peace with people one regards as damned."[4] Some would go so far as to say that religion should therefore not even be a part of our public deliberations, the civil conversation I have been advocating.

In this chapter, I will explain why arguments of this kind represent a misreading of both American history and constitutional law—to say nothing of a misunderstanding of religion itself. Yet, there are ways in which religion, sincerely held, *is* a threat to some understandings of civility. Paradoxically, the student of civility should cherish these aspects of religion because, without them, we would have no democracy worth speaking of.

RELIGION'S BOGUS DANGERS

. . . .

Let us begin with a simple concession: religionists are capable of just as much incivility—just as much nastiness and contempt—as their secular counterparts. Consider the pro-life side in the abortion battle. The pro-life movement is dominated by devout Christians, and yet many pro-life activists behave and speak in ways that are decidedly uncivil. Some who have committed acts of terror have claimed to be doing so in God's name. So it is important to confess that religious belief alone does not provide an inoculation against incivility. Religious people of all faiths and all political stripes engage in demonizing of those who disagree with them, even though they are nearly all members of traditions that command them not to. But, as a Christian, I have special confessing to do, for my co-religionists are frequently uncivil.

Christians, who understand God as stern but ultimately loving, should have a civility advantage over most people: the command to love the neighbor is so unequivocal that it should lead Christians to approach others with a sense of awe in this fresh aspect of God's creation. As a Christian, I would like this to be true. But it too often isn't. So we witness, for instance, the Reverend Jerry Falwell relentlessly trumpeting ridiculous charges that President Clinton arranged murders when he was governor of Arkansas. Or the booing of Democratic Party head David Wilhelm when, addressing the Christian Coalition, he issued a call for greater civility. Or the death threats received by the evangelist Louis Palau after he reminded his radio audience that their obligation to pray for the leaders of their country certainly includes the President of the United States.

The media, biases ever to the fore, tend to focus on these conservative misdeeds. But liberal religious leaders fare no better on the issue of awe. A pro-life friend of mine, a member of the United Church of Christ, was advised by her pastor that, because of her views on abortion, she should think about joining another church. Or take the case of John Shelby Spong, a bishop of my own Episcopal Church, who is quite sure that most other Christians have misread the Bible, overlooking, for example, the point that Mary, far from being a virgin who gave miraculous birth, might have been a teenaged rape victim.[5] Disagree with him? Think just maybe the Bible is true? According to Spong, this might make you a "fundamentalist" who has to "park your brain at the door of the church."[6]

I do not mean to suggest that most religious believers are uncivil, and I wish the media would cover more of those who are not. (An example: The tennis star Michael Chang gets virtually no news coverage for his regular prayers, respect for his opponents, and Christian lifestyle, whereas players who run their mouths constantly are featured prominently. Why is Chang not a story? Writes one journalist, with unusual frankness, "Simply put, Jesus isn't good copy."[7]) Nor do I mean to suggest that the religious, as a group, are less civil than the nonreligious. Still, so many prominent religionists are uncivil that the student of civility must concede that a belief in one's possession of the truth can lead to a disrespect for fellow citizens who disagree. This is the point of Rousseau's infamous observation that it is difficult to live in peace with people one regards as damned. I do not think Rousseau was wrong so much as underinclusive: it is hardly the religious alone who have trouble living in peace with those who are on the wrong side of truth. Too often, it seems to be all of us, religious or secular, who are ready to consign those who take positions different from our own to the inner circles of Hell. After all, it is a lot easier than trying to convince them . . . or letting them try to convince us.

This brings us to the concerns raised by Stanley Fish and others on the potential dangers religion poses to civility. The critics are of the view that religions, by nature, encourage incivility. The arguments are of two kinds: appeals to the damage religion has done in history and appeals to the special characteristics of religion that make it unfit for public debate. Let us consider each in turn.

A remarkable number of theorists support a strict separation of religion from politics that has never been the American tradition, and they do so on the basis of historical claims that seem shaky at best. For example, Kathleen Sullivan of Stanford Law School warns, with what I take to be a straight face, that in the absence of a strict separation, the United States might wind up looking like Bosnia or Lebanon.[8] In other words, the reason to prohibit establishments of religion is that otherwise the various religious groups would go to war with each other. But is this true? Many (by some measures most) nations of the world have established state-supported churches, but few of them have lately rejoiced in religious warfare. As the political scientist Samuel Huntington has pointed out, the bitter ethnic and religious conflicts around the globe have stemmed not from efforts to acknowledge and mediate deep differences but from efforts to suppress them.[9]

A second form of the historical argument focuses on the many people who have died in religious wars. But the statement that wars have been fought in the name of God is a non sequitur. As the theologian Walter Wink once pointed out, more people have died in the twentieth century's secular wars than in the preceding *fifty centuries* of fighting combined.[10] In this century, neither Stalin nor Hitler nor Mao needed a religious justification to act—in fact, they spoke in glowing terms of freedom and justice—and yet the three of them were responsible for the deaths of close to one hundred million people. No religious war in history, not all the religious wars of history added together, did as much damage as this century's wars of nationalism and ideology. So if we are to ban religious sentiment from public life because it has been responsible for so much horror, let us not forget to ban advocacy of freedom or justice as well.*

---

* One might answer that a Stalin, for example, did not really believe in justice but only used the term for his ends. What this objection really says is that Stalin did not mean by justice what we mean by justice. Similarly, I suppose that what the Crusades meant by Christianity we do not mean by Christianity.

A further point. Although there have been eras in history when religious leaders commanded armies, by as early as the Middle Ages the princes commanded the armies, and if they sought blessings from God for their warlike endeavors, the endeavors themselves were nevertheless wars by states, or near-states, for reasons of state. Even the Crusades were, for the princes, about resources and markets, not about spreading the faith. (Nobody tried to convert the conquered Moslems.)[11] In any event, since the temporal power of the organized church was shaken by the rise of the nation-state, it has been nations, exclusively, that have made war. So, if religion is dangerous because it has led to so many wars, the nation-state, which has led to many more wars, is even more dangerous. Consequently, theorists who want to bar religion on this ground should be equally ready to dismantle the state—and if they are not, it seems perfectly fair to accuse them of hypocrisy.

The second common academic argument against the participation of religion in public life is that aspects of religion itself make it an obstacle to civility. Some dislike what might be perceived as religion's politics: that is, religion is seen, rightly or wrongly, as presenting an essentially conservative political agenda.[12] This argument has been pressed with particular force by feminist interpreters who contend that the Bible of the Jewish and Christian traditions is often used to further the oppression of women.[13] But, quite apart from the fact that the Judeo-Christian tradition can be, and often is, interpreted to carry the seeds of women's equality, it seems rather a weak and uncivil argument to propose banning a position from public argument on the ground that you disagree with it.

The more interesting point (and the one advanced by Fish) is that religion itself, whatever its politics, possesses features that make it a poor participant in public debate. As set forth by Fish, these features boil down to three: religion is intolerant of disagreement; all it wants is to win; and it is not open to rational debate. The first two prongs of the argument—the alleged intolerance and the desire for victory—need not long detain us, because they are characteristic of every interest group that rushes to politics to obtain the benefits its members want. I am not conceding that religions necessarily possess those traits; but, even if they do, that is no more a reason to ban religion from public debate than it is a reason to ban Planned Parenthood, the American Association of Retired Persons, or the National Rifle Association.

Consequently, the claim of a special problem with religion must rest on the notion that religionists are not open to rational persuasion. Many theorists believe exactly that. The legal philosopher Thomas Nagel, for example, sees religion as too dogmatic to be a proper participant in public debate, a debate that requires justifications that all can accept.[14] Worse, this irrationality supposedly leads to undemocratic results. Thus, Amy Gutmann, arguing against parental control of the education of children, insists that many religious parents teach their children "disrespect for people who are different."[15] But Gutmann offers no evidence to support her stereotyping, and Nagel does not successfully distinguish religious dogma from the dogmas of any interest group that refuses to listen to the reason of its opponents. Besides, in a nation where most citizens claim to be greatly influenced by their religious beliefs, it is a peculiarly undemocratic (and uncivil) task to try to construct public dialogues from which the language most people find most comfortable and comforting is forbidden.[16]

Or it may be that religionists are thought to be irrational in the sense that they are under orders, that when a religious leader commands them to march—or to vote—they will, without further reflection, do so. It is difficult to imagine, however, that anybody can believe this any longer, especially after the work of Sydney Ahlstrom and Nathan Hatch on the democratization of religion in American history.[17] The dissenting tradition runs deep in the American religious psyche and has plainly invaded even religions (like Catholicism) that strike outsiders as purely hierarchical.[18]

But I do not want to press the point too far, because I actually wish the critics were right. I wish the religiously faithful were more of a problem for America. I wish religious people would spend more time judging America's values according to their beliefs, and less time judging their beliefs by America's values. (Martin Luther King, fortunately, got the equation right—at a time when America's values were very different from God's.) I wish religionists would more often adopt in public debate an epistemology that liberalism would find troubling, an understanding that both begins and ends with faith in a transcendent God. This, of course, would give Nagel and other theorists something to worry about. But there is little evidence that it happens very often. On the contrary, no matter how little the secular side of society may want to accommodate itself to the religious, the religious side of society continually and somewhat pitifully accommodates itself to the secular. Religions are constantly apologizing for their religiosity, and they take desperate measures to show that their tenets are after all consistent with liberal theory. The desperation is a sign of the loss of religious confidence—and, in the absence of that confidence, religions can hardly afford the kind of irrationality that Nagel suggests is the rule.[19]

This is not to say that nobody who is religious is capable of the nasty dismissal of others that marks American political life. But the claim that religious people are more likely than others to behave this way is an empirical claim—and so far, no evidence but a handful of antireligious stereotypes has been introduced to show that it is true.

PROSELYTIZING

. . . .

And yet there are aspects of America's religiosity that do present challenges to civility. Perhaps the most obvious is that many religions try to persuade others to join. Why should this be troubling to the student of civility? The reason, as the sociologist Nancy Ammerman has pointed out, is that efforts to proselytize, by their nature, tend to breach the very barriers that civility tries to enforce.[20] Civility, the reader will recall from chapter 4, sometimes requires us to leave other people alone, which suggests that *not* spreading our message when we would like to do it is one of the sacrifices we make for others. Indeed, to press our message where it is not wanted can violate the privacy of others, and privacy, as we have seen, is a concept at the very heart of civility.

But once you decide that it is time to get the message out, gaining an audience often requires that you begin by addressing unwilling listeners. There is little point, says the old adage, in preaching to the choir. You must preach to those you want to reach. The process is the same whether you are electioneering, collecting for charity, or gathering signatures on a petition . . . or trying to persuade others that you possess a religious truth that they lack. It is small wonder that so much evangelizing is attempted in busy airports: to paraphrase the bank robber Willie Sutton, that's where the people are.

Not every religious tradition requires efforts to convert others. Judaism, for example, does not. Christianity does. The Gospel instruction is seen by most Christians as quite unequivocal.[21] One of the tragedies of contemporary Christianity is that so many believers seem more embarrassed by than proud of their faith. But millions of Christians wear their faith in Jesus Christ proudly, and they spend many a waking hour witnessing to others, in the hope that they too will join the flock. Sometimes this work carries a special symbolism of hope and redemption, as when white evangelicals witness across racial barriers. Sometimes it is irritating, as when believers arrest our progress through airports or along sidewalks. And sometimes (Ammerman's central concern) it raises the most profound questions of history and conscience, as in Christian efforts to convert Jews.

The image of Christians proselytizing Jews raises an issue that many Christians prefer not to confront. Much of Christian history has involved efforts to eradicate Judaism, one way or another, from the face of the earth. The centuries of preaching against Jews as "Christ killers" took a bloody toll—without regard to where one stands on the issue of Christian responsibility for the Holocaust. Although the last two decades have seen a significant thaw, Christian history, like American history, has been almost unrelentingly anti-Semitic.[22] So no matter how loving Christians might believe their message to be, one can hardly be surprised when Jews view Christian efforts at proselytizing as essentially hostile.

My own view—not universally shared among Christians, I know—is that trying to convert Jews is a theological error, because Christ did not disturb the special covenantal relationship between God and the Jewish people. (See, for example, Romans 11:26–29.)[23] For those who disagree, who believe that the Gospel message is universal in the sense that nobody who does not accept it will be saved, it would plainly be unloving—uncivil—not to propagate it.

Integrity would permit nothing else. And the same is true for every other religion whose adherents accost strangers in an effort to win converts. Doubtless these efforts are irritating, and at times they may be frightening. Nevertheless, as Martin Marty has argued, those who would proselytize (and maybe the rest of us as well) should give thanks for the fact of living in a society so secure that it is able to protect both their freedom to try to convince others and the freedom of others to refuse to be convinced.[24]

But there is another, rarely mentioned sense in which proselytizing poses a risk to civility. If a sacrificial civility tries to knit us into a single people, the civil religion—the public, vaguely patriotic, non-theological religious observances in which political candidates glory—can play an important role. But, as the theologian (and sometime president of Rice University) George Rupp has pointed out, religions like Christianity, Islam, and Buddhism, because they make universalist claims, are different: "Unlike civil religion, appeals to the absolute authority of religious experience or revealed truth have no intrinsic or necessary relationship to a single society or nation."[25] In other words, the very missionary spirit that leads believers to spread the message can also lead them to ignore the idea of nationhood that helps give civility its meaning. But that, too, is a risk that a free society should embrace.

RELIGION, POLITICS, AND CIVILITY

. . . .

We often hear it said that religion, quite apart from any deficiencies it might have, is a private matter, not a public one, and for that reason should be forever separate from politics. We hear these words recited, for example, whenever religious people offer religious reasons for limits on abortion. (We did not hear them when the Catholic bishops called for a more equitable sharing of the nation's wealth or a ban on nuclear weapons.) But nothing in the Constitution or our history suggests that excluding religious voices from our public debates is actually a good idea. Democratic politics without the active participation of the religious voice is a politics without the source of social meaning to which most Americans say they turn. We do not demonstrate the value of religion by rendering it invisible, because the public space we then create is oddly illiberal and intolerant, perhaps totalitarian: a state that tells people what they may value and what they may not.

The student of civility must begin to worry whenever dialogue is deadened by removing from the conversation potential sources of dissent. In a democratic polity, religions serve the important societal function of resistance: standing up for the possibility that life itself has different meanings than those the dominant culture tries to create. This function of religions, says the theologian David Tracy, accounts for their subversive nature.[26] For that matter, in its own backhanded way, the Supreme Court appears to agree. In 1879, in explaining why the Mormon religious belief in polygamy was insufficient to shield Mormons who married multiple wives from prosecution, the justices referred to the Mormons as "subversive of good order"[27]—meaning that their insistence on living a moral understanding different from that of the mainstream threatened the orderly day-to-day operation of the society.[28]

Although I think the Court made a legal mistake in giving insufficient weight to the claims that religion makes on the conscience, I think the Court's social analysis was precisely on point: religions *are* often subversive of good order. The true believer often *will* act in ways that others consider bizarre or even immoral. Such activity *does* threaten to unweave the fabric of the society.[29] Indeed, I often think that it is this very subversive nature that leads to the suspicion about religion that even today is too often seen in liberal politics.[30] Nobody much likes subversives, of course, which is one reason that religions are so often slapped down by legislatures and courts alike—and why the power of faith is often needed to help them to stand back up.

When religious believers do stand up, they often mark themselves as different from everybody else. And if they take their religion seriously, religious believers *are* different from everybody else.[31] The religionist should place faith in God ahead of faith in fallible human institutions, and often slights his own religion when he tries too hard to conform. And the effort to conform—to show that religion does not truly affect who we are—is nowadays all too common. One saw this, for example, in the 1980s when the

Roman Catholic bishops' call for a more equitable sharing of the nation's wealth was answered by a group of lay Roman Catholics who issued their own dissenting document arguing that capitalism is morally neutral and its inequalities economically inevitable.

Yet religionists are truest to themselves, and to the nation's traditions, when they refuse to conform their behavior and attitudes to the expectations of others. And the student of civility appreciates this point:

> *Religions do their greatest service to civility when they preach not only love of neighbor but resistance to wrong.*

Preaching of this kind helps give the religious believer the strength to be different, in the small as well as the large. When the Amish refuse to use modern equipment of any kind, or Orthodox Jews refuse to engage in any of the categories of proscribed work on the Sabbath, they are not simply insisting on the right to practice their religion; they are proclaiming their differences through their conduct, and doing so in a symbolic voice far too loud to ignore. And so they behave subversively, insisting on behaving as God commands rather than abandoning God's will to follow secular trend.

This subversive behavior might strike the reader as uncivil: have I not argued from the beginning that civility requires us to discipline our desires for the sake of living in community with others? How is the Islamic student demanding to be excused from class in order to pray different from the student described in chapter 4 who does not want to be excused but does want to wear droopy pants?

The difference is sufficiently profound that it is difficult to describe. One is reminded of Søren Kierkegaard's admonition to Christians never to defend their faith, lest they reduce it to the status of a thing that needs their defense. A divine call is an injunction, not a desire, and although the choice to obey it remains just that, a choice, the choice to follow God is not the same as the choice to follow a whim. The centrality of religion in our history and in the public mind today refutes any claim of sameness. The fact that religion is specially protected in the Constitution—that it is, indeed, the first subject of the First Amendment—is simply further evidence that the need for the religionist to behave differently from others has always been a cherished part of our traditions.

There is another difference, a vital one. Religion is not like any other human activity. Religion proposes a transcendence, the existence of a greater reality. Religion stretches the soul in a direction that nothing else does—the direction of considering the purpose of human existence. In particular, the Western religious traditions, by positing that we have been created by God, propose that our lives belong to God, not to ourselves. This understanding in turn generates propositions about what we should and should not value. If believers accept what their religions teach about what to value, it changes who they are. Of particular concern to the student of civility, it strengthens the believer's resistance to the values of politics and the market that are sweeping all else before them. Although a variety of philosophies and ideologies might try to do the same job, capitalism tends to subvert them; they lack the sheer staying power of religions that have survived for centuries—or millennia. And religions, because they emphasize the eternal and the transcendent, propose the relative unimportance of (for example) fame or wealth. The Western religions, by preaching love of neighbor, offer a realistic possibility of creating new and different people who can rescue us yet—that is, who can rescue us if they turn out to be consumers and voters who have not internalized the self-seeking so characteristic of our age.

Often the willingness of the religious to be subversive in the face of official and unofficial pressures has made the nation better. The abolitionist and civil rights movements, both of which were openly and proudly religious, provide strong evidence, if any is needed, for the importance of these religious institutions that subvert the established meanings of the society. Had the nation been persuaded in the 1850s or the 1960s by the argument that religious dissenters are so dangerous that they must be suppressed, two glorious and redemptive chapters in the nation's history might never have been written.

Today's strict separationists would prefer not to consider this history, but it is there nevertheless. In the years before the Civil War, defenders of slavery often accused abolitionist preachers of improperly mixing politics and the pulpit. A decisive answer came from one O. T. Lanphear, the antislavery pastor of High Street

Church in Lowell, Massachusetts, in the course of an 1856 sermon on the abolitionists' favorite New Testament verse: the unequivocal command to love our neighbors.

Lanphear railed against "any third or fifth rate civilian" who chose "to blame the pulpit for being an agitator because it cries out against oppression." Reminding the world of its moral errors, Lanphear argued, is exactly what the church is for:

> Shall the pulpit therefore betray its high trust by refusing to point out the connection between politics and theological truth? Shall it cringe and accept the tame and servile position which the Douglases of our time are pleased to propose?[32]

The reference to Douglas was, of course, to Stephen Douglas, the Illinois congressman who had argued that antislavery preachers should stop trying to enforce their own morality on everybody else. And the reference to tameness and servility is, even now, very much to the point. The advocate of religious freedom can never accept the idea that the separation of church and state implies an elevation of the state above the church.

RELIGIOUS FREEDOM

. . . .

So the student of civility, hoping to prevent the state from swamping the church, will naturally be an advocate of a robust religious freedom, the creation of a sphere where citizens are free to practice their diverse faiths without official interference. Of course, in principle, everybody is in favor of religious freedom. It is only the specifics that get us confused. The particular form of religious freedom that the student of civility will necessarily support is religious autonomy.

When I say *autonomy*, I have in mind a space in which to behave as though one is truly private, that is, unregulated. This may seem an odd formulation. But it actually makes sense. We talk a great deal nowadays about the right to privacy in a variety of contexts, but we hardly ever really mean it—not in the traditional sense, the right to be left alone and even undiscovered.[33] Modern America simply leaves us too little private space. But autonomy is the functional equivalent of privacy. A respect for autonomy allows people and institutions, in certain settings, to behave in ways that people *do* notice, and yet with which people are unable to interfere.

To take the most obvious example, given our subject, the right to worship God freely in whatever way I choose is part of my autonomy. We might say, colloquially, that it is part of my privacy, but that is a misuse of the word, because we do not require that those whose mode of worship may be unfamiliar or unpopular keep it to themselves in order to enjoy the protection of our political and constitutional traditions. A Sikh who wears his turban, an Orthodox Jew who wears his tallith and his yarmulke, the Catholic who wears ashes on her forehead on the first day of Lent, all are exercising an autonomy that cannot be violated, even though everybody sees them do it. Similarly, a religious institution's right of autonomy does not depend principally on whether anybody (including its members) is affected by its "private" actions, still less on whether anybody happens to approve of them. The autonomy is a matter of fundamental right.

This autonomy may sometimes lead to the violation of laws that others willingly obey. The Supreme Court has lately been hostile to this vision of religious autonomy, rejecting, for example, the request by a Muslim prisoner to attend services required by his faith but not held in the maximum-security wing of the prison where he was incarcerated—even though Christian inmates in the wing had all their religious needs met.[34] The Court's position has been that the Free Exercise Clause protects only against intentional discrimination by the state against a religion,[35] an interpretation that renders the clause a superfluity in light of the Equal Protection Clause. This line of cases has reduced the Free Exercise Clause from a guarantee of autonomy, with the robust religious pluralism that the term implies, to a guarantee that the religious may believe what they like as long as they do not try to do anything about it—a secularized version of nineteenth-century Protestantism, masquerading as constitutional principle.

The student of civility must rigorously defend this autonomous space—for religious institutions as much as for religious individuals—even when the courts do not. In the law, such a space is known as an *accommodation* of religion—allowing religious people and institutions, because of their beliefs, to do things that other people and entities may not. For example, when an Orthodox Jew seeks to wear a yarmulke while serving in military uniform—an act that would otherwise be a violation of regulations—he is asking for an accommodation.[36] The theory behind granting accommodations is that they are required by the First Amendment, that without them, religions that lack the political clout to protect themselves in the legislative process would, over time, disappear. Why? Because the state would adopt regulatory laws without considering the religion's interests.

Nobody argues that accommodations should always be granted. The test most popular among accommodationist scholars is that when defiance of a law is religiously motivated, the state may enforce it against the religionist only by demonstrating that the law is narrowly tailored to serve a compelling interest. In theory, this is a sensible test. In practice, it has all the well-known flaws of balancing tests: it is relatively standardless, and so the outcomes of concrete cases are not predictable. The Congress tried to force the courts to apply the compelling interest test by adopting the Religious Freedom Restoration Act in 1993, and the Supreme Court four years later held it unconstitutional on that very ground—that the legislature cannot tell the courts how to decide cases.

Consider a concrete example, a lawsuit that Georgetown University lost. The suit was aimed at forcing the school to grant official recognition of an organization of gay students. The denial was challenged under the District of Columbia's human rights law, which forbids discrimination on the basis of sexual orientation. Georgetown, a Catholic school, argued that because homosexual conduct is considered sinful by the Catholic Church, the school's religious freedom protected it from suit. Because civility requires the protection of spaces within which to develop dissenting values, this argument has obvious appeal. But the student of civility might protest that antidiscrimination laws are special, because they are aimed at forcing us to do precisely what discrimination denies, to see and be awed by the presence of God in those who are very different from us. This, too, is a strong argument, and that is why the equities of the Georgetown case are so balanced.

The Georgetown case, like so many tough cases, presents a clash of rights, not of wrongs—that is, there is something of the side of the angels in each of the competing positions. It involves two different kinds of civility: welcoming the stranger, whether we want to or not, and deferring to religion as the place where new social meanings are created, whether we want to or not. What religious freedom requires in such a case is that we take care that the secular zeal for civility of the first kind does not eradicate the ability of religion to do the second.

.　.　.　.　.　.　.　.　.　.　.　.　.　.

The alternative meanings presented by a religion can help the religious believer decide what it is that God believes is right, but the answer to that question cannot, by itself, determine when the believer should enlist the power of the state to enforce that decision on others. To answer "never" is to slight the achievements of the abolitionists, who not only enlisted the state in aid of their religious campaign but finally provoked a war, and of the civil rights movement, which inspired an uncertain nation to enact a set of terribly coercive but utterly just laws against racial discrimination. To answer "always" is to miss the lessons that Kierkegaard drew from the ascent of Christendom—that the church that merges its identity with the state loses its best self, for it can no longer fashion separate dissenting meanings for believers. This last danger is particularly acute in a country like the United States, where most citizens identify themselves as Christians. How the student of civility who happens to be a Christian avoids this particular pitfall is the subject of the next chapter.

15
· · · · · · · · · · · · ·
Civility and the Challenge
of Christendom

C HRISTIANS in America often think of themselves as the norm and others as the variants from it, but this is both an empirical and a theological error. It is an empirical error because the percentage of Americans who describe themselves as Christians has been falling steadily in recent decades. Some of the loss comes because other religious traditions have gained, but much of it comes because more and more Americans describe themselves as not particularly religious.

It is a theological error because Christians are not supposed to be just like everybody else. As John Murray Cuddihy pointed out twenty years ago, if by civility we mean inoffensiveness, it would be a grievous wrong for Christians to be civil.[1] Christians live in a tradition whose teachings on subjects from sexuality to wealth to war might make the secular world uncomfortable, but if Christians believe the teachings of the faith to be correct, it would be bizarre not to share them. We do no justice to our faith, and show little respect for our fellow citizens, by muting our voices so that others will not be offended. (Nothing in this argument turns on what one thinks traditional Christian teachings actually are.)

I do not take Cuddihy to mean that Christians should strive for active incivility in dialogue, that Christians should ignore the admonition to love the neighbor. I think he means—or at least I want him to mean—that Christians should not be reluctant to stir things up. Christians should never see themselves as servants of the

265

secular order. They should not feel the need to apologize for their convictions and should avoid becoming the captive army of a political party. They should not allow themselves to be domesticated and thus should not be tricked into conversations about whether one can be a good Christian and also believe in liberal democracy. The entire point of being a committed Christian is that nothing else is of comparable importance; that is, there is no other standard but the will of God by which Christians should be prepared to judge themselves. This, then, is another sense in which Christians should be subversive, endlessly and creatively and energetically subversive, of the existing order, whether that existing order calls itself liberal, conservative, or even Christian. Christians should follow the lead of Robert McAfee Brown, who observed during the Vietnam War that "the minute we Christians begin to sound just like everyone else, we've lost the ball game."[2] Unfortunately, we Christians too often take the opposite position: so determined are we to fit in that we try to pretend that our faith makes us like everybody else—or that everybody else should be just like us. And therein lie any number of challenges.[3]

THE CHRISTIAN NATION

. . . .

The first challenge that the Christianness of the American majority poses to civility is reflected in the intermittent effort to proclaim America a "Christian nation." Some groups that use the phrase—principally those affiliated with the Reconstructionist movement—are quite serious about establishing a Christian theocracy in the United States. But the term *Christian nation* has become a lively part of the political language, slipping into the speeches of politicians and activists who scarcely seem to know what they are saying. The phrase may be meant as a description of an admirable source of ethics, but it promises, in practice, to work a sharp religious discrimination. When one religion is made suddenly official, others just as suddenly exist by sufferance of the true American faith. That is not genuine religious freedom.

I do not mean to suggest that no nation with an established

church can be civil: most countries in the world have an official church or at least government support of religion, and we do not seem ready to cut off relations with any of them on the ground that a connection between church and state is a violation of fundamental human rights. No matter how many philosophers assert the contrary, I suspect that our fervent anti-establishment sentiment is more a historical accident than the outcome of any careful process of reasoning. The sentiment is surely a product of our national circumstance—the nature of our founding and the nature of the welcome we have traditionally proclaimed to the world. Nevertheless, we are lucky that the accident happened.

Americans have always guarded jealously the ability to worship freely. The framers were mostly Christians, and they believed themselves guided by God, but they did not establish the United States as a Christian nation in any strongly theological sense. As the historian Jon Butler has shown, the idea that the United States is, or should be, or ever was a Christian nation actually stems only from the middle of the nineteenth century.[4] This is not to say that most Americans were not Christians before that—they always have been and certainly will be for many years to come, perhaps as long as the nation endures—but rather that the nation seemed to lack a consciousness of itself as distinctively Christian. The Christian nation movement was in large measure a response to immigration, which many American Protestants saw as bringing un-American religions (by which they meant Roman Catholicism and Judaism) to the nation's shores. If you travel the nation's backroads—or just travel the Web—you quickly find that there are many Americans who believe this still.

A nation in which most citizens identify themselves as Christians must be especially careful to avoid any suggestion that this majority sentiment justifies an official endorsement of Christian revelation. Religious freedom is a part of the foundation of the republic, and to cast it aside, even through inadvertence, is to make a radical and very uncivil break with our nation's difficult but ultimately admirable history. The United States of America is a deeply religious nation, but we are, I hope proudly, a religiously diverse nation too. When we proclaim an official religion, we pressure the American people to follow that approved route to God—

which has the uncivil effect of reducing the ability of the religions to create alternative centers of meaning, the basis of democratic resistance to the values of the dominant culture.

At the same time, precisely because so many Americans call themselves Christians, the Christian churches must be careful not to become fat and lazy. They must not stop struggling to live according to the will of God rather than the will of man, and they must not stop trying to persuade others (by word and example) of the truth and value of their faith. Christians must also struggle not to let their faith become the creature of the majority—or of the government. If Christian churches gain secular power, they lose the glorious and redemptive power of resistance: they cannot stand outside the dominant culture, offering moral criticism of its excesses and its failures, if instead they *are* the dominant culture. Fortunately—as so often in American history—the famous sectarianism of American Christianity helps defeat the project of creating a national religion. Four out of five Americans may claim to be Christians, but the notion that four out of five Americans agree on very much theology is laughable. (There are plenty of self-described Christians who even doubt the divinity of Christ.) The nation's sharp diversity of Christian opinion has helped preserve our tradition of protecting religious freedom by removing most of the temptation to impose religious worship by secular fiat.

This does not mean that every proposal to give any aid to religious activity is a threat to these traditions. For example, government assistance to religiously run social welfare organizations should be perfectly acceptable as a constitutional matter, despite some grumbling from strict separationists who seem to think that religious freedom requires treating religious organizations worse than others.[5] Indeed, I do not believe that there is even a constitutional problem with vouchers to aid parents who wish to send their children to private religious schools. In both cases, to deny aid to religious groups when secular groups can get it strikes me as a form of antireligious discrimination. This is not to say that parents, or religious groups, should *accept* government assistance; the potential for dependency should be scary to anybody who believes that freedom requires independence. But certainly there is nothing in our nation's traditions, and nothing in the nature of civility, that forbids it.

THE PROBLEM OF CHRISTMAS

. . . .

But what about the Christmas tradition, which permeates the culture every December? Does it represent an endorsement of a particular religious tradition? Is it civil? Uncivil? Is it an inseparable part of American history and culuture, or a backdoor effort to enforce a vision of Christian nationhood? Let us take a moment and think it through.

When I was a public school child in the 1960s, the Christmas pageant was simply another part of the school year. We thought nothing of it. We sang religious Christmas songs, we sang secular Christmas songs, and, at the end, the three kings always made an appearance onstage. It was great fun for us Christian kids—but how painful it must have been for children of other faiths. There were, as I recall, only a couple of Jewish children at my elementary school, and I am pretty sure they did not opt out of the festivities, but I wonder, now, what must have gone through their minds (and their parents' minds) as they stood alongside the rest of us to sing "We Three Kings of Orient Are" and "Silent Night." I think how I as a parent would feel if my children attended a school that insisted on a joyful celebration of a single religious holiday that commemorated nothing I wanted them to believe: I would be simply furious.

Moved by these concerns, many public schools in recent years have tried to compromise, either by holding a Christmas pageant but eliminating specifically religious music—"Santa Claus Is Coming to Town" replaces "We Three Kings of Orient Are"—or by holding what they call a winter pageant, and including seasonal music and stories from several different cultural and religious traditions. So now, when I talk to audiences about religion and the public schools, I encounter Christian parents who do not care whether there is prayer in the classroom but do want to hear their children sing "O, Little Town of Bethlehem" in the Christmas pageant. And I encounter Jewish parents who are irritated that the schools celebrate Christmas at all.

Yet both of these compromises are both civil and sensible—and much more complicated than they may first appear. It is in the nature of a compromise that nobody is fully satisfied. Consider the

Supreme Court's all-too-brief effort to find compromise on the question of whether a crèche—a nativity scene—may be erected on public land. The Court originally held that a crèche was allowable on public land if erected with private funds. This rule steered a middle way between pro-crèche forces (who thought public support of a crèche just fine) and anti-crèche forces (who thought a crèche, no matter who paid for it, should not be on public land). It left neither side quite satisfied, but both sides appeared willing to live with it. And then, without warning, the justices decided that a crèche was allowable as long as it existed in a setting that did not constitute an endorsement of the religious aspects of the Christmas holiday—evidently meaning that Santa and his reindeer stood alongside the baby Jesus and His family.[6]

Critics have forcefully questioned this "endorsement" test. Michael Paulsen argues that "it is no test at all, but merely a label for the judge's largely subjective impressions."[7] Mark Tushnet has asked how judges who are Christians will be able to tell whether a display endorses Christianity.[8] And some critics think the problem was the original compromise. Thus, Jonathan Sarna has questioned whether the state should be allowed to engage in any official notice of Christmas at all, whether obviously religious or arguably secular. Says Sarna: "None of the justices really came to grips with the fact that Christmas alone of all national holidays celebrates a religious event that many Americans do not recognize."[9]

But this fact is not quite a fact. For me as a Christian, the Christmas that I celebrate with my family is undeniably religious. But Christmas, for better or worse, is also a secular event, one that nearly all Americans, including the great majority of Americans who are not Christians, also recognize. In fact, Christmas is celebrated by 96 percent of Americans.[10] This figure is usefully compared to the roughly 80 percent who describe themselves as Christians, a figure that, as sociologists of religion tirelessly remind us, includes millions who may have some Christian heritage but are not observant in any measurable sense.

The religious Christmas that Christians observe is a celebration of the nativity of Jesus Christ, who is, Christians believe, the Son of God and the Savior of all humanity. Although many Christians traditionally exchanged token gifts at the time, as symbols of joy at

Christ's birth, it was the retail trade—not the churches—that began, during the nineteenth century, to transform the holiday into an occasion for national giving. The decision to borrow the story of Saint Nicholas (which was not a Christmas story) and transform him into a red-suited old man who gives presents to children was a deliberate marketing decision by a small group of wealthy Americans, in league with the writer Washington Irving, to persuade the public to buy. Nicholas (who lived in the fourth century) was said to have been kind to children, so some Christians gave gifts on his feast day—not on a feast day celebrating the birth of Jesus Christ. The *Oxford Dictionary of Saints* summarizes further evolution this way: "[I]t attained its present form in North America, where the Dutch Protestants of New Amsterdam united it to Nordic folkloric legends of a magician who both punished naughty children and rewarded good ones with presents."[11]

But even in America, where modern Christmas was born, the celebration was not a central part of the Christian calendar (especially among Protestants) until *after* it became a popular secular holiday; that is, the decision by the churches to make Christmas a special day *followed* the decision by American shopkeepers to turn it into a scheme for selling their wares.[12]

The secular Christmas that we nationally celebrate—egged on by greeting card makers, toy companies, and the shopping mall industry—is very different from the religious holiday that Christians value. Indeed, many evangelical Christians believe that it smacks of paganism to tell children that a fat man in a red suit flies through the air, aided by reindeer, delivering presents to children around the world. The legend of Santa Claus has an undeniable Christian provenance in the life of Saint Nicholas, but it is not, as understood in the United States, a Christian legend. The traditional children's bedtime story "The Night Before Christmas" (originally "A Visit from Saint Nicholas") is not in any sense a Christian story; neither is the popular 1994 film *The Santa Clause*. The conclusion has nothing whatsoever to do with endorsement and everything to do with the distinction between what a religion actually teaches and what commerce decides to borrow.

That Christmas is a key part of the civil religion is beyond peradventure. It is a national holiday, the public schools are not in session, the President typically issues a Christmas message, and the season brings broad and often successful appeals for charitable giving, somehow tapping into a vein of generosity that is moribund much of the rest of the year.* Moreover, the cheery and generous ardor that has become known as the "Christmas spirit" exemplifies the United States as most of us wish it would more often truly be, thus serving the aspirational function that the civil religion performs. (I am reminded of a lecture by the Jewish legal scholar David Bleich, who argued with devastating casualness that the problem with America is not that it is a Christian nation—but that too often it isn't.)

That does not mean that everybody celebrates Christmas or even likes the season, and a number of non-Christian writers have told moving tales of exclusion and alienation. Indeed, some Jewish scholars complain that the national celebration of Christmas has had a distorting effect on Judaism because of the elevation of Hanukkah into a more important observance than it should be, only so that Jewish children will not feel excluded. (This parallels the disturbance of some evangelical parents over the celebration in the schools of Halloween.)

My point, however, is not that Christmas causes no discomfort, but that the Christmas hegemony is not a Christian hegemony. It is a part of the larger commercial hegemony. Christmas as now celebrated in America is simply another triumph for the values of the market—the *I want*, the *you need*—over the values of the spirit, and is, in that sense, a defeat for Christianity. Indeed, one might argue for a ban on Christmas pageants not because some religious parents object but because the pageants in their current form are often nothing but a paean to Madison Avenue: Santa Claus is as much a marketing tool as Mickey Mouse or Michael Jordan, but, unlike Mickey or Michael, he possesses no independent cultural importance. In the Christmas culture, Santa is *only* a marketing tool. The student of civility, as we have seen, must always be alert for the invasion of other spheres of life by the forces of the market. When we organize our public school calendars around the desire

---

* Or we might be more cynical and propose that the charitable giving that gathers such steam in December is fueled less by the Christmas spirit than by the looming deadline of December 31 for contributions that will be tax-deductible in the current year.

of manufacturers to sell consumer products, and use a school assembly to welcome their symbol—Santa—into our children's midst, we are proclaiming that the market values have already won. A celebration so crass is neither civil nor Christian.

But the Christmas celebration in our civil religion is unlikely to go away anytime soon. The President will continue to put up a tree at the White House, just as he will host an Easter egg roll, another non-Christian tradition—indeed, a deeply pagan one. (To the devout Christian, for whom Christ's death is a more important symbol than Christ's birth, telling children about a rabbit at Easter may be even worse than telling them about the fat man with the red suit at Christmas.) Cities will still decorate their downtowns, villages will decorate their squares. And, of course, the stores will still have their sales. Public school children, no matter what educators choose to do about it, will be well aware that the Christmas season has, once more, seized the nation. So we might as well make the most of it.

Where does this leave us? With compromise—which is precisely what civility often demands. And it is in the nature of compromise that neither side gets exactly what it wants. So parents who long for the return of the religious Christmas pageants they remember from the schools of their childhoods, with wise men and the baby Jesus and "O, Little Town of Bethlehem," rather than the deification of Santa, will not get it. Parents who long to banish any mention of Christmas from the public schools will not be satisfied either. Schools, rather, will be free—should they wish!—to hold the watered-down, quasi-secular pageants that are characteristic of life in a time of market domination and religious caution. Parents who like the idea of this limited celebration should certainly fight for it. But Christians, quite apart from the risk of using the schools to ram Christian culture down the throats of non-Christians, should be wary of the threat the secular Christmas poses to the integrity of *Christian* faith. Thus, Christians should be wary of cooperating with the market's theft of a Holy Day and its transformation into a secular national holiday. In the meantime, schools could profitably use the pendency of the Christmas season, whether they choose to celebrate Christmas or not, to remind children of the importance of generosity toward others, of sacrifice, of giving rather than getting—that is, the importance of civility.

RELIGION AND INTEGRITY

. . . .

Having twice mentioned integrity, I should say a word about what, for the religious, it entails. In my book *Integrity*, I define the concept as having three steps: taking the time to be deliberate in figuring out what is right; doing that right thing even when there is a cost; and being willing to say what you have done and why you have done it. For the person of faith, the first step is guided by an understanding of God's will. Living that faith may require sacrificing the good opinion of others—or sacrificing wealth, or sexual freedom, or other things that our culture holds dear.

For example, the person who joins a holy order that requires vows of poverty and chastity is sacrificing things that are valued in this world, the better to serve God. The vows do not kill the desire for either material wealth or sexual pleasure; but the integrity of the faith guides the continuing choice to give them up. Or consider the twenty-four colleges of the Mennonite tradition, most of which do not seek endowment funds, preferring to rely, in the Mennonite tradition, on the kindness of strangers. At the same time, Mennonite schools push the traditional Anabaptist notions of internationalism, by seeking students from abroad and by preparing young Americans for missions abroad, and community, by placing special emphasis on the Christian responsibilities that teachers, staff, and students all share toward one another.[13] The colleges, while seeking to educate their students, also make affirmative efforts to stand in the world as examples of the principles of the faith.

Living faith with integrity today is difficult, because the religions are pressed from all sides: from an American left that views religion as a purely private matter, from an American right that views religion as genuine only when it agrees with the conservative program, and even from within, where the religions are pressed to change with the times, reworking God's word to fit political fashion. Too many members of the clergy seem to have accepted the view that God wants human beings to be comfortable with who they are, that the purpose of a worship service is to reassure the members of the congregation that they are indeed doing what God wants them to do. In my own denomination, the Episcopal

Church, the leadership has lately announced (to simplify matters a bit) that there are no significant restrictions on what one may believe in order to be an Episcopalian. In particular, there are no significant standards of personal rectitude, even for clergy. Nobody is called upon to sacrifice the fulfillment of any desire for anybody else. This staggering pronouncement transformed a powerful eighteenth-century ideal about the ability of the believer, armed with a conscience guided by Scripture and powerful preaching, to come to his or her own understanding of the will of God, into a bleary late-twentieth-century moral relativism.

Such an approach is unhelpful in the reconstruction of civility, which needs religions willing to challenge the faithful to adopt values different from those of the larger political and market cultures that are drowning democracy. Small wonder that the Episcopal Church has an oversupply of priests and an undersupply of parishioners. Protestants seem to be voting with their feet, avoiding those denominations that are collapsing into training grounds for what Saul Bellow memorably termed sheriffs of ghost towns.

One of the most instructive documents in understanding how integrity answers these pressures is the Barmen Declaration, issued at one of the bleakest moments in history. The Barmen Declaration was a joint 1934 statement by several German Protestant churches, challenging the effort by the Nazi regime to eliminate the traditional denominations and impose in their stead a state-mandated version of Christian doctrine. Barmen has lessons for today's shortsighted abusers of religion, from the strict separationists on the left to the new theocrats on the right, and to those on both sides of our politics who believe in bending Christ's message to fit the needs of the present political moment or, just as sinful, their own ideological stances.

To the strict separationists, who would render religion a private matter, and deprive the church of its vital role as a mediating institution between citizen and government:

We reject the false doctrine, as though the State, over and beyond its special commission, should and could become the single and totalitarian order of human life, thus fulfilling the Church's vocation as well.

To the theocrats, who see politics marching in lockstep with their religious understandings:

> We reject the false doctrine, as though the Church, over and beyond its special commission, should and could appropriate the characteristics, the tasks, and the dignity of the State, thus itself becoming an organ of the State.

And to those who urge the churches to change with the times, to affirm the moral and political beliefs of the congregation, or to follow where popular consensus leads:

> We reject the false doctrine, as though the Church were permitted to abandon the form of its message and order to its own pleasure or to changes in prevailing ideological and political convictions.[14]

These are hard teachings, but the churches that signed the Barmen Declaration faced hard times. Many German Protestants caved in to Nazi pressure, when standing up for Christ might have slowed or even stopped the Holocaust.

My attraction to the Barmen Declaration, I think, helps explain why my most joyful memories of American Christianity are of another era, the late 1950s and early 1960s, when thousands of white preachers consciously chose to challenge wary and sometimes hostile congregations to love their neighbors who happened to be black. The mirror-image preaching—the preaching that made the Civil Rights Movement a moral force before it was a political one—was the message of thousands of black preachers who called upon their congregations to love even those who were oppressing them. The gospel of love, in short, was not limited either to those the members of the congregation happened to like or those who happened to like the members of the congregation. And the obligation of the faithful to follow these often hard teachings had nothing to do with what the faithful wanted to do. On this point, integrity and civility coincide: our duty to do what is right does not turn on our instincts or desires.

16

. . . .

The Etiquette of Democracy

I~N THE END,~ of course, the student of civility wants to know
what can be done. In the first six chapters of the book, I presented
a set of rules to govern the sacrificial civility that the ethic of neighbor-love requires. From chapter 7 onward, I have tried to offer
concrete suggestions for the reconstruction of civility. The time has
come to look back over what we have learned . . . and to see where
it leads. I said at the outset that the book is a kind of prayer. Let us
now be very clear about what the prayer is for.

THE PEOPLE WE CAN BE

. . . .

At the beginning of the book, the reader will recall, we examined
briefly the work of Norbert Elias, the Swiss sociologist who did the
first important scholarship on the history of civility. As we reach·
the end, it is useful to go back and reconsider his ideas, now from a
slightly different angle.

Rules of civility, we know from Elias's research, began to
develop in Europe at the same time that the church began to yield
its authority to the nation-state, and they served the important
function of teaching the importance of gaining control over our
instincts. People could no longer kill others with whom they had
grudges, and they could no longer urinate where they chose; the
relationship between the two is that both are natural urges, and
both had to be cabined, if only for the society to survive. But there

was a moral aspect as well: the ability to discipline the desires of the animal self, argued Erasmus of Rotterdam in the first treatise on civility, distinguishes the civilized person from the barbarian.

Nowadays, when we look back on the days when Europeans ate with their hands from a shared plate or drank from a common cup, we shake our heads at their backwardness. But it may be, Elias suggests, that we are not looking deeply enough:

> People who ate together in the way customary in the Middle Ages, taking meat with their fingers from the same dish, wine from the same goblet, soup from the same pot or the same plate, with all the other peculiarities of which examples have been and will further be given—such people stood in a different relationship to one another than we do.

That much, perhaps, seems obvious. The interesting question is how the relationship was different. Elias tells us:

> [T]his involves not only the level of clear, rational consciousness; their emotional life also had a different structure and character. . . . What was lacking in this *courtois* world, or at least had not been developed to the same degree, was the invisible wall of affects which seems now to rise between one human body and another, repelling and separating.[1]

In other words, the Europeans of the Middle Ages lacked our modern sense of the self as radically separate from every other self. Rather than our norms of individualism, they perceived themselves as part of a larger whole. And if in this belief they often went too far, persecuting and even killing in the effort to keep the world homogeneous, we who fancy ourselves more civilized may go too far in the other direction, insisting on an individualism so stultifying that to talk about community or obligation is almost to state an evil.

We cannot return to a world in which individual identity was subsumed within a larger and often brutal whole, although some Enlightenment thinkers—notably Hobbes—seemed to think this a wonderful idea, and Marxism, along with other totalizing ideologies, believes it even today. What we can do is try, within the limits of democracy, to construct a civility that will lead future generations to admire what we tried to do for civilization rather than condemn us for our barbarism.

And where do we begin? Back in chapter 2, we happened across a line from the British historian Andrew St. George, who—following de Tocqueville's famous observation—proposed that democracy itself "can be seen not only as a type of government but as a system of manners, a form of social life."[2] So let us review what we have seen so far in our study of civility, in order to figure out just what we might list as these democratic manners—what we might call *the etiquette of democracy.*

Over the course of the book, I have highlighted a set of fifteen rules that should guide us in reconstructing our civility. Let us take a moment now to review them, and to consider, very briefly, the application of each to the manners of democracy.

> *Our duty to be civil toward others does not depend on whether we like them or not (chapter 2).*

As a matter of democratic politics, this rule is perfectly sensible. Whatever may be the rights and obligations that we distribute in a democracy, we should not limit them to the people who happen to be our friends or who think as we do. This suggests in turn that even politicians mired in difficult campaigns, or activists fighting their desperate battles, should take care to show others the respect that fellow citizens deserve. Otherwise, we are kidding ourselves if we imagine that the step from disrespecting those we dislike to disrespecting the electoral process in which they, rather than we, emerge victorious is a particularly large one.

> *Civility requires that we sacrifice for strangers, not just for people we happen to know (chapter 4).*

Civility, I said at the outset, is principally an ethic for strangers. In a democracy, especially a large one, we are most of us strangers to each other. And so the struggle to protect the democratic freedoms of those we know well should not be different from the struggle to protect the democratic freedoms of those we do not know at all. Our views on every issue—crime, free speech, taxes, whatever—should not turn on the accident of how we and our immediate friends happen to be affected by the policy in question. Civility supposes an obligation to a larger if anonymous group of fellow citizens.

> *Civility has two parts: generosity, even when it is costly, and trust, even when there is risk (chapter 4).*

This principle is uncomplicated. In our politics, we should look forward to the chance to be generous, and we should not hesitate to take risks. There are lessons here for conservatives and liberals alike. Conservatives worry about liberals throwing money at problems, but, while nobody likes to waste precious dollars, we should not be miserly. Liberals, on the other hand, are always suspicious of conservative proposals to experiment with everything from welfare reform to charter schools. Civility proposes that we should take more chances.

The ideal of trust has another political implication. Too often, activists in one cause or another justify imposing a single, Washington-centered answer on the ground that the states or local communities or individual people cannot be trusted to do it right (whatever "it" may be). Civility proposes, instead, that we should trust that the judgment of others is as good as our own.

> *Civility creates not merely a negative duty not to do harm, but an affirmative duty to do good (chapter 4).*

We cannot reconstruct civility if citizens take the view that they have fulfilled their obligation to others simply by not harming them. The affirmative duty to do good for others—whether through volunteerism, charitable contributions, or the simple kindness of carrying sandwiches across the street—is at the heart of the love of neighbor on which a sacrificial civility properly rests.

> *Civility requires a commitment to live a common moral life, so we should try to follow the norms of the community if the norms are not actually immoral (chapter 5).*

The trust that civility requires of us sometimes means that we must accept the moral judgments of others. This may seem antithetical to freedom but actually is essential to it. Freedom avoids anarchy when we agree, across a wide range of subjects, that the community norms will govern our behavior. This does not mean we should never mark ourselves as different; but, for each of us, the question of when to be different and when to be guided by others should be a matter of careful and prayerful consideration. When we flout the norms of our community just for the sake of flouting them, we may believe we are somehow actualizing our selves, but we are, in truth, simply engaging in the same incivility as the rich man who will not give his money away and the driver who considers nobody's comfort but his own.

Of course, if we are to follow most of the norms of our community, we must also take a hand in shaping them, through moral conversation, and the community itself must welcome conversation about moral truth, in order to create a moral world in which most citizens will want to participate. And so civility requires that we talk to each other about matters of importance, and that we welcome those who seek to talk to us.

We must come into the presence of our fellow human beings with a sense of awe and gratitude (chapter 6).

We will never be able to reconstruct civility—we will never be able even to follow the simple rules I here set out—unless we first rethink the manner in which we approach others. We must not encounter our fellow citizens with suspicion or pessimism or hostility; we must encounter them with the realization that they are as fully remarkable as we are, and so must be grateful for the opportunity.

In practical terms, this means we must avoid such uncivil attitudes as racial or religious bigotry. It means that members of the Christian Coalition must search for the face of God in the leaders of the gay rights movement—and also that the leaders of the gay rights movement must search for the face of God in members of the Christian Coalition.[3] And it means that the strangers we meet on the street or our opponents in a debate are as entitled to our respect—to that sense of awe—as the people we love most in the world.

Civility assumes that we will disagree; it requires us not to mask our differences but to resolve them respectfully (chapter 8).

We must never make the mistake of supposing that democracy requires consensus. It does not. It requires debate, which in turn presupposes that we do indeed have disagreements. But civility demands of us that we not allow those disagreements to push us into words or acts of sharp offense or violence. I do not mean that nothing is worth fighting for—only that the number of things worth *fighting* for should, in a democracy, be small. If the number seems large, it is unlikely that democracy is any longer the proper word for our society.

Civility requires that we listen to others with knowledge of the possibility that they are right and we are wrong (chapter 8).

This process, which I call civil listening, is at the heart of the dialogue that allows democracy to function. The function of debate in a truly civil society is not only to prevail; the function is to allow the best idea to win out. Therefore, no matter how certain I may be that I am right, unless I give you a genuine and open opportunity to persuade me of my errors, I cannot seriously expect you to give me a genuine and open opportunity to persuade you of yours.

Civility requires that we express ourselves in ways that demonstrate our respect for others (chapter 9).

So much for negative campaigning. And demonizing our opponents. And adopting, in everyday language, the habit of using violent or offensive words and phrases. We show respect for ourselves and others when we trouble ourselves to think carefully about what we say, rather than grabbing for the first expletive that comes to mind.

To speak respectfully when respect is difficult to feel is not the same as lying, unless we view all manners as dissembling. As the journalist E. J. Dionne puts the point: "Fake courtesy is unseemly, especially when it looks fake. But overdosing on sincerity and authenticity is unwholesome and unwise."[4]

> *Civility requires resistance to the dominance of social life by the values of the marketplace. Thus, the basic principles of civility—generosity and trust—should apply as fully in the market and in politics as in every other human activity (chapter 10).*

Perhaps the greatest threat to reconstructing civility is the tendency in recent decades of the values of the market (and, to a lesser extent, of politics) to dominate the rest of social life. First and worst among these values is the proposition that the desires of the individual are of paramount importance. One who believes in civility as sacrifice can never accept this proposition, and therefore will insist on nurturing in the social world potential centers of resistance, places capable of developing and actually implementing alternative social meanings. The nation's churches, synagogues, and mosques are in the best position to do this, for they would be doing only what religions at their best have always done: subverting the established order—in this case, the values of the marketplace.

The accident of the line of work in which you find yourself is almost never an excuse for incivility, with the exception, perhaps, of those who must defend our country (and sometimes our streets) from violent assaults and therefore must be prepared to be violent in return. But the old saw that some professions—law, for example, or journalism—require incivility is no more than an excuse for moral laziness.

> *Civility allows criticism of others, and sometimes even requires it, but the criticism should always be civil (chapter 12).*

This rule, I hope, speaks for itself.

> *Civility discourages the use of legislation rather than conversation to settle disputes, except as a last, carefully considered resort (chapter 12).*

In contemporary America, we tend to rush toward legislation and regulation—in short, toward coercive means of correction—whenever we spot a problem and believe we have found the solution. Conservatives seem to think that only liberals do this, and vice versa, but the truth is that everybody does. The practice is quite uncivil, however, for it often stifles debate and always assumes that those who disagree cannot be trusted to do what is right. When we legislate as soon as we think we have the answer, we forget to engage in civil listening.

Sometimes, of course, an evil is so great or a risk so large that legislation is the only reasonable path. But we must be wary of supposing that this is so whenever we happen to think that we are right. For that is the path away from democracy and toward autocracy.

> *Teaching civility, by word and example, is an obligation of the family. The state must not interfere with the family's effort to create a coherent moral universe for its children (chapter 13).*

The family is the place where all moral instruction begins. In order to teach civility, the adults in the family must both talk about and live an ethic of sacrifice. This is no easy thing, but there is no alternative. Because the family is prior to the state, the state must not invade its sacred sphere except for the strongest of reasons. And so the parents must be free—must be *trusted*, the student of civility might say—to make wise and loving decisions for their children about everything from which religious tradition is the right one to which forms of discipline are appropriate, to which school the children should attend. The fact that we might disagree with the choices parents make is not an argument against allowing parents to choose, unless we think the state has a monopoly on wisdom.

> *Civility values diversity, disagreement, and the possibility of resistance, and therefore the state must not use education to try to standardize our children (chapter 13).*

The education of children is of vital importance, but raising smart children is no substitute for raising moral children. It is for the family, not the state, to decide which moral principles children ought to learn. When the state uses its schools to place impediments in the path of this parental choice, it betrays a deep mistrust of the ability of parents to make right judgments, and it places itself in opposition to religious traditions—the entities most likely to develop the different social meanings that help us to resist the incursion of the values of politics and the market into other areas of social life.

> *Religions do their greatest service to civility when they preach not only love of neighbor but resistance to wrong (chapter 14).*

Religions that simply try to conform, and to make their believers comfortable, are not true to the best self of religion and certainly are useless in the effort to reconstruct civility. Religionists who are afraid of being thought different from everybody else will never be able to engage in serious acts of resistance and therefore will be unable to counter the values of the market with an alternative set of understandings. The recent Protestant tendency to worry more about filling the seats than challenging the congregation is a particular threat to civility.

. . . .

These rules suggest the possibility of judging the civility not only of ourselves, as human beings and citizens, but of the country we have inherited and are (one hopes) laboring together to improve. One might reasonably ask, for example, how we as a nation treat the worst off among us—people whom, under the command to love our neighbors, we are instructed to love. As Richard John Neuhaus has pointed out: "It is not a Marxist but a biblical insight that a society is judged along its fault lines, that we are judged by our relationship to the vulnerable, to the marginal, to those whom many view as expendable."[5] And so civility provides a standard by which to judge not only our personal but our national morality.

That is not to say that we cannot have sharp and firm (and civil) disagreements over which policies best implement the goals that civility requires us to seek. But these fifteen rules at least help us to know what it is we should be trying to do.

. . . .

But civility, as I have explained from the outset, will always have its critics. In 1997, when New York's chief judge proposed rules requiring lawyers on opposing sides to be civil to each other, the prominent divorce lawyer Raoul Felder wrote a caustic response in the *New York Times*. "[I]f lawyers truly care about the causes they represent, they should, on occasion, get hot under the collar, raise their voices, become pugnacious," he wrote. Conflict, argued Felder, is what the legal profession is about. Civility, he concluded, "may not always be the right reaction in an adversarial courtroom."[6]

This argument reminds me of the commentary by Ed Rollins (see p. 121) that it was his job to diminish the reputation of his client's opponent. Nastiness, in other words, is not merely the option but the responsibility of the political profession. The legal profession too: "I have never heard a client complain that his or her lawyer was rude," Felder tells us. In both cases, law and politics, rudeness is evidently justified on the ground that rudeness is what the client is paying for.

As any student of civility would, I find this a fascinating notion: that there are professions for which incivility is a requirement. I suppose I disbelieve it; or, rather, if there are such professions, I am skeptical of their morality, because they fail to convey a message that we are, all of us, not lone drivers but fellow passengers. It may be that law and politics seem so dismally rude because their principal ethic is merely one of victory, an ethic materially enriching and emotionally satisfying, but morally unimportant. If lawyers are paid to be rude and political consultants to be nasty, and if their incivility is linked to the fact that they are also paid to win, we should scarcely be surprised that professional athletes find it comfortable to brawl with fans, spit on umpires, take bites out of ears, and, in one unfortunate case nicknamed "Assassin," specialize in injuring fellow football players. After all, the athletes want to win too.

Some etiquette. Some democracy.

17
. . . .

Coda: The Civility of Silence

Wher I was a child, my tired father would return home from a day at the office, and he and my mother, equally exhausted from a day of coping with the house and five children, would sit alone in the living room, enjoying what came to be called their "quiet time." They would sometimes, but rarely, speak; more often, they simply sat there, perhaps sipping martinis, certainly unwinding together. We children well understood that these precious minutes were inviolable. We were not to interrupt for any cause short of broken bones. Not because my parents did not love us. Not because they did not want to be with us. But because they needed a period of peace, a moment of silence, to renew their energies—especially their emotional energies—before resuming the exhilarating, debilitating routine stress of being responsible for five fragile human lives.

The student of civility should value silence too. The sound, the noise, the sheer unrelenting *loudness* of our world combine to make civility difficult to achieve. The challenge of contemporary life is not so much that we are busy as that we are blasted around the clock with the sounds of our society: raucous music, insistent telephones, cynical newscasts, angry traffic. Small wonder that we seem so selfish. Small wonder that the polls say people think incivility is growing worse.[1] Our world is too loud to grant us the life space to remember our duties to others: we seem to spend all of our time searching for bits of peace and quiet for ourselves.

And yet if we lose the vast silences that help define the sounds that fall between them, we may lose the ability to appreciate the transcendent. In a world full of noise, it is remarkably easy to

287

imagine that we are alone—or, more particularly, that we humans, material, tangible, and loud, are all that truly exists. The quiet spaces help to remind us of who and whose we truly are. Lying on one's back in the deep of a silent night, gazing for an hour at a sky brilliant with sharp, white stars, it is difficult to resist the tug of God. There are reasons, my wife often reminds me, that deep religiosity thrives in the open spaces of the South and the West and seems endangered in the crowded, noisy urban caverns we have built along our coasts, our rivers, and our lakes.

We have seen that our reconstruction of civility, and thus the salvation of our civilization, requires an appreciation of the transcendent—whether or not stated in explicitly religious terms. The task will require finding, and helping others to find, the silences in which we can catch our emotional breath and take our moral bearings, remembering, at peace, what we owe, and to whom . . . and remembering that a part of our obligation is simple gratitude for the gifts of life and of our fellow humans. Sometimes the need is for a physical space in which to find peace, which is why it is so outrageous that most of our churches keep their doors closed most of the week—and why the last part of the local budget to be cut should be funding for libraries, museums, and parks, the places where we can share the silence with our fellow citizens.

A couple of years ago, stranded in San Antonio by a New England snowstorm that had canceled all flights, I wandered into the Alamo. A sign at the door calls for silence. Men are asked to remove their hats. Walking the grounds of the old, broken fort in peace, it is easy to conjure visions of the war that made the building famous. It matters little who was on the side of right or even what really happened: we know that lots of people, many of them women and children, died there. The mandatory silence is a signal of respect for the dead; sharing it with my fellow tourists also created a powerful commonality, a sense that we were mourning together, and that the event we were mourning was the result of a great sacrifice. In the loud, glitzy heroism of Hollywood, where the good guys always live to fight another day (see chapter 9), such sacrifices are unthinkable. But in the silence of the Alamo, it is easy to imagine sacrificing oneself for a great good.

One can gain something of the same sense of the beauty of tran-

scendent duty in a thousand other ways—walking a Civil War battlefield, hiking a little-used trail through the woods, rafting
through a canyon, even reading a wonderful book—but perhaps
the most powerful is prayer. Recently I heard a story about Mother
Teresa, and although I cannot remember it word for word, the gist
of it was this:

Mother Teresa was asked by an interviewer what she says to
God when she prays.

"I don't say anything," she replied. "I just listen."

So the interviewer asked her what God says to her.

"He doesn't say anything," said Mother Teresa. "He just listens."
And before the astonished interviewer could press her further, she
added, "And if you don't understand that, I can't explain it to you."

If Mother Teresa could not explain it, I am confident that I can't
either. But I think I understand it. I only wish that I could emulate
it. Somehow, whenever I lie still and pray, no matter how hard I
try to be silent and listen, my inner voice begins to intrude, and
my effort at civil listening—civilly listening to God—is broken.
But when I walk a vast, silent space, I feel that God is close to me,
and I know that the duties I owe others because of God's command are every bit as real and solid and unchanging as the next
stone on the path.

SILENT MOMENTS

· · · · · · · · · · · · ·

This raises a question about the public schools. I quite understand
that it is too late in history to ask the schools to resume teaching
classes on "manners and deportment." (See chapter 4.) And yet it
does seem to me that the education of children is woefully incomplete unless it helps them to understand that living in a civilized
community imposes obligations other than the pursuit of self-
interest. Given what I have already written, the reader will not be
surprised to learn that I believe the only way to do this is to give
children the opportunity to strive, if just for an instant, for that
sense of transcendence, of peace, that we find only in the quiet
spaces so difficult to find in the hurly-burly of the day.

Ah, but how to do it? I have always been a skeptic on classroom prayer, although most of the Western world seems to manage with it. But what about what has come to be called the moment of silence? Civil libertarians are against it: should the student of civility join them? I recognize that quite a few scholars (and not a few judges) are concerned that a moment of silence to begin the school day would have an effect on nonpraying students, who might feel pressured by their knowledge of the religion that others are exercising during the morning's brief silence. The pressure of this knowledge, it is said, the Constitution forbids.[2]

But this cannot be a serious objection. If children have the constitutional right to pray silently—and they do—it would be bizarre to suggest that the state cannot be aware of the right and the desire to exercise it and take steps to make it easier. If a program making it easier for children to pray is wrong because some might not want to do it, then the same objection should attach to, for example, a program making it easier for children to have sex. Young people may (and should) choose not to have sex. And yet the fact that some young people might feel that birth control information or condom distribution in the schools signals state approval of sexual activity seems not sufficiently weighty for the public schools to decide not to do it. (Which is another reason my wife and I would rather not, thank you, send the state our children to educate.) Quite the contrary: anybody who suggests that schools should, perhaps, not be the purveyors of sexual information and pressure is dismissed as narrow-minded, fanatical, and most certainly illiberal. But it is difficult to see why the no-birth-control-information type of fanatic is more dangerous than the no-classroom-prayer type.*

Besides, the objection that some children would know that

---

* As on prayer itself, there is a racial divide on the moment of silence. White Americans are more or less split on the practice, but black Americans favor it overwhelmingly. A few years ago, the Democratic mayoral primary in Washington, D.C., featured three candidates, all African Americans, all committed to either school prayer or a moment of silence to open the school day. This should scarcely have been surprising. The black church tradition is generally evangelical, and evangelicals tend to support classroom prayer. The reason is not a desire to have the state proselytize on their behalf. The reason is that evangelicals have long been suspicious of external powers—including the power of the schools—that might try to wean their children from their faith. That white liberals continue to ignore these deep religious aspirations in the black community simply adds to the deep cynicism that so many African Americans feel, believing, as many do, that the Democratic Party feels entitled to their votes but has no interest in their dreams.

other children were praying is a non sequitur. If my children's knowledge of your children's silent prayers raises a constitutional problem, we face an insurmountable paradox. A legend about the brilliant Slovenian chess master Aron Nimzovich illustrates the point. As the story is told, Nimzovich was playing in the great 1927 tournament at New York City, when his opponent, Milan Vidmar, lit up a cigar. An irritated Nimzovich immediately complained to the tournament director that the fumes were distracting him. The director had a chat with Vidmar, who good-naturedly agreed to put the cigar out.

A few minutes later, an agitated Nimzovich was once more standing before the director.

Puzzled, the director peered over at the table. "But, Master Nimzovich," he pointed out, "your opponent isn't smoking!"

"I know, I know," Nimzovich is said to have replied. "But he looks as if he wants to!"

All of which leaves us with the ball perhaps somewhat advanced over where we started. It may be that the moment of silence is itself an important part of our reconstructed civility, as children and teachers alike begin the day in contemplation—*quiet* contemplation—before beginning the school day. School is a busy time, a competitive time, a time during which children are all too often encouraged to think only of themselves and their own needs and desires. When the state announces that it wants everybody to pause and reflect before that busy day begins at its public schools, some children, it is true, will decide to pray, which is perfectly fine, and others will know of their prayers—but all children will receive the message that peace, quiet, and patience are also among the virtues of civilized life.

. . . .

Just about the time I was finishing this manuscript, my wife and I took our two children for a walk at the New Haven Burial Ground, more commonly known to those at Yale University (right across the street) as the Grove Street Cemetery. The cemetery is the final resting place for members of many old New Haven families, including most of the presidents of Yale and such other luminaries as Noah Webster and Charles Goodyear. Our son wanted to see the grave of Eli Whitney, one of many Whitneys interred at the Burial Ground, which prides itself on being the first cemetery in America to be divided into family plots.

I have always enjoyed cemetery walks. A cemetary reminds us of the impermanence of mortal life, suggesting a need for dispatch in fulfilling our moral obligations; but it also reminds us of the durability of faith, which suggests that these obligations themselves are transcendent, not contingent. Like the Alamo, like a national park, like a moment of silent prayer, a cemetery helps us to find the peace within which we remember that we do not belong entirely to ourselves.

Although it was a July morning, the cemetery was peaceful and cool. We took our time, following the twisting pathways, deciphering the fading inscriptions on the headstones, enjoying the sacred silence. During our walk, and quite by accident, I stumbled across the grave of Kingman Brewster, former president of the university as well as ambassador to the Court of Saint James. The inscription on the fine stonework, drawn from Brewster's voluminous writings, was startling for one who was trying so hard to understand our attraction to the ideal of civility:

> The presumption of innocence is not just a legal concept. In commonplace terms it rests on that generosity of spirit which assumes the best, not the worst, of the stranger.

To which I can only add: don't forget the cream cheese and jelly sandwiches.

Amen.

NOTES

1. Barbarians Running Late

1. A marvelously informative account of the early years of the railroads is Sarah H. Gordon, *Passage to Union: How the Railroads Transformed American Life, 1829–1929* (Chicago: Ivan R. Dee, 1996).

2. See, for example, the discussion of the views of European travelers to the United States in John F. Kasson, *Rudeness and Civility: Manners in Nineteenth-Century Urban America* (New York: Hill & Wang, 1990), pp. 57–60, 219–22.

3. Quoted in Andrew St. George, *The Descent of Manners: Etiquette, Rules and the Victorians* (London: Chatto & Windus, 1993), p. 165.

4. Gordon, *Passage to Union,* p. 247.

5. St. George, *The Descent of Manners,* p. 165. Although St. George is British, he made this comment specifically about the United States.

6. Quoted in "Man Skips Security, Jams Up Houston Airport," *Austin American-Statesman,* July 21, 1995, p. B3.

7. Quoted in "Late Passenger Grounds IAH Flights," *Houston Chronicle,* July 21, 1995, p. A29.

8. See Timothy Jay, *Cursing in America: A Psycholinguistic Study of Dirty Language in the Courts, in the Movies, in the Schoolyards, and on the Streets* (Philadelphia: J. Benjamin, 1992).

9. See the FBI data reported in Jerry Seper, "Almost 8,000 Hate Crimes Reported Last Year, FBI Says," *Washington Times,* November 5, 1996, p. A4.

10. See, for example, Jennifer Steinhauer, "Whatever Happened to Service?" *New York Times,* March 4, 1997, p. D1. For an argu-

ment that part of the service decline is related to the lack of a common language, see Gary Strauss, "Consumers Frustrated by Verbal Gridlock," *USA Today*, February 28–March 2, 1997, p. 1A; Daniel Pederson, "Dissing Customers," *Newsweek*, June 23, 1997, p. 56.

11. Although the weird liberal celebration of "The People v. Larry Flynt" generated much critical comment (from liberals) for its sanitizing of the magazine's content, the initial shot across its bow was probably Gloria Steinem's article, "Hollywood Cleans Up Hustler," *New York Times*, January 7, 1997, p. A17.

12. These and other stories are reported in Edwin McDowell, "The Arrival of Uncivil Aeronautics," *New York Times*, April 30, 1997, p. D1.

13. "Failure to keep in proper lane or running off road" is a factor in 28 percent of fatal accidents. "Driving too fast" is a factor in 20 percent. U.S. Department of Transportation, National Highway Traffic Safety Administration, *Traffic Safety Facts 1994* (Washington, D.C.: NHTSA, 1995), p. 96.

14. Robert D. Putnam, "Bowling Alone: America's Declining Social Capital," *Journal of Democracy* 6 (January 1995): 65.

15. See the figures cited in "The American Uncivil Wars," *U.S. News & World Report*, April 22, 1996, p. 66.

16. See Jennifer Bradley, "Civility Brief Outlines Steps for Being Nice," *Roll Call*, March 10, 1997.

17. See, for example, Jill Lawrence, "Excuse Me, but . . . Whatever Happened to Good Manners?" *USA Today*, December 16, 1996, p. 1A.

18. See Antonia Barber, "Rough Language Plagues Schools, Educators Say," *USA Today*, March 11, 1997, p. 6D, citing a telephone poll by the National Association of Secondary School Principals.

19. Arthur M. Schlesinger, *Learning How to Behave: A Historical Study of American Etiquette Books* (New York: Macmillan, 1946), pp. 64–65.

20. See the discussions in Kasson, *Rudeness and Civility*; and St. George, *Descent of Manners,* passim.

21. See the fascinating stories in William Lee Miller, *Arguing About Slavery: The Great Battle in the United States Congress*

(New York: Knopf, 1996); the Sumner story, quite a famous one, appears on p. 486.

22. Kasson, *Rudeness and Civility*, pp. 222–28.

23. See Norbert Elias, *The Civilizing Process* [1939], tr. Edmund Jephcott (New York: Pantheon, 1978, 1982), pp. 153–88. On the matter of the soiled chair, see p. 123. The first volume is entitled *The History of Manners*, the second, *Power and Civility*. Elias's reviewers, although generally quite favorable, warned that he ignored the ability of many non-European peoples to discipline their bodily functions long before Europeans decided that the failure to do so meant one was uncivilized. See, for example, Keith Thomas, "The Rise of the Fork," *New York Review of Books*, March 9, 1978, p. 78.

24. Ibid., p. 53.

25. A particularly pointed discussion of the gendered nature of some rules of civility is found in Carol Brooks Gardner, *Passing By: Gender and Public Harassment* (Berkeley: University of California Press). Although I by no means endorse all that Gardner has to say, I do think she makes valuable and clear points about the way that etiquette, even unintentionally, can serve as an obstacle to justice. Gardner argues that we should preserve rules of civility that promote equality or "ensure fulfillment of special needs"—her example is special consideration for the elderly and the disabled—but insists that we should reject rules of civility that promote inequality. She warns that even behaviors that seem helpful on their face—the male instinct to come to the aid of women in trouble, for instance—might, in particular instances, actually perpetuate images of women as generally less competent than men (pp. 64–75). Writes Gardner:

> Inasmuch as the requirements of etiquette demand that women demonstrate their gender in public places in ways that have connotations of, for example, frailty, incompetence, and subordination, the individual who complies implies (or is willing for the moment to seem to imply) a larger belief in the present system of gender relations as well. (P. 18)

Gardner thoughtfully details ways that many small, seemingly polite behaviors arguably promote inequality. Much of her book is about sexual harassment, but she is also concerned about comments that do not amount to harassment but are nevertheless potentially harmful. Even well-intended compliments on a woman's physical appearance or attire, says Gardner, might pressure women to dress in ways that will draw similar compliments in the future (pp. 158–98). Gardner probably sweeps two much social behavior into her critique, but her model is an enormously helpful one.

26. 163 U.S. 537 (1896).
27. See Putnam, "Bowling Alone," pp. 70–71.
28. See Robert E. Goodin, *Manipulatory Politics* (New Haven: Yale University Press, 1980), chap. 2.

2. Do Manners Matter?

1. *Bipartisan Congressional Retreat Fact Sheet*, p. 1.
2. "Bipartisan Retreat Scheduled to Help Congress Work Better," *Congressional and Presidential Activity*, Bureau of National Affairs (BNA), December 13, 1996, p. F1.
3. See, for example, Richard Sennett, *The Fall of Public Man: On the Social Psychology of Capitalism* (New York: Vintage, 1978), and Lyn H. Lofland, *A World of Strangers: Order and Action in Urban Public Space* (New York: Basic Books, 1973).
4. Both quoted in Ernie Freda, "On Washington: Another Senator Bowing Out," *Atlanta Constitution*, March 11, 1997, p. 4A.
5. Michael J. Sandel, "Making Nice Is Not the Same as Doing Good," *New York Times*, December 29, 1996, sect. 4, p. 9.
6. See Ellen Goodman, "Little Acts Rebuild Civility," *Boston Globe*, January 2, 1997, p. A15.
7. See the discussion in Gertrude Himmelfarb, *The De-Moralization of Society: From Victorian Virtues to Modern Values* (New York: Knopf, 1995).
8. Benjamin DeMott, "Seduced by Civility: Political Manners and the Crisis of Democratic Values," *The Nation*, December 9, 1996, p. 11.
9. For a forceful (but often unpersuasive) argument that the idea that we should unite for common goals is often oppressive, see Iris Marion Young, *Justice and the Politics of Difference* (Princeton, N.J.: Princeton University Press, 1990).

10. Michael Reagan, "Reagan: 'Bye to GOP," *USA Today*, April 17, 1997, p. 15A.

11. Maureen Dowd, "Bubba Don't Preach," *New York Times*, February 9, 1997, p. 15.

12. Charles P. Flynn, *Insult and Society: Patterns of Comparative Interaction* (Port Washington, N.Y.: Kennikat Press, 1977), pp. 101, 103.

13. See the discussions of the value to democracy of opposition in Mary P. Ryan, *Civic Wars: Democracy and Public Life in the American City During the Nineteenth Century* (Berkeley: University of California Press, 1997), and Iris Marion Young, *Justice and the Politics of Difference* (Princeton, N.J.: Princeton University Press, 1990). I discuss the same theme in some detail in my book *The Dissent of the Governed: A Meditation on Law, Religion, and Loyalty* (Cambridge, Mass.: Harvard University Press, 1998).

14. St. George, *The Descent of Manners*, p. xv. See also his more detailed explication of this point in chapter 4.

15. See the discussions of the importance of democratic dissensus in Ryan, *Civic Wars*. Ryan argues for the importance of what she calls "heterogeneous democracy." The student of civility would of course agree.

16. James Q. Wilson, *The Moral Sense* (New York: Free Press, 1993), p. 83.

17. See, for example, the discussion in Penelope Brown and Stephen Levinson, *Politeness: Some Universals in Language and Usage* (London: Cambridge University Press, 1987); see also Ken-ichi Ohbuchi, Sachiko Chiba, and Osamo Fukushima, "Mitigation of Interpersonal Conflicts: Politeness and Time Pressure," *Personality and Social Psychology Bulletin* 22 (1996): 1035. See also Deborah Tannen, "When You Shouldn't Tell It Like It Is," *Washington Post*, March 1, 1987, p. D3.

18. Charles Taylor, *Sources of the Self: The Making of the Modern Identity* (Cambridge, Mass: Harvard University Press, 1989), p. 55.

19. Arthur M. Schlesinger, *Learning How to Behave: A Historical Study of American Etiquette Books* (New York: Macmillan, 1946), pp. 70–71.

20. Norbert Elias, *The Civilizing Process* [1939], tr. Edmund Jephcott (New York: Pantheon, 1978, 1982). The first volume is

entitled *The History of Manners*, the second *Power and Civility*.

21. Kasson, *Rudeness and Civility*, p. 193.

22. Elias, *The Civilizing Process*, vol. 1, p. 121.

23. Martin Luther King, Jr., *Why We Can't Wait* (New York: Harper & Row, 1964), pp. 92–99.

24. Albert J. Raboteau, "Martin Luther King, Jr., and the Tradition of Black Religious Protest," in Rowland A. Sherrill, ed., *Religion and the Life of the Nation* (Urbana: University of Illinois Press, 1990), pp. 46, 57.

25. For a dated but sturdy discussion, see William A. Gamson, "Violence and Political Power: The Meek Don't Make It," *Psychology Today* (July 1974): 35.

26. See, for example, Martin Luther King, Jr., "Pilgrimage to Nonviolence," in James Melvin Washington, ed., *A Testament of Hope: The Essential Writings of Martin Luther King, Jr.* (San Francisco: Harper & Row, 1986), p. 35. For a powerful exposition of the religiosity of the marchers, see Charles Marsh, *God's Long Summer: Stories of Faith and Civil Rights* (Princeton, N.J.: Princeton University Press, 1997).

27. Stanley Fish, "Why We Can't All Just Get Along," *First Things* (February 1996): 18.

28. Wendy Kaminer, "The Last Taboo," *The New Republic*, October 14, 1996, p. 24.

29. Indeed, when religion becomes entangled with nationalism, incivility, and even violence, will often be the result—a proposition as true for the United States, which set out to conquer for God at the end of the nineteenth century, as it is for many a small but angry country today. For a perhaps overly pessimistic account of some contemporary ethnic divisions in which religion plays a nasty part, see Chris Hann, "The Nation-State, Religion, and Uncivil Society: Two Perspectives from the Periphery," *Daedalus* (Spring 1997): 27.

30. Richard J. Mouw, "Religious Conviction and Public Civility," in Joseph Runzo, ed., *Ethics, Religion, and the Good Society* (Louisville, Ky.: Westminster/John Knox Press, 1992), pp. 95, 107. Mouw is specifically addressing Christianity, because of the power of its eschatological yearning, but the point has broader religious application.

---

31. Quoted in Pope John Paul II, *The Gospel of Life* (New York: Times Books, 1995), p. 39.
32. For example, my Yale colleague Bruce Ackerman's book *Social Justice in the Liberal State* (New Haven: Yale University Press, 1980) takes as a starting point the liberal proposition that no one of us is inherently more deserving of resources than any other and spins from that premise a detailed and often fascinating ethical system. But as Ackerman himself has admitted elsewhere, this sensible and morally appealing starting point must be assumed, not argued for. See Bruce Ackerman, "Why Dialogue?" *Journal of Philosophy* 86 (1989): 5.
33. The incident provoked considerable, and rather sarcastic, news coverage. Typical was the story in the *New York Times*, which began: "So much for the spirit of Hershey, candy kisses and civility in the House of Representatives." Adam Clymer, "Bloom of Bipartisanship Quickly Wilts in House," *New York Times*, April 10, 1997, p. A26.
34. Flynn, *Insult and Society*, pp. 39–60.
35. Ibid. This dismissal is an illustration, within the workplace, of what Lyn Lofland, in another context, calls "spatial segregation." See Lofland, *A World of Strangers*.
36. See St. George, *The Descent of Manners*, pp. 139, 175.
37. Ibid., pp. 158–66.
38. Christopher Clausen, "How to Join the Middle Classes: With the Help of Dr. Smiles and Mrs. Beeton," *American Scholar* 62 (Summer 1993): 403.
39. Ibid., p. 405.
40. Goodman, "Little Acts Rebuild Civility."

3. The Death of the Golden Age

1. Stephen Budiansky, "1953: Home, Hearth, and Heretics," *U.S. News & World Report*, October 25, 1993, p. 28. (The survey in question was conducted in 1953.)
2. See Garry Wills, *John Wayne's America: The Politics of Celebrity* (New York: Simon & Schuster, 1997).
3. *United States v. St. Clair*, 291 F. Supp. 122, 124 (S.D.N.Y. 1968).
4. The original classroom prayer cases are *Engel v. Vitale*, 370

U.S. 421 (1962), which struck down a state-composed prayer, and *Abington School District v. Schempp*, 374 U.S. 203 (1963), which struck down a program in which the state permitted Bible verses to be read.

5. For a fascinating speculation on the relationship between changes in the Vietnam-era draft laws and student participation in antiwar demonstrations, see Lewis A. Kornhauser, "The Great Image of Authority," *Stanford Law Review* 36 (1984): 349.

6. See E. J. Dionne, *Why Americans Hate Politics* (New York: Simon & Schuster, 1991).

7. See *Palmer v. Thompson*, 403 U.S. 217 (1971).

8. See *Griffin v. County School Board of Prince Edward County*, 377 U.S. 218 (1964).

9. This case is discussed in Emily Field Van Tassel, "Why Judges Resign: Influences on Federal Judicial Service, 1789–1992," in *Research Papers of the National Commission on Judicial Discipline and Removal*, vol. 2 (Washington, D.C.: 1993), p. 1137.

10. Quoted in John Hart Ely, *Democracy and Distrust* (Cambridge, Mass.: Harvard/Belknap, 1980), p. 60.

11. John Courtney Murray, *We Hold These Truths: Catholic Reflections on the American Proposition* (New York: Sheed and Ward, 1960), p. 11.

12. I. R. Hall, *Christian Unity: The Source of Brotherly Love* (Oxford: John Henry Parker, 1840), p. 9.

13. Kasson, *Rudeness and Civility*, p. 258.

14. See Ryan, *Civic Wars*, esp. chaps. 2, 3, and 7. In particular, Ryan tries to show that black people and women were more directly involved in urban politics in the middle of the nineteenth century, before the rise of bureaucracies stressing conformity, than they were by the middle of the twentieth.

15. See the discussions in Robert Wright, *The Moral Animal* (New York: Pantheon, 1994), and Wilson, *The Moral Sense*, passim.

16. For particularly poignant (if sometimes self-serving) discussions by gang members of the needs their gangs fulfill, see Yusuf Jah and Sister Shah'Keyah, *Uprising: Crips and Bloods Tell the Story of America's Youth in the Crossfire* (New York: Scribner's, 1995).

17. One need not be religious in the traditional sense to appreciate this point. See the discussion in Mortimer J. Adler, *How to Think About God: A Guide for the Twentieth-Century Pagan* (New York: Collier, 1992).

18. See the discussion in my book *Integrity* (New York: Basic Books, 1996), pp. 224–26.

4. Welcoming the Stranger

1. Michael Alexander, "Computer Security: How Much Backup Is Needed?" (book excerpt), *Computer Reseller News*, August 19, 1996, p. 164.

2. See Adrian Mars, "Keys to the Plague," *Guardian Online* (May 1, 1997),URL:http://go2.guardian.co.uk/computing/archive/863011510virus.html.

3. Quoted in ibid.

4. Richard Sennett, *The Fall of Public Man: On the Social Psychology of Capitalism* (New York: Vintage, 1978), p. 3.

5. Benton Johnson, "Modernity and Pluralism," in Martin E. Marty and Frederick E. Greenspahn, eds., *Pushing the Faith: Proselytism and Civility in a Pluralistic World* (New York: Crossroad, 1988), pp. 10, 17.

6. John Murray Cuddihy, *The Ordeal of Civility: Freud, Marx, Lévi-Strauss, and the Jewish Struggle with Modernity* (New York: Basic Books, 1974), p. 12.

7. Robert Coles, *The Moral Intelligence of Children* (New York: Random House, 1997), p. 96.

8. The newest entrant is Ryan, *Civic Wars*. See also the discussions in Kasson, *Rudeness and Civility*; and Lofland, *A World of Strangers,* passim.

9. Stanley Milgram, *The Individual in a Social World: Essays and Experiments* (Reading, Mass.: Addison Wesley, 1977), p. 29.

10. Milgram discusses a number of these studies in his book. A more recent, and more comprehensive, review of similar, and equally depressing, studies is Thomas Gabor, *"Everybody Does It!": Crime by the Public* (Toronto: University of Toronto Press, 1994), esp. chap. 3.

11. Milgram, *The Individual in a Social World,* p. 29.

12. Quoted in Kasson, *Rudeness and Civility*, p. 82.

13. St. George, *The Descent of Manners*, p. 161.

14. See the citations in Schlesinger, *Learning How to Behave*, p. 83, n. 12.

15. Kasson, *Rudeness and Civility*, p. 44.

16. See the discussion in Schlesinger, *Learning How to Behave*, pp. 30–31.

17. See "The American Uncivil Wars: How Crude, Rude and Obnoxious Behavior Has Replaced Good Manners and Why That Hurts Our Politics and Culture," *U.S. News & World Report*, April 22, 1996, p. 66.

18. For disheartening discussions, see Mary Ann Glendon, *Rights Talk: The Impoverishment of Political Discourse* (New York: Free Press, 1991), and Michael J. Sandel, *Liberalism and the Limits of Justice* (Cambridge: Cambridge University Press, 1982). A more recent, and slightly more polemical, treatment of some similar issues is Jean Bethke Elshtain, *Democracy on Trial* (New York: Basic Books, 1995).

19. James Q. Wilson, *Thinking About Crime* (New York: Random House, 1975), p. 236.

20. For further discussion along this line, see Glendon, *Rights Talk*.

21. 403 U.S. 15 (1971).

22. For a discussion of the dramatic change in mores regarding spoken language during the 1960s, see Kenneth Cmiel, "The Politics of Civility," in David Farber, ed., *The Sixties: From Memory to History* (Chapel Hill: University of North Carolina Press, 1994), p. 263.

23. See, for example, the argument presented in Alexander Bickel, *The Morality of Consent* (New Haven: Yale University Press, 1975).

24. See, for example, the thoughtful, scholarly, and occasionally disturbing discussion in Marianna Torgovnick, *Primitive Passions: Men, Women, and the Quest for Ecstasy* (New York: Knopf, 1997), pp. 189–207.

25. See the discussion in Rabbi Zelig Pliskin, *Love Your Neighbor: You and Your Fellow Man in the Light of the Torah* (Brooklyn: Aish HaTorah, 1977).

26. Dennis Rodman, with Michael Silver, *Walk on the Wild Side* (New York: Delacorte Press, 1997).

27. For an analysis of this proposition, see Richard A. Posner, *The Economics of Justice* (Cambridge, Mass.: Harvard University Press, 1981), pp. 102–10. Posner once argued that we should be allowed to sell ourselves into slavery; see ibid., p. 86. I might add that I have always suspected that Professor (now Judge) Posner, a great believer in economic efficiency, was playing a role more than offering a serious argument when he wrote this.

5. The Embarrassment of Free Will

1. See Steven Waldman, "The Tyranny of Choice: A Consumer Revolts," *The New Republic*, January 27, 1992, p. 22.

2. See Robert V. Levine, "Is Love a Luxury?" *American Demographics* (February 1993): 27.

3. Jane M. Johnson, Interim Co-President, Planned Parenthood, letter to the editor, *The New Republic*, November 13, 1995, p. 4.

4. Although pro-choice advocates often argue for abortion rights on the ground that they are important in protecting women's health or to avoid pregnancies from rape or incest, the great majority of abortions are apparently for what amounts to birth control. See the data discussed in "Abortion Battles: More in Common Than We Think," *USA Today*, August 13, 1996, p. 17A.

5. See Stanley Hauerwas, *Dispatches from the Front: Theological Engagements with the Secular* (Durham, N.C.: Duke University Press, 1994), pp. 10–15.

6. See Orlando Patterson, *Freedom*, vol. 1, *Freedom in the Making of the Western Culture* (New York: Basic Books, 1991). Patterson puzzles over why the ideal of individual freedom took hold first in the West and why it is in the West that it has had the greatest staying power and is exalted over such competing values as nationalism, family, and tradition. His controversial answer is that although the origins of the concept can be traced to ancient Greece, it was Christianity that institutionalized our understanding of freedom—but that the understanding was shaped, always, by the opposition of freedom and the very ancient and universal human practice of slavery.

7. See Glendon, *Rights Talk*, and Amitai Etzioni, *The New Golden Rule: Community and Morality in a Democratic Society* (New York: Basic Books, 1996).

8. Lynne McFall, "Integrity," *Ethics* 98 (October 1987): 5. I discuss McFall's work in my book *Integrity*, pp. 23–25.

9. See Jaroslav Pelikan, *The Vindication of Tradition* (New Haven: Yale University Press, 1984), p. 65. For a similar argument on the need to respect traditions and, simultaneously, to evaluate them, see Alasdair MacIntyre, *After Virtue: A Study in Moral Theory*, 2d. ed. (South Bend, Ind.: University of Notre Dame Press, 1984).

10. Samuel Fleischacker, *The Ethics of Culture* (Ithaca: Cornell University Press, 1994), p. 70.

11. See, for example, the research collected in Tom R. Tyler, *Why People Obey the Law* (New Haven: Yale University Press, 1990).

12. See the discussion in Allan Gibbard, *Wise Choices, Apt Feelings: A Theory of Normative Judgment* (Cambridge, Mass.: Harvard University Press, 1990). See also Lisa Bernstein, "Social Norms and Default Rules Analysis," *Southern California Interdisciplinary Law Journal* 3 (1993): 59.

13. See Lisa Bernstein, "Opting Out of the Legal System: Extralegal Contractual Relations in the Diamond Industry," *Journal of Legal Studies* 21 (1992): 115.

14. See Robert Ellickson, *Order Without Law: How Neighbors Settle Disputes* (Cambridge, Mass.: Harvard University Press, 1991). For a suggestion that we are often better off when our norms carry no legal power, see Richard A. Epstein, "Enforcing Norms: When the Law Gets in the Way," *The Responsive Community* (Fall 1997): 4.

15. Kasson, *Rudeness and Civility*, pp. 157–61.

16. See generally the discussion in Stephen Ansolabehere and Shanto Iyengar, *Going Negative: How Attack Ads Shrink and Polarize the Electorate* (New York: Free Press, 1995).

17. See the useful discussion in Stephen D. Sencer, "Read My Lips: Examining the Legal Implications of Knowingly False Campaign Promises," *Michigan Law Review* 90 (1991): 428.

18. The question of American exceptionalism—whether American institutions and people are fundamentally different from

those in other countries—has obsessed the nation since its founding. In the nineteenth century, the answers possessed a decidedly Protestant cast, and the doctrine of Manifest Destiny was one of its creations. The years after World War II saw a consensus that the exceptionalism thesis was true, and, among scholars, a surge in interest in finding an explanation for it. This period produced some of the best-known work on the subject, including, among other books, Stephan Thernstrom's *Poverty and Progress* (1964); Seymour Martin Lipset's *The First New Nation: The United States in Historical and Comparative Perspective* (1963); Louis Hartz's *The Liberal Tradition in America* (1955); and David Potter's *People of Plenty: Economic Abundance and the American Character* (1954). Our more skeptical age has seen yet another awakening of interest in the problem, but without the enthusiasm of past generations. See, for example, Seymour Martin Lipset, *American Exceptionalism: A Double-Edged Sword* (New York: Norton, 1996), and Michael Kammen, "The Problem of American Exceptionalism," *American Quarterly* 45 (1993): 1.

19. See, for example, Sydney E. Ahlstrom, *A Religious History of the American People* (New Haven: Yale University Press, 1972). Whether or not most scholars believe this, most voters certainly do, and they tend to turn against candidates who seem to deny it. The (perhaps unfair) perception that Michael Dukakis was not particularly religious, according to Garry Wills, was a principal cause of his heavy defeat by George Bush in the 1988 presidential election. See Garry Wills, *Under God: Religion and American Politics* (New York: Simon & Schuster, 1990).

20. For an amusing, if occasionally too bitter, discussion of the lack of military service in Vietnam by leading Republicans, see John Gregory Dunne, *Crooning* (New York: Simon & Schuster, 1990).

21. See, for example, the data collected in David Blankenhorn, *Fatherless America: Confronting Our Most Urgent Social Problem* (New York: Basic Books, 1995).

22. See generally the essays in Robert N. Bellah, Richard Madsen, William M. Sullivan, Ann Swidler, and Steven M. Tipton,

eds., *Individualism and Commitment in American Life* (New York: Harper & Row, 1987), especially the splendid essay by Swidler entitled "Love and Adulthood in American Culture."

6. Sacrifice and Neighbor-Love

1. Luther Willson, *The Character and Effects of Christian Love: A Sermon Occasioned by the Death of Mrs. Martha Williams* (Providence: Goddard & Mann, 1816), p. 5.
2. Ibid., p. 6.
3. Quoted in Rabbi Zelig Pliskin, *Love Your Neighbor: You and Your Fellow Man in the Light of the Torah* (Brooklyn: Aish HaTorah, 1977), pp. 229–30.
4. Dietrich Bonhoeffer, *Ethics*, tr. Neville Horton Smith (New York: Touchstone, 1995). The book was first published in 1949, a few years after Bonhoeffer's execution by the Nazis.
5. Readers who are skeptical of the proposition that our duty to our family is not dependent on how happy we are may consult the argument in chaps. 3, 8, and 9 of my book *Integrity*.
6. Charles G. Finney, "On Love to Our Neighbor," in Louis Gifford Parkinson, ed., *Principles of Love* (Minneapolis: Bethany House, 1986), pp. 195, 201.
7. See, for example, Aaron Hutchinson, *A well tempered Self-Love a Rule of Conduct towards others: a Sermon Preached at Windsor, July 2, 1777* (Dresden, [Vt.?]: Judah-Paddock and Alden Spooner, 1777).
8. Quoted in Richard Lovelace, "The Bible in Public Discourse," in Rodney L. Peterson, ed., *Christianity and Civil Society* (Maryknoll, N.Y.: Orbis Books, 1995), pp. 62, 72.
9. See Robert Coles, *The Moral Intelligence of Children* (New York: Random House, 1997), pp. 16–30.
10. A very thoughtful effort to work out the legal implications of the command to love the neighbor is Anthony E. Cook, "The Death of God in American Pragmatism and Realism: Resurrecting the Value of Love in Contemporary Jurisprudence," *Georgetown Law Journal* 82 (April 1994): 1431.
11. See Jürgen Habermas, *The Theory of Communicative Action*, vol. 2, tr. Thomas McCarthy (Boston: Beacon Press, 1984).
12. See, for example, Thomas Nagel, "Moral Conflict and Political

Legitimacy," *Philosophy and Public Affairs* 16 (1987): 215. See also Bruce Ackerman, *Social Justice and the Liberal State* (New Haven: Yale University Press, 1980); and Amy Gutmann, *Democratic Education* (Princeton, N.J.: Princeton University Press, 1987).

13. See, for example, Robert N. Bellah, "How to Understand the Church in an Individualistic Society," in Peterson, *Christianity and Civil Society*, p. 1; MacIntyre, *After Virtue*; and Hauerwas, *Dispatches from the Front*, esp. the introduction and chap. 4.

14. Andrew Hacker, "Good or Bad, Greed Is Often Beside the Point," *New York Times*, June 8, 1997, sect. 4, p. 3. Christian ethicists, of course, could have a grand argument over just how big a difference.

15. Here one might usefully compare John Winthrop's sermon on "A Model of Christian Charity," in which he offered the famous image of the Massachusetts Bay Colony as "a city upon a hill, the eyes of all people . . . upon us." In that sermon, Winthrop argues that God is indifferent as to whether we are rich or poor, but cares only that we be willing, should the need arise, to sacrifice all we have for others.

16. Unfortunately, the social science evidence is at best equivocal, and may even cut slightly the other way. For a critical review of the literature, see Peter M. Shane, "School Desegregation Remedies and the Fair Governance of Schools," *University of Pennsylvania Law Review* 132 (1984): 1041. As Shane points out, most of the literature is so methodologically weak that the careful reader will hesitate to draw broad conclusions.

17. See the discussion in Pliskin, *Love Your Neighbor*, pp. 278–92.

18. For the proposition that most Americans believe that young people are getting out of control, see "Americans Down on Youth," *U.P.I.*, June 25, 1997 (available on Nexis).

19. See Cynthia Tucker, "Rap Lyrics Mock Family Values," *Montgomery Advertiser*, March 31, 1997, p. 6A.

20. Carter, *Integrity*, pp. 238–41.

7. The Demon on the Other Side

1. I discuss some examples of this censorship in my article "Let Us Pray," *The New Yorker*, December 5, 1994, p. 60.

2. See, for example, the discussion in Stephen Ansolabehere and

Shanto Iyengar, *Going Negative: How Attack Ads Shrink and Polarize the Electorate* (New York: Free Press, 1995). Journalists noted the change at the time. See, for example, the discussion in Martin Dyckman, "Focus Groups Cloud Our Political Vision," *St. Petersburg Times*, November 6, 1988, p. 5D.

3. See Roderick P. Hart, *Seducing America: How Television Charms the Modern Voter* (New York: Oxford University Press, 1994), p. 4.

4. See survey data discussed in "The American Uncivil Wars," *U.S. News & World Report*, April 22, 1996, p. 66.

5. See Ansolabehere and Iyengar, *Going Negative*. According to the authors' data, one bad effect of negative advertising is its tendency to shrink voter turnout. Some earlier work reached contrary results, finding no effect on turnout. See Gina Garramone, "Effects of Negative Political Advertising on the Political Process," *Journal of Broadcasting and Electronic Media* 34 (1990): 299. Garramone's study, however, involved college students who were subjected to hypothetical advertisements by fictitious candidates.

6. Stephen Bates, *Battleground* (New York: Poseidon Press, 1993).

7. See Norton Epstein and Sondra Krakower, "A Measure of Verbal Aggression," *Perceptual and Motor Skills* 39 (1974): 215.

8. 347 U.S. 483 (1954).

9. I discuss some this history in Stephen L. Carter, *The Confirmation Mess: Cleaning Up the Federal Appointments Process* (New York: Basic Books, 1994).

10. Ibid., pp. 65–73.

11. Support for all of this may be found in the journalist Ethan Bronner's thoughtful and evenhanded book about the Bork hearings, *Battle for Justice: How the Bork Nomination Shook America* (New York: Norton, 1989). See also Carter, *The Confirmation Mess*, pp. 47–53.

12. Hart, *Seducing America*, p. 83.

13. Peter Sloterdijk, "Cynicism—The Twilight of False Consciousness," *New German Critique* 33 (1984): 197; quoted in Hart, *Seducing America*, p. 83.

14. Quoted in "The GOP Feeding Frenzy Is Far from Over," *Business Week*, June 19, 1989, p. 36.

8. The Varieties of (Not) Listening

1. Hendrik Hertzberg, "The Era of Sour Feelings," *The New Yorker*, February 3, 1997, pp. 7, 8.

2. I discuss this problem in chapter 14. For more detail, see my book *The Culture of Disbelief: How American Law and Politics Trivialize Religious Devotion* (New York: Basic Books, 1993).

3. I do not mean that nobody has the right to challenge, for example, equal opportunity or private property. I only mean that the dominant norms of our conversations make the arguments difficult to raise (as racists and Marxists alike frequently discover) and therefore make the arguments difficult to win. For a defense of the idea that a liberal democracy must screen some ideas out of its dialogues on self-governance, see Stephen Holmes, "Gag Rules or the Politics of Omission," in Jon Elster and Rune Slagstad, eds., *Constitutionalism and Democracy* (New York: Cambridge University Press, 1988), p. 19.

4. I discuss this proposition in considerable detail in my book *The Dissent of the Governed: A Meditation on Law, Religion, and Loyalty* (Cambridge, Mass.: Harvard University Press, 1998).

5. See Stephen L. Carter, "A Curse on Both Tents," *New York Times*, August 13, 1996, p. A17.

6. See the discussion of this problem in Albert O. Hirschman, *Exit, Voice, and Loyalty* (Cambridge, Mass.: Harvard University Press, 1970).

7. Stephen Holmes, "Gag Rules or the Politics of Omission," in Jon Elster and Rune Slagstad, eds., *Constitutionalism and Democracy* (New York: Cambridge University Press, 1988), p. 19.

8. Willson, *The Character and Effects of Christian Love*, p. 11.

9. This is not to say that there are *no* opinions that a person of true integrity cannot hold. But the number should be small. The more we think that all people of integrity must hold the same political convictions (ours), the closer we verge toward political fanaticism. See the discussion in Carter, *Integrity*, esp. chaps. 3 and 14.

10. Willson, *The Character and Effects of Christian Love*, p. 11.

11. Michael J. Perry, *Love and Power: The Role of Religion and*

Morality in American Politics (New York: Oxford University Press, 1991).

12. St. George, *The Descent of Manners,* pp. 54–62.

13. Willson, *The Character and Effects of Christian Love,* p. 15.

14. Donald W. Shriver, Jr., *An Ethic for Enemies: Forgiveness in Politics* (New York: Oxford University Press, 1995), p. 9; see also his chap. 3.

15. Charles G. Finney, "On Love to Our Neighbor," in Louis Gifford Parkinson, ed., *Principles of Love* (Minneapolis: Bethany House, 1986), pp. 195, 200.

16. For discussions of Eliot's anti-Semitism, see, for example, Lee Smith, "Memory and Desire: Reports of Eliot's Anti-Semitism Are Hardly News," *Village Voice*, June 18, 1996, p. 63; and Christopher Hitchens, "How Unpleasant to Meet Mr. Eliot," *The Nation*, August 12, 1996, p. 8. For forceful but inadequate defenses, see Craig Raine, "T. S. Eliot: Guilty by Association?" *Financial Times* (London), May 18, 1996, p. 14, and "Eliot's Black Humor," *Daily Telegraph*, August 26, 1996, p. 17. All of this heated argument was occasioned by the publication of Anthony Julius's 1996 book *T. S. Eliot: Anti-Semitism and Literary Form*, which argues that Eliot's anti-Semitism infects his entire oeuvre. On the overall issue of Eliot's anti-Semitism, I cast my lot with Hitchens, who writes: "Was T. S. Eliot an anti-Semite? What a question! Of course he was an anti-Semite, if the term retains any of its meaning." Hitchens, I should add in fairness, makes clear in his essay that he does not think much of Julius's book.

17. Michiko Kakutani, "Culture Zone: Bigotry in Motion," *New York Times Magazine*, March 16, 1997, p. 24.

18. Shriver, *An Ethic for Enemies,* p. 9.

19. Lewis B. Smedes, *The Art of Forgiving: When You Need to Forgive and Don't Know How* (Nashville, Tenn.: Moorings, 1996), p. 151. See also the essays collected in Amitai Etzioni and David E. Carney, eds., *Repentance: A Comparative Perspective* (Lanham, Md.: Rowman and Littlefield, 1997).

20. Willson, *The Character and Effects of Christian Love,* p. 19.

21. Frederick Schauer, "Formalism," *Yale Law Journal* 97 (1988): 509, 539.

9. Fighting Words

1. Quoted in Curry Kirkpatrick, "He's Just Old Enough to Drive the Lane," *Newsweek*, December 4, 1995, p. 72.

2. Paul Vitello, "Test Your Political Savvy," *Newsday*, November 5, 1995, p. A6.

3. See, for example, Manuel Schiffres, "7 Great Small Stocks," *Kiplinger's Personal Finance Magazine* (October 1996): 36 ("Buy the right stock at the wrong time and you can get handed your head"); "Capital Punishment: Retirees Who Aim to Spend Only the Income Generated by Investments Can Lose out to Inflation," *Chicago Tribune*, September 22, 1996, business sect., p. 3 ("All too often, these poor folks get their heads handed to them").

4. *Gross v. Burggraf Construction Co.*, 53 F.3d 1531 (10th Cir. 1995).

5. See, for example, Carroll E. Izard, *The Psychology of Emotions* (New York: Plenum Press, 1991).

6. See, for example, "USA Should Put Own House in Order Before Attacking Human Rights in China," Xinhua News Agency, Beijing (broadcast transcript), in *BBC Summary of World Broadcasts*, March 5, 1997 (available on Nexis).

7. See, for example, Carol Z. Stearns and Peter N. Sterns, *Anger: The Struggle for Emotional Control in America's History* (Chicago: University of Chicago Press, 1986).

8. See, for example, Izard, *The Psychology of Emotions,* pp. 241–47.

9. Hannah Arendt, *On Violence* (New York: Harcourt Brace, 1970).

10. Quoted in "Short Stuff," *Raleigh News and Observer,* June 1, 1996, p. A2.

11. See, for example, J. D. Considine, "Keep Assets out of a Sling," *Baltimore Sun*, February 18, 1997, p. 1D.

12. See "Canada's 'Christian Soldiers' Get Marching Orders," *Daily Telegraph*, June 10, 1995, p. 11.

13. "Top 10 Hits," *Atlanta Journal and Constitution*, July 23, 1994, p. E6, which discusses a survey of 3,000 readers of *The Anglican Digest*, who were asked to select their favorite hymns. In the survey, "Onward, Christian Soldiers" finished tenth.

14. Readers interested in the serious philosophical and theological

debate over whether warfare itself is ever just might usefully compare Grady Scott Davis, *Warcraft and the Fragility of Virtue* (Moscow: University of Idaho Press, 1992), which argues yes, with James W. Douglass, *The Non-Violent Cross* (New York: Macmillan, 1968), which basically argues no.

15. Dave Grossman, *On Killing: The Psychological Cost of Learning to Kill in War and Society* (Boston: Little, Brown, 1995), p. 87.

16. Historically, this has been particularly true of women, who, barred from actual service, have often been the most adamant and aggressive supporters of the war itself. See Jean Bethke Elshtain, *Women and War* (New York: Basic Books, 1987).

17. See, for example, Paul Ramsey, *The Just War: Force and Political Responsibility* (New York: Scribner's, 1968).

18. Grossman, *On Killing,* p. 92.

19. Quoted in Barton J. Bernstein, "Smithsonian Decision Not Americans' Views on War," *Daily Yomiuri,* February 3, 1995. Professor Bernstein taught me American history at Stanford back in the seventies, and I first encountered the Truman letter in one of his classes. I should add that I am not questioning Truman's decision to drop the bomb, only the justification offered in the letter.

20. Surgeon General's Scientific Advisory Committee on Television and Social Behavior, *Television and Growing Up: The Impact of Television Violence* (Washington, D.C.: U.S. Government Printing Office, 1972).

21. Brandon S. Centerwall, "Television and Violence: The Scale of the Problem and Where to Go from Here," *Journal of the American Medical Association* 267 (1992): 3059. It should be noted that even those who agree with Dr. Centerwall's basic analysis are skeptical of the claim that without television there would be ten thousand fewer homicides and seventy thousand fewer rapes each year. See, for example, the discussions in Mark M. McCarthy, "Broadcast Self-Regulation: The NAB Codes, Family Viewing Hour, and Television Violence," *Cardozo Arts and Entertainment Law Journal* 13 (1995): 667; and Harry T. Edwards and Mitchell N. Berman, "Regulating Violence on Television," *Northwestern University Law Review* 89 (1995): 1089.

22. See, for example, the data discussed in Jonathan D. Klein, Jane D. Brown, Kim Walsh Childers, Janice Oliveri, Carol Porter, and Carol Dykers, "Adolescents' Risky Behavior and Mass Media Use," *Pediatrics* 92 (July 1993): 24; Kenneth D. Gadow and Joyce Sprafkin, "Field Experiment of Television Violence with Children," *Pediatrics* 83 (March 1989): 399; and L. Rowell Huesmann, "Television Violence and Aggression: The Causal Effect Remains," *American Psychologist* 28 (1973): 617.

23. This is the implication, for example, of Jerome L. Singer and Dorothy G. Singer, *Television, Imagination, and Aggression: A Study of Preschoolers* (Hillsdale, N.J.: Lawrence Erlbaum Associates, 1981).

24. See the discussion in Anne-Claude Bernard-Bonnin, Sophie Gilbert, Elizabeth Rousseau, Pierre Masson, and Brigitte Maheux, "Television and the 3- to 10-Year-Old Child," *Pediatrics* (July 1991): 48.

25. Milton Chen, "Exploding 3 Myths about Tykes and TV," *TV Guide*, March 10, 1997.

26. Neil Postman, *The End of Education: Redefining the Value of School* (New York: Knopf, 1995), p. 85.

27. See Kenneth J. Gergen, "Aggression as Discourse," in Amélie Mummendey, ed., *Social Psychology of Aggression: From Individual Behavior to Social Interaction* (Berlin: Springer-Verlag, 1984), p. 51.

28. A useful summary of the research, as well as a presentation of findings that tend to corroborate this traditional dichotomy, is Mary B. Harris, "How Provoking! What Makes Men and Women Angry?" *Aggressive Behavior* 19 (1993): 199.

29. I couch the text in guarded terms because I have read only press reports on the research. See, for example, "If You Must Insult Someone, Pick a Northerner, Michigan Study Finds," *Los Angeles Times,* September 15, 1996, p. A23.

30. See, for example, Meri Matsuda, "Public Response to Hate Speech: Considering the Victim's Story," *Michigan Law Review* 87 (1989): 2320.

31. See *Chaplinsky v. New Hampshire*, 315 U.S. 568 (1942).

32. Owen M. Fiss, *The Irony of Free Speech* (Cambridge, Mass.: Harvard University Press, 1996), p. 14.

33. The sociologist Charles Flynn, whose work we discussed in chapter 2, points out that the utility of racial epithets is principally the maintenance of racial caste: they remind blacks and whites alike of the correct racial pecking order. Insult, he reports, is a vital means of social control in every divided society. See Flynn, *Insult and Society*, pp. 39–60. Even when the system supported by the insults is swept away, the epithets may retain a controlling function: racism has less bite when it is not supported by law, but that does not mean it has no bite at all.

34. But see the discussion in James Q. Wilson, *The Moral Sense*, pp. 29–54.

35. The economist would argue that if Alan gives up his seat to Beatrice and Carlos does not, the reason must be that Alan gains satisfaction (derives utility, in the jargon) from doing the deed, and Carlos does not. In other words, giving up the seat is worth more to Alan, but keeping the seat is worth more to Carlos. If this is so, then the task of those who would reconstruct civility is to change the preferences of people who would prefer not to yield their seat. If the habits of politesse are learned, it is vital that we find places to teach them.

10. Market Language and the Linguistics of Incivility

1. "Has Nice Finally Replaced Nasty?" *Fort Lauderdale Sun-Sentinel*, July 20, 1996, p. 1D.

2. Debbie Salamone, "Judicial Races Too Nasty, Defense Lawyers Say," *Orlando Sentinel*, October 28, 1996, p. C1.

3. Mark Kiszla, "Sordid Cowboys Sullying Name, Game," *Denver Post*, January 2, 1997, p. C4.

4. Sandy Coleman, "Majoring in Street Smarts," *Boston Globe*, September 25, 1996, p. D1.

5. Browser Lets Parents Set Usage Standards," *Dubuque Telegraph Herald*, September 1, 1996, p. A12.

6. This is, of course, a very old point, and it has often been made by economists, going all the way back to Adam Smith. Recent warnings about the tendency of the market sphere to swamp the rest of

human life have been sounded by such prominent economists as Arthur Okun (in *Equality and Efficiency: The Big Tradeoff*), Charles Lindbloom (in *Politics and Markets*), and, of course, John Kenneth Galbraith, as well as by social critics galore.

Needless to say, there are dissenters. For a forceful and fascinating but ultimately unsuccessful effort to restate all of morality in terms of efficiency, see Richard A. Posner, *The Economics of Justice* (Cambridge, Mass.: Harvard University Press, 1981).

7. E. F. Schumacher, *Small Is Beautiful: Economics as if People Mattered* (New York: Harper & Row, 1973).

8. Don E. Eberly, *Restoring the Good Society: A New Vision for Politics and Culture* (Grand Rapids, Mich.: Hourglass Books, 1994), p. 72.

9. Pontifical Council for Social Communication, *Ethics in Advertising* (1997), reprinted in *Advertising Age,* March 10, 1997, p. 26.

10. Both quoted in Tamar Charry, "The Roman Catholic Church Gets Mixed Reviews on Its Foray into Advertising's Big Issues," *New York Times*, March 31, 1997, p. D9.

11. Quoted in Carol Krol, "Pontifical Council Sets Guidelines for Making Ads: Vatican Values Leave U.S. Admen Unimpressed," *Advertising Age*, March 3, 1997, p. 37.

12. See, for example, William Landes and Richard Posner, "Trademark Law: An Economic Perspective," *Journal of Law and Economics* 30 (1987): 265. The proposition that advertising should be treated (in economic terms) as information is associated with the work of Phillip Nelson. See, for example, Nelson, "Information and Consumer Behavior," *Journal of Political Economy* 78 (1970): 311; and Nelson, "The Economic Consequences of Advertising," *Journal of Business* 48 (1975): 213.

13. *Ethics in Advertising*.

14. Quoted in Melanie Wells, "Vatican: Thou Shalt Not Make Ads False or Sexy," *USA Today*, February 26, 1997, p. 1B.

15. See "Pope Warns on Lust in Marriage," *New York Times*, October 10, 1980, p. 3. If the argument seems counterintuitive, consider Matthew 5:28: "I say to you that everyone who looks at a woman with lust has already committed adultery in his heart."

Jesus' words here make no exception for the woman's husband. The point, however, must surely be that the adultery comes when a man looks at his wife *only* with lust, seeing her only as a sexual being, and desiring that being, rather than desiring the whole complex person to whom he is actually committed in marriage. For Pope John Paul II's earlier and detailed views on the complexities of sexual desire (written long before his papacy), see Karol Wojtyla, *Love and Responsibility*, tr. H. T. Willets (New York: Farrar, Straus & Giroux, 1994). The book was first published in 1960.

16. *Ethics in Advertising.*

17. See the discussion in chapter 13. A more detailed explication of my objections to the current liberal theory of education may be found in Stephen L. Carter, "Parents, Religion, and Schools: Reflections on Pierce 70 Years Later," *Seton Hall Law Review* (forthcoming, 1998).

18. See, for example, Cass R. Sunstein, "Naked Preferences and the Constitution," *Columbia Law Review* 84 (1984): 1689.

19. See, for example, Alan R. Andreasen, *Marketing Social Change: Changing Behavior to Promote Health, Social Development, and the Environment* (San Francisco: Jossey-Bass, 1995).

20. See the data collected in Stephen Hart, *What Does the Lord Require? How American Christians View Economic Justice* (New York: Oxford University Press, 1992).

21. See the discussion in Stephen L. Carter, "Nativism and Its Discontents," *New York Times*, March 8, 1992, p. 15.

22. The sociologist Peter L. Berger's early warnings about this problem have proved particularly prophetic. See, for example, his books *The Noise of Solemn Assemblies* (New York: Doubleday, 1961), and *Facing up to Modernity: Excursions in Society, Politics, and Religion* (New York: Basic Books, 1977).

23. The 70 percent figure comes from a survey of 1,008 adults reported in Richard Morin, "Unconventional Wisdom," *Washington Post*, August 27, 1995, p. C7. In the same survey, 65 percent said they believe in Satan. On the question of whether people answer for their sins on Judgment Day, 77 percent of mainline Protestants and 42 percent of Jews believe the answer is yes, according to a Pew Research Center survey reported in

Gustav Niebuhr, "Survey Finds Wide Variation in the Intensity of Faith," *New York Times*, June 25, 1996, p. A18. But no matter how many of us believe in Judgment Day, only 8 percent of us, according to the Harris poll, worry a lot about whether we are going to Hell or not. See Joe Pisani, "Eternity Hardly Troubles Us," *Tampa Tribune*, October 15, 1995, p. 5.

24. Quite apart from collective action problems, the theory that the consumer will decide assumes a concentrated rationality that simply does not attach to all purchase decisions. In particular, laboratory research has made clear that people try to simplify their choices by using decision rules that, unfortunately, create systematic and predictable errors in the decisions themselves. See, for example, Richard Nisbett and Lee Ross, *Human Inference: Strategies and Shortcomings of Social Judgment* (Englewood Cliffs, N.J.: Prentice-Hall, 1980), and the articles collected in Daniel Kahneman, Paul Slovic, and Amos Tversky, eds., *Judgment Under Uncertainty: Heuristics and Biases* (Cambridge: Cambridge University Press, 1982).

25. Azizah al-Hibri, "On Being a Muslim Corporate Lawyer," *Texas Tech Law Review* 27 (1996): 947, 960.

26. An excellent and nearly contemporaneous retelling of the Beech-nut tale is James Traub, "Into the Mouths of Babes," *New York Times Magazine*, July 24, 1988, p. 18. An example of the incorporation of the story into a business school case study format is Julianne Nelson, "The Market Ethic: Moral Dilemmas and Microeconomics," *Journal of Business Ethics* 11 (1992): 317. For a thoughtful discussion of why firms choose to conceal bad news—and how they suffer for the choice—see Robert R. Kerton and Richard W. Bodell, "Quality, Choice, and the Economics of Concealment: The Marketing of Lemons," *Journal of Consumer Affairs* 29 (1995): 1.

Perhaps because the behavior of management was so bizarre, the Beech-nut case has also found its way into psychology textbooks. See, for example, Philip G. Zimbardo and Michael R. Leippe, *The Psychology of Attitude Change and Social Influence* (1991), pp. 120–21.

27. For a fascinating discussion of the link between sexual harassment and incivility, see Carol Brooks Gardner, *Passing By:*

Gender and Public Harassment (Berkeley: University of California Press, 1995), pp. 64–75, 158–98.

11. Some Technologies of Incivility

1. See Robert A. Nisbet, *A History of the Idea of Progress* (New York: Basic Books, 1980).
2. See *The Telephone Cases* 126 U.S. 1 (1888).
3. See Sennett, *The Fall of Public Man*; and Lofland, *A World of Strangers.*
4. Quoted in Pamela McCorduck, "Sex, Lies, and Avatars," *Wired* (April 1996): 108. For a fuller statement of Sherry Turkle's views on the contingent nature of information following the cyber revolution, see her book *Life on the Screen: Identity in the Age of the Internet* (New York: Simon & Schuster, 1995).
5. Kurt Andersen, "The Age of Unreason," *The New Yorker*, February 3, 1997, pp. 40, 41.
6. For an amusing discussion of the commercial aspects of push and pull, see James Gleick, "Pushy, Pushy," *New York Times Magazine*, March 23, 1997, p. 32.
7. *Gertz v. Robert Welch, Inc.*, 418 U.S. 323 (1974).
8. For a lively if disturbing discussion of morphing online, see Mark Dery, *Escape Velocity: Cyberculture at the End of the Century* (New York: Grove Press, 1996), pp. 202–3 and, especially, chap. 6.
9. Word-stuffing takes advantage of the relative lack of sophistication of the computer programs that drive Internet search software. These programs, known as search engines, work in the same way: when the user requests a list of Websites on a specific subject—wine, for example, or dating—the search engine searches all the sites to which it can gain ready access and provides to the user a list of sites on which the key word appears. Most search engines rank the sites in order, according to the frequency with which the key word is mentioned. For example, if the user is searching for Websites that specialize in wine, the first one on the list will be the one in which the word *wine* occurs most often.

Word-stuffing does just what the name implies: the key word is scattered all over the Website, perhaps hidden in graphics or even inside other words, so that the search engine records a large number of repetitions and ranks the site very high, perhaps at the top. (Hiding a word in graphics is no big deal. Imagine a piece of plain red paper on which you write the word *wine* perhaps fifty times using red ink. The result appears to the unaided eye as a solid red graphic, but the computer has no trouble distinguishing the words from the background and thus reports back a site with an extra fifty repetitions of the word.)

10. Kasson, *Rudeness and Civility,* pp. 99–111.
11. See *Reno v. ACLU*, 117 S. Ct. 3439 (1997).
12. Among the many depressing reports are "Guarding Young Web-Surfers," *Consumer Reports*, September 1997, p. 17, and Nell Minow, "Filtering Filth: Web Filters: Which Ones Work?" *Slate*, posted Aug. 14, 1997, http://www.slate.com/Features/Filth/Filth.asp. The lack of parental ability to use the software may seem a relative small problem, but the blocking programs suffer from other deficiencies as well. Many are easy to spoof: for example, in some cases one can get around the blocking through a simple renaming of certain files on the hard drive. Others block too much: Minow reports that some, for example, will block the poetry of Anne *Sex*ton. And many young people report that stealing their parents' password, enabling them to unlock the blocking program is . . . well . . . child's play. (One easy way to steal passwords is to insert a simple program that records all the keystrokes of other users.)
13. Michael L. Dertouzos, *What Will Be: How the New World of Information Will Change Our Lives* (New York: HarperEdge, 1997), pp. 64–80.
14. President William J. Clinton, State of the Union Address, U.S. Capitol, February 4, 1997 (official text as released by the White House).
15. Marilyn Gell Mason, "The Yin and Yang of Knowing," *Daedalus* (Fall 1996): 161, 171.
16. Leon Festinger, Henry W. Riecken, and Stanley Schachter, *When Prophecy Fails* (New York: Harper & Row, 1956), p. 28.

Festinger's better-known book, *A Theory of Cognitive Dissonance* (Evanston, Illinois: Row & Peterson, 1957), was not published until the following year.

17. Lawrence Lessig, "The Path of Cyberlaw," *Yale Law Journal* 104 (1995): 1743, 1745.

18. Lewis Thomas, "To Err Is Human," in *The Medusa and the Snail: More Notes of a Biology Watcher* (New York: Viking, 1979), p. 36.

19. I discuss this study in Stephen L. Carter, "Scientific Liberalism, Scientistic Law," *Oregon Law Review* 69 (1990): 471.

20. John I. Thornton, "Uses and Abuses of Forensic Science," in William A. Thomas, ed., *Science and Law: An Essential Alliance* (Boulder, Colo.: Westview Press, 1983), pp. 79, 88.

21. See *Brown v. Board of Education*, 347 U.S. 483 (1954). The social science research appears, without comment or analysis, in footnote 11 of the Court's opinion.

22. See Stephen Galebach, "A Human Life Statute," *Human Life Review* 7 (1981): 3. The Human Life Bill survived subcommittee hearings in the Senate but never escaped the Judiciary Committee. I discuss the constitutionality of the proposal in Stephen L. Carter, "The Morgan 'Power' and the Forced Reconsideration of Constitutional Decisions," *University of Chicago Law Review* 53 (1986): 819.

23. For a powerful example of a pro-life argument that does not turn on the humanity of the fetus, see Bonhoeffer, *Ethics*, pp. 171–77.

24. See, for example, Chandler Burr, *A Separate Creation: The Search for the Biological Origins of Sexual Orientations* (New York: Hyperion, 1996).

25. See Byron York, "Hyping the Gay Gene," *Forbes Media Critic* (Spring 1996): 89.

26. See *Bowers v. Hardwick*, 478 U.S. 186 (1986).

27. One need not consider homosexuality inborn to accept the proposition that discrimination against homosexuals is wrong. For example, black Americans are far less likely than any other group (whether we divide by race, sex, religion, income, region, or education) to believe homosexuality to be innate, but far more likely than almost every other group to support legislation barring employment discrimination on the basis of

sexual orientation. See Gallup poll, January 1, 1997 (available on Westlaw/Polls Database).

12. Law, Tolerance, and Civility's Illusions

1. See William Lee Miller, *Arguing About Slavery: The Great Battle in the United States Congress* (New York: Knopf, 1996).
2. 491 U.S. 397 (1989).
3. On the unconstitutionality of hate speech codes, see, for example, *Doe v. University of Michigan*, 721 F. Supp. 852 (E.D. Mich. 1989).
4. A forcefully argued but nevertheless disturbing example is Meri Matsuda, "Public Response to Racist Speech: Considering the Victim's Story," *Michigan Law Review* 87 (1989): 2320.
5. Michael W. McConnell, "America's First 'Hate-Speech' Regulation," *Constitutional Commentary* (Winter 1992): 17.
6. I discuss this case in *Integrity*, pp. 219–20.
7. Quoted in "Most in Presidential Race Urge Tougher, Stronger Crime Policies," *Minneapolis Star Tribune*, February 9, 1996, p. 7A.
8. For useful discussions of Locke's limited views of tolerance, see, for example, Paul Johnson, *A History of Christianity* (New York: Atheneum, 1976), pp. 337–40; Michael W. McConnell, "The Origins and Historical Understandings of Free Exercise of Religion," *Harvard Law Review* 103 (1990): 1409; and Suzanna Sherry, "An Essay Concerning Toleration," *Minnesota Law Review* 71 (1987): 963.
9. Well, maybe it has some. See Glenn Tinder, *Tolerance and Community* (Columbia, Mo.: University of Missouri Press, 1995).
10. See the discussion in Pliskin, *Love Your Neighbor*, pp. 278–92.
11. A 1996 Gallup poll, for example, found nearly seven of ten Americans opposed to abortion as a means of birth control. See Dennis Byrne, "Rigid Abortion Plank Weakens Platform," *Chicago Sun-Times*, May 9, 1996, p. 35.
12. I am including as "birth control" the following reasons, which appear to be the most common ones for which abortion is sought: a fear that the baby will change the woman's life, a

belief that the baby will be too expensive, and a sense that an important relationship will change (including a concern about raising a child alone). See the data presented in visual form in "Abortion Battles: More in Common Than We Think," *USA Today*, August 13, 1996, p. 17A.

13. A 1996 Gallup poll found 71 percent opposed to partial-birth abortion. See "Abortion Battles," p. 17A. Another survey found opposition at a smaller but still substantial 54 percent. See "Pew Research: Majority Support 'Partial-Birth' Abortion Ban," *Abortion Report*, May 23, 1997. I have heard pro-life politicians and activists cite figures as high as 90 percent in opposition to the practice, but I am aware of no data supporting their claims. The wording of the questions no doubt accounts for some of the differences, but scholars who study attitudes on abortion are always reminding us that public opinion on this issue is remarkably volatile.

14. See "Abortion Battles."

15. See Naomi Wolf, "Our Bodies, Our Souls," *The New Republic*, October 16, 1995, p. 26. Wolf's sharpest line: "How can we charge that it is vile and repulsive for pro-lifers to brandish vile and repulsive images if the images are real?"

16. This is the burden of, for example, Ronald Dworkin, *Life's Dominion: An Argument About Abortion, Euthanasia, and Individual Freedom* (New York: Knopf, 1993), and Laurence Tribe, *Abortion: The Clash of Absolutes* (New York: Norton, 1990). A strong majority of the American public, however, sharply disputes the notion that the freedom to choose abortion should not depend on the reason the choice is made.

17. Legal interpretation, wrote Cover, is "designed to generate credible threats and actual deeds of violence." Robert M. Cover, "Violence and the Word," *Yale Law Journal* 95 (1986): 1601, 1610.

18. 410 U.S. 113 (1973).

19. A quite readable, if slightly dated, summary of the empirical research is Tom R. Tyler, *Why People Obey the Law* (New Haven: Yale University Press, 1990).

20. Samuel Seabury, *A Discourse on Brotherly Love* (New York: Gaine, 1777), pp. 8–9.

21. Tyler, *Why People Obey the Law,* p. 65.
22. Seabury, *A Discourse on Brotherly Love,* p. 9.
23. Ibid., p. 14.
24. Ibid., p. 12.

13. Where Civility Begins

1. For recent discussions of the literature, see Robert Coles, *The Moral Intelligence of Children* (New York: Random House, 1997), pp. 61–166; and James Q. Wilson, *The Moral Sense* (New York: Free Press, 1993), pp. 141–63.
2. For strong support of explicit character education, see, for example, the data cited in Tamara Henry, "The Problems with Schools / Poll Says It's Violence, Fighting, Lack of Discipline," *USA Today,* August 26, 1994, p. 7D. The poll found, for example, that 97 percent support teaching honesty and 93 percent support teaching democracy.
3. Joseph Cardinal Bernardin, *The Gift of Peace* (Chicago: Loyola Press, 1997).
4. See the figures quoted in Anne Lindberg, "Choosing School Not as Easy as ABC," *St. Petersburg Times,* January 1, 1997, p. 1.
5. For a similar idea of deliberation in teaching children right and wrong, see Coles, *The Moral Intelligence of Children,* passim.
6. Kasson, *Rudeness and Civility,* pp. 157–61.
7. See, for example, the discussion in Flynn, *Insult and Society,* pp. 36–38.
8. The most important contemporary defender of this view is, of course, Alasdair MacIntyre, especially in his classic work *After Virtue,* 2d ed. (Notre Dame, Ind.: University of Notre Dame Press, 1984).
9. See John McKnight, *The Careless Society: Community and Its Counterfeits* (New York: Basic Books, 1995).
10. Elias, *The Civilizing Process,* pp. 170–73.
11. I discuss this episode in chapter 9 of *The Culture of Disbelief.*
12. *Pierce v. Society of Sisters,* 268 U.S. 510 (1925).
13. Michael Eric Dyson, *Between God and Gangsta Rap: Bearing Witness to Black Culture* (New York: Oxford University Press, 1996), pp. 13–16.

14. See *Ware v. Valley Stream High School,* 75 N.Y.2d 114, 550 N.E.2d 420 (N.Y. 1989).
15. See, for example, the data and sources discussed in Rebecca R. S. Socolar and Ruth E. K. Stein, "Spanking Infants and Toddlers: Maternal Beliefs and Practice," *Pediatrics* 95 (January 1995): 105.
16. Dyson, *Between God and Gangsta Rap,* p. 15.
17. See, for example, Bruce Ackerman, *Social Justice and the Liberal State* (New Haven: Yale University Press, 1980), pp. 150–60; Amy Gutmann, *Democratic Education* (Princeton, N.J.: Princeton University Press, 1987), pp. 1–70; Stephen Macedo, "Liberal Civic Education and Religious Fundamentalism: The Case of God vs. John Rawls," *Ethics* 105 (1995): 468; Ira C. Lupu, "The Separation of Powers and the Protection of Children," *University of Chicago Law Review* 61 (1994): 1317. Somewhat more sympathetic to parents, but still in its way quite troubling, is Suzanna Sherry, "Responsible Republicanism: Educating for Citizenship," *University of Chicago Law Review* 62 (1995): 131.

    A thoughtful response to much of this body of work is Stephen G. Gilles, "On Educating Children: A Parentalist Manifesto," *University of Chicago Law Review* 63 (1996): 937. A sobering discussion of the practical side of this argument is James Davison Hunter, *Culture Wars: The Struggle to Define America* (New York: Basic Books, 1991). See also Stephen Bates, *Battleground*; Robert Wuthnow, *The Struggle for America's Soul: Evangelicals, Liberals, and Secularism* (Grand Rapids, Mich.: William B. Eerdmans, 1989); and Stephen L. Carter, *The Culture of Disbelief,* ch. 9.
18. Amy Gutmann, *Democratic Education,* pp. 1–70.
19. Ackerman, *Social Justice and the Liberal State,* pp. 150–58.
20. Bruce Ackerman, in *Social Justice in the Liberal State,* does not quite specify who will run his "liberal schools," and does not really tell us what role he thinks private schools should play, but it is difficult to resist the conclusion that he imagines liberal schools run by the state, and considers private schools to be of questionable value.
21. Ira C. Lupu, "The Separation of Powers and the Protection of

Children," *University of Chicago Law Review* 61 (1994): 1317, 1353.

22. Sherry, "Responsible Republicanism," pp. 160–61.
23. Ackerman worries about parents who will "force-feed their children without restraint." Ackerman, *Social Justice in the Liberal State,* p. 160. Gutmann insists that many religious parents teach their children "disrespect for people who are different." Gutmann, *Democratic Education,* p. 31.
24. *Ware v. Valley Stream High School,* 75 N.Y.2d 114, 550 N.E.2d 420 (N.Y. 1989).
25. Bonhoeffer, *Ethics,* pp. 172–73.
26. Paula M. Cooey, *Family, Freedom, and Faith: Building Community Today* (Louisville, Ky.: Westminster John Knox Press, 1996), p. 45.
27. All of these data are drawn from a *USA Today*/CNN/Gallup poll reported as a table under the headline "Family Values: Some Surprises," *USA Today,* March 11, 1997, p. 6D.
28. See Bickley Townsend and Kathleen O'Neil, "American Women Get Mad: Women's Attitudes Are Changing," *American Demographics,* (August 1990): 26. The authors discuss a 1990 poll by the Roper Organization indicating that 53 percent of women surveyed prefer a "shared" marriage and 38 percent prefer "a traditional marriage in which the husband is the sole breadwinner and the wife cares for the home and children." I have not been able to uncover any more recent data.
29. See the data collected in David Blankenhorn, *Fatherless America: Confronting Our Most Urgent Social Problem* (New York: Basic Books, 1995); and Judith S. Wallerstein, "The Long-Term Effects of Divorce on Children: A Review," *Journal of the American Academy of Child and Adolescent Psychiatry* 30 (1991): 349.
30. Readers who find this point perplexing should examine the two chapters I devote to the question of marriage in *Integrity.*

14. Uncivil Religion

1. For an impressive demonstration of the proposition that Christianity has always existed in tension with other forces

(and within itself) in the United States, see Jon Butler, *Awash in a Sea of Faith* (Cambridge, Mass.: Harvard University Press, 1990).

2. Richard Lovelace, "The Bible in Public Discourse," in Peterson, *Christianity and Civil Society*, pp. 62, 69.

3. On the measurement problem, see, for example, Wade Clark Roof and William McKinney, *American Mainline Religion: Its Changing Shape and Future* (New Brunswick, N.J.: Rutgers University Press, 1987); and Robert Wuthnow, *The Struggle for America's Soul: Evangelicals, Liberals, and Secularism* (Grand Rapids, Mich.: William B. Eerdmans, 1989).

4. Quoted in Richard J. Mouw, "Religious Conviction and Public Civility," in Joseph Runzo, ed., *Ethics, Religion and the Good Society* (Louisville, Ky.: Westminster/John Knox Press, 1992), p. 97*n*9.

5. See John Shelby Spong, *Born of a Woman: A Bishop Rethinks the Birth of Jesus* (San Francisco: Harper San Francisco, 1992). For effective criticism of Spong's methodology, see Luke Timothy Johnson, *The Real Jesus: The Misguided Quest for the Historical Jesus and the Truth of the Traditional Gospels* (San Francisco: Harper San Francisco, 1996).

6. Quoted in Lela Garlington, "Spong Urges Reading Bible with Jewish Eyes," *The Commercial Appeal* (Memphis), September 16, 1996, p. 1B.

7. Tom Weir, "Chang Moves in Range of World's Top Ranking with Quiet Efficiency," *USA Today*, September 5, 1996, p. 14C.

8. Kathleen Sullivan, "God as a Lobby," *University of Chicago Law Review* 61 (1994): 1655.

9. See Samuel P. Huntington, *The Clash of Civilizations and the Remaking of World Order* (New York: Simon & Schuster, 1996).

10. Walter Wink, *Engaging the Powers* (Philadelphia: Fortress Press, 1992), p. 233.

11. See Paul Johnson, *A History of Christianity* (New York: Atheneum, 1976), pp. 247–50.

12. On this point, it is useful to compare the argument pressed by Mary E. Becker, "The Politics of Women's Wrongs and the Bill of 'Rights': A Bicentennial Perspective," *University of Chicago*

Law Review 59 (1992): 453, that religion, for just this reason, should not be rewarded with specially enhanced constitutional protection.

13. Not all feminists identify the same solution to this problem. The leading positions, even after the passage of two decades, probably remain that of Mary Daly, who would eliminate the biblical text altogether on the ground that it is hopelessly patriarchal and create in its stead a new, "post-Christian" religion, and Phyllis Trible, who believes biblical tradition to be valuable but also thinks sensitive interpretive tools are required to avoid oppression. Compare Mary Daly, *Beyond God the Father: Toward a Philosophy of Women's Liberation* (Boston: Beacon Press, 1973) with Phyllis Trible, *God and the Rhetoric of Sexuality* (Philadelphia: Fortress Press, 1978). For me as a Christian, the weakness of Daly's position is that it ultimately views religion as simply created by the faithful rather than encountered by them, denying altogether that religious knowledge is given from God. What I find appealing in Trible—even though I do not always agree with her—is that she begins where I think the believing Christian always must, with an appreciation of the biblical text itself.

A more recent and very controversial synthesis, emphasizing the connection between the equality of women and larger questions of social justice, is Elisabeth Schussler Fiorenza, *In Memory of Her: A Feminist Theological Reconstruction of Christian Origins* (New York: Crossroad, 1983).

14. Thomas Nagel, "Moral Conflict and Political Legitimacy," *Philosophy and Public Affairs* 16 (1987): 215.

15. Gutmann, *Democratic Education*, p. 31.

16. I discuss this point in more detail in *The Culture of Disbelief*, esp. chaps. 3 and 11.

17. See Sydney Ahlstrom, *A Religious History of the American People* (New Haven: Yale University Press, 1972), and Nathan Hatch, *The Democratization of American Christianity* (New Haven: Yale University Press, 1989).

18. This is not to concede the suggestion of Harold Bloom that, in effect, America reduces all religions to one form or another of gnosticism. See Harold Bloom, *The American Religion: The*

Emergence of the Post-Christian Nation (New York: Simon & Schuster, 1992).

19. For a frank acknowledgment of both the loss of confidence and the sense that the church cannot afford to seem "theocratic," see Leander E. Keck, *The Church Confident* (Nashville, Tenn: Abingdon Press, 1993).

20. Nancy T. Ammerman, "Fundamentalists Proselytizing Jews: Incivility in Preparation for the Rapture," in Martin E. Marty and Frederick E. Greenspahn, eds., *Pushing the Faith: Proselytism and Civility in a Pluralistic World* (New York: Crossroad, 1988), p. 109.

21. This reading of Scripture is not unchallenged. For a brief discussion of its complexities, see Martin E. Marty, "Proselytism in a Pluralistic World," in Marty and Greenspahn, eds., *Pushing the Faith*, p. 155.

22. For a scholarly if depressing chronicle, see Leonard Dinnerstein, *Anti-Semitism in America* (New York: Oxford University Press, 1994).

23. I recognize that my opposition to the proselytizing of Jews probably places me in a minority of Christians, but I consider the relevant passages in Romans to be less ambiguous than many of my coreligionists believe. Theologically, the question is not whether Jesus Christ is the Savior of Jews—Christians believe that He is the Savior of all human beings—but rather whether Jews, despite their special Covenant with God, must profess faith in Christ in order to be saved. Many Christians answer *Yes.* I answer *No.* I should emphasize, however, that I do not consider the effort to convert Jews to be anti-Semitism, because a disbelief in the truth of someone else's religious convictions is not the same as a hatred for that person. Nevertheless, as I note in the text, the long Christian history of vilification and persecution of Jews creates a special obligation of caution when considering efforts to convert Jews. For a surprisingly delicate examination of the fissures on this issue, see James Sibley, "Some of Their Best Friends Are Jews," *New York Times Magazine*, March 16, 1997, p. 42. See also the discussion in Richard John Neuhaus, "Jews for Jesus, Established A.D. 32," *First Things*, December 1996, p. 48.

24. See Martin E. Marty, "Proselytism in a Pluralistic World," in Runzo, *Ethics, Religion, and the Good Society*, p. 155.

25. George Rupp, "From Civil Religion to Public Faith," in W. Lawson Taitte, ed., *Religion and Politics* (Austin: University of Texas Press, 1989), pp. 171, 185.

26. See David Tracy, *Plurality and Ambiguity: Hermeneutics, Religion, Hope* (Chicago: University of Chicago Press, 1987).

27. *Reynolds v. United States*, 98 U.S. 145 (1879).

28. For a critical but fascinating discussion of the history (and fate) of the Mormon belief in plural marriage, see D. Michael Quinn, "Plural Marriage and Mormon Fundamentalism," in Martin E. Marty and R. Scott Appleby, eds., *Fundamentalisms and Society* (Chicago: University of Chicago Press), p. 240.

29. For liberal defenses of the subversive nature of religion, see, for example, Hauerwas, *Dispatches from the Front*, and Elizabeth Mensch and Alan Freeman, *The Politics of Virtue: Is Abortion Debatable?* (Durham, N.C.: Duke University Press, 1993).

30. See the discussion in Carter, *The Culture of Disbelief*, pp. 35–41.

31. C. S. Lewis once commented that Christians should view the world as "enemy-occupied territory." C. S. Lewis, *Mere Christianity* (New York: Walker and Company, 1987 [1943]), p. 67. Although Lewis was referring, quite literally, to the Devil, the student of civility can see in the phrase an emphasis on the true religious believer's radical disconnection from the world and its values. Whatever their flaws, the various fundamentalist movements that seem to follow the introduction of modernity in every religion emphasize the preservation of that distinction. Lewis argued, correctly, that many forces in the world combine to try to wean believers from their faith, and he worried, sensibly, that each compromise faith makes with the world makes faith less faith and more world.

32. O. T. Lanphear, *Thou Shalt Love Thy Neighbor as Thyself: A Discourse Delivered at the United Service of the Congregational Churches in Lowell* (Lowell, Mass.: Brown & Morey, 1856).

33. The originating article is Samuel D. Warren and Louis D. Brandeis, "The Right to Privacy," *Harvard Law Review* 4 (1890): 193.

34. See *O'Lone v. Estate of Shabazz*, 482 U.S. 342 (1987).

35. See *Church of the Lukumi Babalu Aye v. City of Hialeah*, 508 U.S. 520 (1993).

36. The Supreme Court rejected this particular claim in the case of *Goldman v. Weinberger* 475 U.S. 503 (1986), and was overruled by the Congress in 10 U.S.C. § 774.

15. Civility and the Challenge of Christendom

1. See John Murray Cuddihy, *No Offense: Civil Religion and Protestant Taste* (New York: Seabury Press, 1978).

2. Quoted in Alan P. F. Sell, *Aspects of Christian Integrity* (Louisville, Ky.: Westminster/John Knox Press, 1990), p. 74.

3. For a readable and often exquisite account of the struggles of the early Christians with the same problem—the clash between God's word and the desire to fit in—see Wayne A. Meeks, *The Origins of Christian Morality: The First Two Centuries* (New Haven: Yale University Press, 1993), esp. chaps. 4, 5, and 6.

4. See Butler, *Awash in a Sea of Faith,* pp. 283–88.

5. See the competing arguments in Joe Klein, "In God They Trust: Washington Faces a New Challenge: Should It Let Churches Take Over the Inner Cities," *The New Yorker*, June 16, 1997, p. 40.

6. To see the shift in the Supreme Court's "crèche" jurisprudence, compare *Lynch v. Donelly*, 465 U.S. 668 (1984), with *Allegheny County v. ACLU*, 492 U.S. 573 (1989). For a thoughtful analysis of the compromise and its collapse, see Alan Dershowitz, *Chutzpah* (Boston: Little, Brown, 1991), pp. 331–34.

7. Michael Paulsen, *"Lemon* Is Dead," *Case Western Reserve Law Review* 43 (1995): 795.

8. Mark Tushnet, *Red, White, and Blue* (Cambridge, Mass.: Harvard University Press, 1988).

9. Jonathan Sarna, in Joseph Runzo, ed., *Ethics, Religion, and the Good Society* (Louisville, Ky.: Westminster/John Knox Press, 1992), p. 166.

10. See Ari L. Goldman, "Religion Notes," *New York Times*, February 27, 1993, p. 9; "Celebrating Christmas," *USA Today*, December 18, 1992, p. 1D (table).

11. David Hugh Farmer, *The Oxford Dictionary of Saints*, 3d ed. (Oxford: Oxford University Press, 1992), p. 355.
12. See Stephen Nissenbaum, *The Battle for Christmas* (New York: Knopf, 1996).
13. For a more detailed discussion of these and other aspects of the Mennonite colleges, see Rodney J. Sawatsky, "What Can the Mennonite Tradition Contribute to Christian Higher Education?" in Richard T. Hughes and William B. Adrian, eds., *Models for Christian Higher Education: Strategies for Success in the Twenty-First Century* (Grand Rapids: William B. Eerdmans, 1997), p. 187.
14. "Text of the Barmen Declaration," reprinted in Hubert G. Locke, ed., *The Church Confronts the Nazis: Barmen Then and Now*, Toronto Studies in Theology, vol. 16 (New York and Toronto: The Edwin Mellen Press, 1984).

16. The Etiquette of Democracy

1. Elias, *The Civilizing Process*, p. 69.
2. St. George, *The Descent of Manners,* p. xv. See also his more detailed explication of the quoted point in chap. 4.
3. Ralph Reed, the former executive director of the Christian Coalition, has offered an explicit and powerful call for greater civility and mutual respect between conservative evangelicals and their opponents—specifically including gay rights activists. See Ralph Reed, *Active Faith: How Christians Are Changing the Soul of American Politics* (New York: Free Press, 1996), pp. 258–67.
4. E. J. Dionne Jr., "Chattering Class," *Washington Post Magazine*, March 30, 1997, p. W02.
5. Richard John Neuhaus, "Democracy, Economics, and Radical Pluralism," in W. Lawson Taitte, ed., *The Citizen and His Government* (Austin: University of Texas Press, 1984), pp. 99, 120.
6. Raoul Lionel Felder, "I'm Paid to Be Rude," *New York Times*, July 17, 1997, p. A23.

17. Coda: The Civility of Silence

1. See the figures cited in "The American Uncivil Wars," *U.S. News & World Report*, April 22, 1996, p. 66.
2. See, for example, David Z. Seide, "Daily Moments of Silence on Public Schools: A Constitutional Analysis," *New York University Law Review* 58 (1983): 364. For a similar argument by a theologian, see the discussion in Cooey, *Family, Freedom, and Faith*, chap. 4.

INDEX